# Reading as Democracy in Crisis

# Reading as Democracy in Crisis

*Interpretation, Theory, History*

Edited by James Rovira

LEXINGTON BOOKS
Lanham • Boulder • New York • London

Published by Lexington Books
An imprint of The Rowman & Littlefield Publishing Group, Inc.
4501 Forbes Boulevard, Suite 200, Lanham, Maryland 20706
www.rowman.com

6 Tinworth Street, London SE11 5AL

British Library Cataloguing in Publication Information Available

**Library of Congress Cataloging-in-Publication Data**

Names: Rovira, James, editor.
Title: Reading as democracy in crisis : interpretation, theory, history / edited by James Rovira.
Description: Lanham : Lexington Books, [2019] | Includes bibliographical references and index.
Identifiers: LCCN 2019006098 (print) | LCCN 2019014418 (ebook) | ISBN 9781498553872 (Electronic) | ISBN 9781498553865 (cloth : alk. paper)
Subjects: LCSH: Literature and society. | Books and reading--Sociological aspects. | Democracy and the arts.
Classification: LCC PN51 (ebook) | LCC PN51 .R34 2019 (print) | DDC 028--dc23
LC record available at https://lccn.loc.gov/2019006098

Printed in the United States of America

For all Bananafishers everywhere, especially our dear departed
Bananafishers, Robert "Scottie" Bowman, Tim O'Connor,
and Will Hochman.

# Contents

# Preface

The idea for this collection began with my dissertation "Kierkegaard, Creation Anxiety, and William Blake's Early Illuminated Books," which was extensively revised into the book *Blake and Kierkegaard: Creation and Anxiety* (Continuum/Bloomsbury 2010). I brought Blake and Kierkegaard together to answer the question, "Why do we fear what we create?," a question I began to ask after seeing the film *The Matrix* and realizing how much it was a retelling of Mary Shelley's *Frankenstein*—and then realizing how many times Shelley's novel was remade, retold, or reimagined long before the Wachowskis made their film. It seemed that whenever we imagine human beings creating a new form of life or intelligence, some independently thinking and willing being, we imagine horrible consequences will follow. The ensuing apocalypse is either personal and familial, as in Shelley's novel or the film *Ex Machina*, or global and widespread, as in the *Terminator* or *Matrix* films.

I was attending Cassandra Laity's Literary Theory seminar at Drew University when the first *Matrix* film came out, so I took that opportunity to acquaint myself with Baudrillard's *Simulacra and Simulation*, an important text to the writers and directors of *The Matrix*, and wrote a short piece about Baudrillard and *The Matrix* that kept getting revised and expanded every time a new *Matrix* film was released. The final version of this essay found its way into *The International Journal of Baudrillard Studies*.[1] The idea would not leave me alone, however, so it became the subject of my dissertation. I eventually named this fearful imaginative landscape "Creation Anxiety." The Romantics were to provide narratives of a fallen creator while Kierkegaard would provide a concept of anxiety.

I originally intended to cover Blake, Mary Shelley, and several other Romantics in my study of Creation Anxiety, but Blake quickly took over.

Once I settled on Blake, I wanted to ground my juxtaposition of Blake and Kierkegaard on historical, philosophical, and textual grounds simultaneously, and I wished for that justification to be an integral part of the answer to my question about the forces driving Creation Anxiety. So the first chapter of *Blake and Kierkegaard* explores the similarities between Blake's England and Kierkegaard's Denmark during their respective lifetimes, and the next two consider how Plato's thought and his presentation of Socrates influenced them both. Chapter 4 extends the previous chapter's discussion of Plato's models of human development to Blake's and Kierkegaard's ideas about generation, which then leads to a discussion of Creation Anxiety in the final chapter. That chapter explores the contours of Creation Anxiety in Blake's *The [First] Book of Urizen* using Kierkegaard's concept of the demonic as found in *Concept of Anxiety*, engaging with the historical context provided by the first chapter as it does so.

A later book chapter considering the implications of Blake's and Kierkegaard's shared Moravian backgrounds appeared in 2018 in the anthology *Kierkegaard, Literature, and the Arts* edited by Eric Ziolkowski for Northwestern University Press. I was invited to contribute this chapter the year after *Blake and Kierkegaard* was published. If I could, I would make it chapter 2 of a second edition of *Blake and Kierkegaard*, as it provides a historical and conceptual link between Blake's and Kierkegaard's similar historical milieus and their similar interests in Socrates via their shared Moravian upbringing. The most important part of this story for my purposes now is that I grounded my use of a theoretical structure to interpret a work of literature on historical and philosophical contexts shared between the literary work and the theoretical paradigm. My theory of choice had historical and philosophical affinities with the literature it was being used to interpret, and those affinities came to be a part of the argument itself. Once I finished revising my dissertation into my book, I realized I wanted to more fully explore the intersections of history and literary theory, so I circulated a CFP for this collection. Years and numerous iterations later, here it is.

The Bananafishers referred to in the dedication were members of a listserv by that name dedicated to the works of J. D. Salinger. It was curated for many years by Tim O'Connor until his death and takes its name from Salinger's story "A Perfect Day for Bananafish," which narrates the suicide of Seymour Glass. Tim tirelessly oversaw a very engaged community of Salinger readers, even hosting a get together for several of its members in New York City on probably more than one occasion. I once met a few members during one of Tim's get-togethers, and on other occasions, and I once joined Chris Kubica, associate producer of the documentary *Salinger* (2013) and coeditor of *Letters to J.D. Salinger* (University of Wisconsin Press, 2014), on a radio program in New York to discuss Salinger. When Tim passed away, the group migrated to Yahoo groups and then to a Google group. It is still active, but barely. Robert "Scottie" Bowman was a longtime listmember and the first of the key members to pass away. A psychologist by profession, he is also the author of *Run to the Sea* (1965) and *The Toy* (1967), both excellent Hemingwayesque novels set in the United Kingdom. Will Hochman, the third person mentioned in the dedication, is the most recent of the Bananafishers to pass away. He was Associate Professor of English at Southern Connecticut State University until his passing, and he was Chris's coeditor on *Letters to J.D. Salinger.* He originally submitted the proposal for the chapter on Louise Rosenblatt, but handed it off to his SCSU colleague Meredith Sinclair when he became ill, who stepped into his place admirably, quickly, and completely on point.

The network of relationships I describe above reflects on my purposes for this collection. The chief premise of this collection is that reading always takes place within specific historical moments that influence its practice. The term "reading practices," of course, can refer to everything from use of print or electronic media to one's physical position and location while reading. So more narrowly considered, this collection argues that we interpret texts as we do because of the historical moment we are in: the people with whom we read, the political and economic situations in which we read, the world pressing in upon us as we read. I met my wife in an AOL book chat while I was part of a book group dedicated to the works of Dostoevsky. She then joined me when I started an AOL book group about Umberto Eco and followed me to my AOL book group about Salinger. Her first gift to me was a paperback copy of Jonathan Carroll's *Outside the Dog Museum.* Before we had children, we had books, and now we are overwhelmed with both children and books. For me, as for many of us, reading is an inherently intimate, personal, and self-defining activity. I think this collection supports the idea that acts of reading and interpretation are also politically self-defining acts, or at least can be. While the ground I describe has long been covered by Reader Response theory, this collection focuses still more narrowly on how we conceptualize our reading practices, and how those conceptualizations are driven by crises in democracy. I argue here that how we conceptualize our interpretive practices are a means by which we try to assert agency over the larger forces that are always encroaching upon us. Our theories of reading are acts of self-definition, acts of self-assertion, and in some of the most private and personal ways, an expression of our deepest political commitments, especially to democracy.

## NOTES

1. James Rovira, "Subverting the Mechanisms of Control: Baudrillard, *The Matrix Trilogy*, and the Future of Religion," *The International Journal of Baudrillard Studies* 2, no. 2 (July 2005): https://www2.ubishops.ca/baudrillardstudies/vol2_2/rovirapf.htm.

# Introduction

## *Interpretation, Theory, History*

## James Rovira

". . . for a man to understand what he himself says is one thing, and to understand himself in what is said is something else."[1]

—Søren Kierkegaard

"Between the too warm flesh of the literal event and the cold skin of the concept runs meaning."[2]

—Jacques Derrida

## INTRODUCTION

Both Søren Kierkegaard and Jacques Derrida in the quotations above seem to suggest that the acts of reading, or of meaning making, or of understanding consist of a threefold dialectical structure. Kierkegaard's "man" stands between the meaning of his words and the self-understanding conveyed by his words, whether he intended them to convey self-understanding or not. Derrida's "meaning" is a meeting place between "too warm flesh"—or materiality—and concept. We see a similar structure fictionalized in Italo Calvino's *If on a winter's night a traveler*. Chapter 8 imagines an author who spends every morning watching a young woman through a spyglass as she reads on her terrace. He watches her before he sits down to work, and as he does so he imagines impossible fantasies, such as the young woman reading a sentence in her book at the same moment he is typing it on his typewriter. When Calvino's fictional author manages to convince himself that this fantasy is true, he jumps up to observe the effects of his words on the woman as she first reads them. But at that moment, he feels the most distance from her: "At times it seems to me that the distance between my writing and her reading is unbridgeable, that whatever I write bears the stamp of artifice and incongruity."[3] When he imagines her, in turn, similarly watching him voyeuristically as he writes, he imagines that "Readers are my vampires," saying that he is "unable to write if there is someone watching me. . . . How well would I write if I were not here!"[4]

In Calvino, voyeurism and vampirism serve as tropes for authorial anxieties as they alternate in focus toward his readers or toward himself as an author. But Calvino's novel, among the most metafictional in print, also posits a dual view of the reading process: more than that, compounded dual views. His male fictional author imagines himself pursuing a female reader as an object of desire, successfully controlling his reader's immediate emotional states through his writing in a way analogous to seductive speech. But this author also imagines himself being observed by the reader, who sees into him and his writing process through the words that connect them both. This dual view of reading of course invites Calvino's own readers to extend this consideration to their own view of Calvino's fictional author and of Calvino himself. What is obscured in this series of representations is the actual fictional reader herself and, by extension, the actual readers of Calvino's novels, who at the moment of reading his words, or for that matter even my own, right now, right here—and yes, I am talking about *you* in particular—are the only elements of presence that exist in relationship to the text. Calvino's author ultimately wishes to efface even his own presence.

Furthermore, Calvino's playful, perverse, imaginative author emphasizes the ways in which our reading practices are both characterized by absence and, simultaneously, an all-too-invasive presence, for while we read we willingly submit to the intrusion of a foreign mind upon our own. This dual experience of presence and absence extends to our experience of the world around us, a world that vanishes as we become engrossed in a book but then finds its way back to us through the book itself. As isolated and disengaged as we may feel while reading—and we often read precisely for this feeling—the world looms large in the background, influencing not only what we choose to read but how we read and how we imagine reading, how we think about the activity of reading itself. To begin to understand how our immediate surroundings might influence the development of our concepts of reading, therefore, is to begin to understand how we consciously take charge of our own most interior lives, both conceptual and emotional, by determining how we respond there to the world around us.

Chapters in this collection engage these dual views of reading by considering how European and North American reading strategies from classical Greece to the present have developed as responses to social, cultural, economic, and political forces. Contributors were asked to articulate a dialectic between the reading strategies explored here and the historical contexts from which these reading strategies arose. While introductions to theory and to major figures in theory anthologies have been providing increasingly suggestive historical contexts for their major figures, Peter Herman's *Historicizing Theory* (2003) is the current volume's only immediate predecessor. It focuses exclusively on historical contexts for theorists writing since the 1960s, engaging Derrida, Foucault, Bloom, Greenblatt, de Man, and Spivak in addition to period- and place-oriented essays.[5] Herman's desire for his anthology was that it would carry out the work of New Historicism, which is to "recover 'the cultural specificity, the social embedment, of all modes of writing,' recognizing that such recovery will inevitably be partial and proceed 'from our own historically, socially and institutionally shaped vantage points.'"[6]

This anthology somewhat shifts Herman's focus from writing to reading and then seeks to suggest reasons for the existence of the theorizing activity itself, in a broad sense of the term, as self-reflection on our reading strategies from Plato to the twenty-first century. As a result, this collection broadens the reach of historicizing approaches to literary studies, and to literary theory, both before and after the key theorists of the 1960s to build on Herman's important and well-executed work of recovery. It seeks to uncover and then explain some of the reasons driving the varieties of our self-reflections on reading, arguing that crises in democracy are the perennial causes, sites, and instigators of all forms of self-reflection on our concepts of reading from the time of Plato and Aristotle to the present, or "the now" in terms of my writing at this moment, in the form of Object-Oriented Ontology. However, democracy has not been just one thing. It has existed in a variety of conditions and has taken a variety of forms, so we will also attempt to register historically inflected differences among these ways of interpreting texts, associating them with some of the material conditions and especially the political contexts that contributed to their development.

Guglielmo Carvallo's and Roger Chartier's anthology *A History of Reading in the West* carries out important work adjacent to the work of this collection but not quite identical to it. In their own words, "Our objective is dual: to recognize the constraints that limit the frequenting of books and the production of meaning and to inventory the resources that can be mobilized by the reader's liberty—a liberty that remains in many ways dependent but is capable of ignoring, shifting about, or subverting the techniques or devices designed to limit it."[7] Their important collection has a much broader scope than this one and a greater emphasis on material culture and its effects on reading practices in a variety of senses. For example, one chapter discusses differences in physical position while reading as a site of historical difference.[8] This collection, comparatively, is only concerned with the "production of meaning" and how it is affected by a specific kind of political pressure, namely, macro or micro level crises in democracy.

Democracy as context for theory or, more generally, for our interpretive practices, bears upon both the immediate social and political context of this writing, on my own personal experiences, and on the development of theory as it came to be known in the late 1960s. Democracy is in crisis around the world at the time of this writing, and I have been personally attuned to its crises in the United States. Aside from a cover of *Time* magazine in which President Donald Trump is pictured gazing at himself in a mirror in which the image reflected back to him is wearing a crown and royal robes,[9] indicators even prior to the election of Donald Trump describe problems with democracy in the United States. *The Economist* reported in a 2016 white paper that the US has been downgraded from a "full" to a "flawed" democracy, citing an "erosion of trust in government and elected officials."[10] Worse, a 2014 study published in *Perspectives on Politics* suggests that "economic elites and organized groups representing business interests have substantial independent impacts on U.S. government policy, while average citizens and mass-based interest groups have little or no independent influence,"[11] implying that the United States is more of an oligarchy than a democracy.[12]

Reaching back a little further, my own earliest political memory is of Watergate, of sitting next to my parents as a seven-year-old while we watched Richard Nixon on television emphatically assert, "I am not a crook."[13] I also remember feeling a widespread, palpable, bitter cynicism toward government after Nixon resigned from office, and even more after he was pardoned by Gerald Ford. I remember the bumper stickers everywhere preceding the 1976 Presidential election that said, next to a picture of Nixon's face, "Would you buy a used Ford from this man?" As we will see later in this collection, Derrida's own trajectory moves from implicit to explicit engagement with politics and biography over the course of his career. Overall, this collection registers milestones from the 30 Tyrants of Plato's time, to the French Revolution in the eighteenth century, to the rise of Nazi Germany in the early to mid-twentieth century, and to the Arab Spring in the twenty-first century. Democracy is seemingly either newly erupting or constantly in crisis by its very nature, as Derrida came to argue late in his career, and theorists of reading and of writing seem always at hand to recover it, extend it, or to challenge it at these key moments in history.

The remainder of this introduction is divided into two parts. I will next consider the implications of the terms "dialectic" and "history" to explain this collection's central methodology, which is to detemporalize history through the practice of condition/response readings of literary and cultural theorists in their historical contexts. While both literary studies and theory have long been engaging historical studies, I attempt here to apply the insights of recent historiography to the study of our reading strategies. I will argue that our meaning-making can be viewed as a series of responses to the conditions suggested by these different figures' historical contexts. My chapter summaries will follow this groundwork chapter by chapter.

I would like to note, however, that this book is about a dialectic between our reading strategies and the historical milieus in which they arose, but I am not claiming that it falls within the purview of literary theory as a more narrowly defined field of discourse. Today, as the title of the most recent *Norton* anthology (and others) suggests, the term "literary theory" refers to all self-reflective reading activities from Plato to the present and is extended to our analysis of all cultural products, not just literature. But the term is more recent than that, and from this point forward I will use it in a narrower sense. "Literary theory," as it came to be known with the rise of French poststructuralism in the 1960s, I am treating as a subset of our reading strategies. It is one that is engaged in a conversation with all past ways of reading and vital to our understanding of the future development of our interpretations of texts, but I don't use the term "literary theory" or "critical theory" or even just "theory" as shorthand for all self-reflection or theorization of our readings throughout history. For example, I will argue that Plato, or Plato's Socrates, was engaged in the metaphysics of reading while Aristotle was not, dividing the metaphysics and *techne* of reading between them. The metaphysics of reading, I will argue, is an impulse opposite writing and reading as *techne* that guided Aristotle to write *Poetics* and *Rhetoric*, which was to subsume the use of words to the controlled purposes of instrumental reason within the contexts of either a stage performance or political oratory.

## DETEMPORALIZING HISTORY

"Dialectic" in some form has been central to the interpretation of cultural products for as long as interpretation has been a self-conscious activity. The practice or concept of dialectic surfaces in Socrates's critiques of Homeric epics in *Republic* and extends into the Middle Ages. During that time (and into the present) dialectic took the form of a catechism and baptismal rites comprised of questions and answers, and then it surfaces again in Hegel's works, which continue to be central to scholarship in many fields. One recent work addressing the significance of Hegel and Hegelian dialectic to theory is Andrew Cole's *The Birth of Theory* (2015).[14] Cole locates the origins of modernity, which he equates with Romanticism, in medieval dialectic. He argues that Hegelian dialectic is a reworking of the medieval dialectic of identity/difference, comparing the identity/difference dialectic to whale vision: because a whale can see on either side of its head simultaneously, it must be able to process two completely different fields of vision at once. The identity/difference dialectic works the same way. Objects considered via this dialectic are seen, simultaneously, through the dual vision of similarity and difference. Cole emphasizes that Hegel's Germany was still a feudal state, so that Hegel was writing near the end of feudalism, and he defines feudalism as "the specific political structure and social arrangement within which modernity and freedom are realized." [15] Cole then suggests that Hegel's identity/difference dialectic transforms into a figure/concept dialect with the onset of theory as it establishes a difference between concrete imagery ("figure") and abstract conceptualizations ("concept") while it attempts to see both simultaneously.

The historiography attempted by this volume synthesizes the figure/concept dialectic by reversing the theorizing act. Authors and artists and filmmakers, at least partly in response to their historical contexts, embed images and figures in their works in ways that imply a conceptual structure, sometimes even with a specific conceptual structure in mind, [16] and theorists respond to these implied conceptual structures with explicit conceptual structures of their own. For example, Northrop Frye read William Blake and responded by reinventing myth criticism in *Anatomy of Criticism* (1957); Stanley Fish read Milton's *Paradise Lost* and then reinvented reader response theory in *Surprised by Sin* (1967); Edward Said read Flaubert, Conrad, Austen, and other nineteenth-century novelists to integrate postcolonial studies fully into the study of English literature with works extending from *Joseph Conrad and the Fiction of Autobiography* (1966) to *Culture and Imperialism* (1993); while Eve Kosofsky Sedgwick developed the concept of homosocial desire from her own reading of nineteenth-century literature in *Between Men* (1985).

Or it could be said that contributions to this anthology attempt to reverse these reading processes, historicizing the conceptual structures developed by theorists. They illustrate how reading strategies developed in response to the historical contexts in which they arose, however those responses are shaped, without claiming that any concept of reading remains in a passive origin/product relationship with their contexts, while the creative works under consideration serve as the grounds on which this dialectic was tested by their acts of interpretation. While none of these chapters seek to subsume our interpretive practices to history, they still affirm the inescapability of history: if a reading strategy attempts to escape history, or even if it succeeds—in which case the reading strategy shapes history more than it is shaped by it—the form of that escape is in part conditioned by the historical context that it rejects. But while I assume it is naïve to think that reading exists independently of historical influence, this assumption does not prohibit contributors from acknowledging every attempt to escape history, however successful or unsuccessful it may be.

To avoid producing intellectual histories that trace only the procession of dehistoricized concepts, our use of the term "history" itself also needs to be clarified, especially when so many later authors respond to very different aspects of the histories of their subjects and even question the possibility of the historical itself. "History," most simply and broadly defined, is the inaccessible sum total of all material events leading up to the present moment. "History" as a discipline, however, is a narrative constructed by the residues of the past remaining in the present, one imposed upon these events after the fact, narratives that follow a number of recognizable patterns both in their identification of patterns within past events and in the ways they register how people think about the past. The most simplistic model of the relationship between later periods, paradigms, or epochs and earlier ones is linear: older paradigms and epochs are completely displaced by newer ones as they arise. Once we identify the start of the postmodern era, for example, modernism has passed or is passing away. Linear models often follow the patterns of apocalyptic literature in which history has a discreet beginning, middle, and end characterized by the revelation or fulfillment of a value system embodied in an ideal future world. Hegel's *Lectures on the Philosophy of History* (1837), for example, establishes dialectical processes as the basis of historical development. In its orientation toward the future, Hegel's concept of history is a linear model that increases in complexity, absorbing older models as it proceeds, and because it culminates in the Absolute Idea, it is a kind of apocalyptic.

Eric Voegelin, in response to Comte's straight linear view in which history in general and disciplinary study in particular proceed through theological and metaphysical phases before moving into the phase of positive science, proposed a model that allows for several paradigms to run concurrently regardless of time of origin or relationship to one another.[17] Because several paradigms exist simultaneously in this model, Voegelin suggests that observers can take "cross cuts" at any given moment to see which paradigms are active at that moment and how they may be interacting. Voegelin's conception of multiple linear models allows us to question the usefulness of the term "residual" to describe a paradigm still adhered to by millions of people however much it may be contrary to educated opinion, which seems to be all that is registered in Comte's view. Raymond Williams's distinctions among dominant, emergent, and residual paradigms improve straight linear models by allowing for overlap and mutual influence as he observes their ongoing transformational processes, but Voegelin allows us to emphasize that what is residual in some communities remains dominant, and persistently so, in others.

The earliest linear models often follow a recurrence pattern when they are not apocalyptic. Polybius articulated a cycle of governments that begins with monarchy and then proceeds through tyranny, aristocracy, oligarchy, and democracy before ending in mob rule, which leads to the restoration of monarchy. His is but one of the recurrence models studied by G. W. Trompf in *The Idea of Historical Recurrence in Western Thought: From Antiquity to the Reformation.*[18] Trompf adds to the cyclical model of recurrence an alternation or fluctuation view, a reciprocal view, a reenactment view, and conceptions of restoration or renaissance.[19] He is careful to affirm that recurrence is almost always thought of as a recurrence of kind or type and not a reproduction of the past, but in any case repeated cycles can still be understood as moving toward a final history. The most recent significant departure from linear historical models are found in Deleuze and Guattari, whose concept of the rhizome decenters approaches to most paradigms that guide either history or our reading practices, to which the breached boundaries of Donna Haraway's "Cyborg Manifesto" is a significant addition. However, the image implied by the rhizome—which is a horizontally growing subterranean stem that sprouts roots and shoots in all directions—still links them all in a continuous and underground present.

Foucault and of course the variety of reading strategies that fall under the umbrella of "New Historicism" account for a significant body of work that historicizes cultural products. Foucault provides genealogies of significant concepts that constitute elements of our reading, but a genealogy itself functions as a kind of linear model. For example, in Foucault the concept of the "homosexual" comes into existence in the nineteenth century with the medicalization of homosexual desire and then continues into the present. While homosexuality is no longer defined as a psychopathology, the words "no longer" place the term "homosexuality" in continuity with a long discourse about homosexuality, a history or genealogy of this discourse. What is a genealogy but a tree, or a complex set of interconnected lines whose outermost branches are its most recent additions? Chapters here might ask of Foucault, "What motivated the concept of a genealogy?" More importantly, this collection calls attention to an additional relationship between paradigms and their historical contexts that can coexist with any variety of linear or rhizomatic models, one that detemporalizes our approach to history and allows for disruptions and discontinuities by seeking out instances of conditions and responses. These condition/response instances are dialectical in form and may be historically continuous with one another or completely discontinuous. The question of historical continuity is not interrogated: just how conditions prompt responses. So when twentieth-century authors engage Plato, to use one example, this volume would suggest that they might do so because the dialogues begin suddenly and urgently to resonate in the present due to similarity of historical circumstance.

Methodologically, then, this volume registers the rise of conditions that correlate with a discreet range of responses. This methodology seeks to escape, at least somewhat, Heidegger's critique of a "vulgar concept of time" that Derrida identified as "time conceived as linear successivity, as 'consecutivity,'" which Derrida says in this context is "what unites [the] metaphysics [and] technics" of the Occident.[20] A condition/response model can account for responses in contemporary texts that resonate with earlier texts even if these earlier texts were unknown to later authors.[21] To elaborate, Clayton Roberts's *The Logic of Historical Explanation*[22] elaborates on the use of condition/response models within the field of historiography. He describes conflicts within historiography from the early twentieth century to the 1970s as characterized by battles between positivist and humanist assumptions. Positivist historiographies employed "covering-law models" in which historical events occur because they follow general laws that govern similar events.[23] According to Roberts, after the 1970s Gadamer, postmodernists such as Hayden White, and post-structuralists such as Derrida changed the terms of the debates within historiography, but "they said little or nothing about the logic that guides the historian in determining why an event occurred."[24] As a result, by the late 1980s historians were moving away from postmodernism and post-structuralism to attempt to resolve some of these central questions again.[25]

Roberts suggests that the new historiographies at the time of his writing asserted that the covering-law model is absurd when applied to macro-level events (such as the French Revolution), but plausible for micro-level events (any of the individual events leading up to the French Revolution, such as food shortages). He calls the process of identifying the micro-events that comprise a macro-event "colligation," and the process of developing covering laws governing these micro-events by comparing them to similar micro-events "correlation," concluding that "Colligation and correlation are the warp and woof from which historians weave their explanations."[26] So in this model, each macro-event is unique and must be understood on its own terms, but micro-events can be compared to similar micro-events to help us understand why they occur.

We can apply this model to the development of reading strategies in two different ways. First, we might view any individual act of reading as a micro-event and the development of any theoretical paradigm of reading as a macro-event. Any one reading of an individual text is like a battle, or a famine, or a plague, or a love affair (depending on the reader's response to the text at hand), while the development of a clearly defined reading strategy is like a revolution, or a new scientific theory, or the founding of a new country. But we can also view these relationships another way: the development of a theory of literature is a micro-event taking place within a broader context, as a response to it, one somewhat conditioned by it but also somewhat defining it. If we combine these two possibilities, any construct that theorizes reading in any sense of the word is the dialectical hinge between individual acts of reading and broader social influences.

Henning Trüper's, Dipesh Chakrabarty's, and Sanjay Subrahmanyam's *Historical Teleologies in the Modern World* provides conceptual structures that can help advance a condition/response model of historicizing reading.[27]

They observe that while teleological thinking had been clearly established by
Aristotle in his study of physics, it did not become a dominant paradigm for
conceptualizing history and many other disciplines until Christian Wolff's
invention of the word "teleology" in 1728 for Diderot's *Encyclopédie*, followed by Kant's subsequent appropriation of the term. The editors modestly
affirm for their anthology that it

> does not mean to argue that it is possible, or impossible, to eliminate teleology,
> or even just tragedy, from history. Neither does it insist that, normatively
> speaking, teleology, historicity or temporality *ought* to be plural. It does, how-
> ever, suggest that historically they have been and that the present-day tendency
> to overlook this plurality is at least in part a product of this very plurality. . . .
> We propose a change of perspective taking into account that its inhabitants and
> modes of habitation have been and are multiple and change in multiple ways;
> that the *polis* subjected to the regime has been and continues to be rather larger
> than smaller, and the regime itself is much less consistent and comprehensive
> than has often been assumed. [28]

"Teleology" in the editors' hands does not necessarily refer to straightfor-
ward linear models because it "does not depend on temporality as pre-given
by, for instance, the phenomenal experience of time." [29] Furthermore, "Teleological directionality was not bound to the future" and is "capable of being
plural." [30] The key aspect of teleology in the editors' view is the burden of the
"requirements of narrative closure," so that teleology constitutes a *poetics* of
historicizing human culture and cultural products rather than a specific temporal framework, meaning in part that thematic or narrative development,
leading to some kind of narrative closure, is emphasized over a temporal
scheme. [31] There is a great deal of sympathy between the work of Trüper,
Chakrabarty, and Subrahmanyam and this collection, whose detemporalizing
work seeks to establish at most a teleology of immediate responses to immediate circumstances, however long those patterns of circumstances and responses persist or however often they undergo disruptions, transformations,
and repetitions. This way of reading texts, furthermore, theorizes them within
their historical contexts, so that the contemporary observer stands in a third
position, one that employs a theoretical model originating in historical conditions similar to the texts under consideration. [32]

This approach, for good or bad, revives the author that was perhaps first
publicly executed in the twentieth century by T. S. Eliot. The goal of this
anthology is to provide a microcorrelation of reading practices with historical
conditions. We can't do so, of course, without reference to the death of the
author which seems to have defined twentieth-century reading practices from
Eliot's "Tradition and the Individual Talent" to the New Critics to Derrida,
postmodernism, and post-structuralism. Derrida himself very directly asserts
that

> The names of authors or of doctrines have here no substantial value. They indicate neither identities nor causes. It would be frivolous to think that "Descartes," "Leibniz," "Rousseau," "Hegel," etc., are names of authors, of the authors of movements or displacements that we thus designate. The indicative value that I attribute to them is first the name of a problem.[33]

I don't believe the work undertaken by this anthology escapes Derrida's critique of the metaphysics of presence: it can only hope to be informed by it. The "authors" we seek to reconstruct in these chapters are of course absent both from our writing about them in the moment of composition and your reading about them now, here, wherever you are, whoever you are. We write about these authors because they are not here, even if they are still living.

The work carried out by these chapters involves seeing the work of interpretation as representing more than just a conceptual problem, but a human one. Our consideration of the history of the reading and writing subject engages identity on multiple levels beyond the conceptual, including politics and affect: fear, hope, love, and rage. The fictional reconstructions revived in these pages, then, become valuable to us as readers to the extent that as writers we engage with them empathetically, combining emotion and desire with *caritas*. So the sympathetic writer of histories is an actor or ventriloquist taking on the name of the author in the living moment of the composition of the text. Whether the authors revived here most resemble living human beings, zombies, or stiff displays in a wax museum depend both upon our skills as writers and readers and on the limitations of all historical study, which this collection does not presume to overcome.

## THE ESSAYS: HISTORY AND OUR READING PRACTICES

In chapter 1, "Democracy as Context for Theory: Plato and Derrida as Readers of Socrates," James Rovira situates the origin of theory in Plato's works, arguing that he was so moved to theorize interpretive practices because political power was distributed among a large governing body that needed to be convinced by verbal argument to make one decision or another. As a result, understanding how words work in a social context became vitally important. Rhetoric is one way of registering this concern. Theorizing our reading and listening practices is another. This chapter therefore engages in a condition/response reading of Plato's dialogues that establish the crisis of democracy that Plato witnessed as the originary context for the theories of reading and language suggested there and for the dialogues' intense concerns about reading, writing, literature, philosophy, and language itself. The first section of the chapter ends with the establishment of a metaphysics/*techne* opposition evident in Aristotle's response to Plato's works that provides the first two categories of responses to the conditions found in a democracy in crisis. The second section of the chapter engages Derrida as a reader of Plato, establishing him as a site of historical and political difference from which he draws conclusions very different from Plato in his reading of Plato's works. It focuses on Derrida's engagement of Plato in his works from 1954 through 1968, encompassing his thesis, his first three books, and then "Plato's Pharmacy," collected in *Disseminations* in 1972 but originally published across two issues of *Tel Qel* in 1968. This reading of Derrida will contextualize his readings of Plato within his post-World War II milieu, his Judaism, and the social conditions in Algeria and then France that surfaced as a crisis of democracy in Paris in May 1968, emphasizing however the influence of the Holocaust on Derrida's thought.

In chapter 2, Aglaia Venters argues that Hegel's work arose from a tension between his Protestant upbringing and the rise and failure of the French Revolution, signaling anxiety over the fact that France's first attempt at democracy was aborted and suggesting that the conditions of the French Revolution caused Hegel to respond with a future that contrasts starkly with the provincial "hometown" world in which he was raised. The French Revolution led Hegel to view history in terms of potentialities that are preconditions for future development and vital to the formation of philosophy. His early works, such as *Phenomenology of Spirit*, emphasize polysemy and argue that language subjects immanent thought to historical biases. Hegel's later *Science of Logic* establishes a dialectic encompassing his entire view of history, setting history and society on a course from slavery to a community of free and equal citizens. The posthumously published *Philosophy of History* proposes an eschatological view of history while addressing his concern for establishing Germany's place in a future characterized by social reform. This chapter therefore engages Hegel's historiography as an act of reading motivated by tensions between Hegel's Protestant upbringing and the new, democratic world he hoped would be brought into being by the French Revolution.

Eric Hood follows with a chapter about Karl Marx, perhaps the most famous neo-Hegelian in history. His chapter examines two of Marx's major contributions to cultural theory: historicism as a methodology and the development of ideology as a concept. Like Hegel, Marx supplies his readers with a way of reading history. This chapter first considers Marx's education and training and the experiences that influenced his thinking over three key periods as conditions for his work. The first period, spent in Bonn and then Berlin, led to his affiliation with the Young Hegelians, who encouraged Marx's materialism. The second was his contact with the socialist circles of Paris where Marx, influenced by his relationships with Proudhon and Engels, focused on political analyses. The third phase occurred in London, where again exiled, Marx responded by taking on the task of examining capitalism as a dynamic economic system rife with internal tensions. The chapter then explores how Marx developed his theories of history and of ideology out of these shifting contexts, and it closes by considering how Marx's understanding of history and ideology work together to suggest both a theory of subjectivity and of cultural production, which ultimately reflects on how human beings read both history and themselves as democratic actors within it.

Steven Wexler's chapter on Wittgenstein shifts the grounds of this discussion to analytic philosophy to advocate for a Wittgensteinian turn in cultural studies. Wexler redefines Wittgenstein's philosophy as "profoundly historical" because it originates in the conditions of a dialectic between certainty and uncertainty waged within the context of the humanist/rationalist contest that began in the seventeenth century. Next, because of Wittgenstein's pragmatism, Wexler argues that what "Wittgenstein ultimately reveals through his moment in the dialectic of uncertainty and certainty is that *pragmatism is naturalism shaped by historical relations but not entirely explained by those relations.*" Rather than presenting an antifoundationalist Wittgenstein, then, Wexler emphasizes Wittgenstein's pragmatism as a kind of naturalism, a response that in his words includes a "whole culture" so can function as a site of meaning-making that includes reference to socioeconomic realities. The rules governing language games, then, are in a pragmatic sense realized in the act of interpretation rather than governing it beforehand. History and culture are embedded within the acts of meaning-making from the start, and in a somewhat Marxist move can extend the logic of democracy both to reading and to political economies.

Cassandra Falke's "Robert Penn Warren: Poetry, Racism, and the Burden of History" begins with a description of Warren's importance to American letters followed by a description of the relative neglect paid to Warren as a critic. Falke then elaborates on the three principles guiding Warren's criticism: "responsibility toward others (including toward authors and readers), a willingness to reckon with complexities without reconciling them, and a striving for awareness of the way one's own interest and attention shape a critical project." These critical principles simultaneously validate the individuality of authors and readers, locating meaning between the two in ways anticipating reader response and deconstructive theory of the 1960s. While Warren is historicized within the context of the rise of New Criticism and his work in *The Kenyon Review*, the most important historical conditions for Warren's work is found in the response of its praxis, namely how his critical principles were realized in his writing about race in the works *Let Us Now Praise Famous Men* and *Who Speaks for the Negro?* as he sought to extend democratic ideals to his analysis of race in the 1960s.

Meredith Sinclair's "Louise Rosenblatt: The Reader, Democracy, and the Ethics of Reading" addresses Rosenblatt's *Literature as Exploration* in its historical moment in 1938, a moment characterized by the conditions of the long-term effects of the Great Depression, the rise of fascism in Europe, and its encroachment into U.S. politics and culture. Rosenblatt's transactional theory of reading, one that anticipates Stanley Fish's variety of reader response theory by almost thirty years, arose as a response to a period when compulsory education was becoming normative in the United States and, with it, competing pedagogical theories. Rosenblatt's transactional theory of reading, in this context, is set against concepts of "schooling" that prepare students to participate in a capitalist economic system by having instilled in them distinctly American cultural values and norms. Rosenblatt's transactional theory of reading instead prepares students to be equal participants in a democracy by being free thinkers and compassionate neighbors. Sinclair's presentation of Rosenblatt does not only see her as concerned with pedagogy, however, but also as a literary theorist, one who supported her pedagogy with a way of reading literature suited for her historical moment, a moment in which compulsory education could support either oligarchy or democracy, which is particularly apropos to the early twenty-first century.

Philip Goldstein's "Aesthetic Theory: From Adorno to Cultural History" examines the effects of identity politics on aesthetic discourse by following a trajectory from Heidegger through Adorno, Foucault, Derrida, and then back to revived interest in Adorno's aesthetics, ending with a description of how some of the tensions within this discourse have been addressed by the work of Frow. Goldstein begins by placing Adorno and Foucault on opposite sides of Heidegger, both agreeing with Heidegger that art retains some autonomy so is able to articulate some socio-historical truths. Foucault, however, dissents by emphasizing that changing historical conditions, not transcendental categories, account for changing discursive modes. Goldstein observes how Derrida then enters this discussion by taking issue with both Foucault's historicizing as well as the autonomy of art as it is supported by either Adorno or Heidegger: Derrida asserts that philosophical constructs rather than socio-historical truths are being represented by these authors. However, Goldstein argues that the rise of identity politics in the 1960s and 1970s changed the terms of this discussion as movements supporting the rights and identities of African Americans, women, gays, lesbians, and other groups called for a re-evaluation of art's autonomy or lack of it, so that this rereading of aesthetics ultimately engages the conditions of democracy and race in the 1960s. He concludes with John Frow's contribution to this discussion, who responded with a resolution of these tensions by arguing that "diverse cultural institutions, regimes, or formations" contribute to the "historical evolution" of the place of art in culture that "explains readers' changing constructions of a text." While criticism since the late 1990s has been increasingly drawn toward Adorno's *Aesthetic Theory* for its potential re-establishment of the autonomy of art, Frow may present a way forward that allows for the continued efficacy of art while acknowledging its contingency as it is interpreted and re-interpreted by ever-changing historical contexts.

Darcie Rives-East's "Judith Butler: A Livable Life" contextualizes Butler's work, generally, within the conditions presented to her by her Jewish background, her lesbian identity, and her observation of her immigrant parents acclimating themselves to U.S. culture as new residents of Cleveland, Ohio, with varying degrees of success. Out of that context, Rives-East arranges Butler's work into three broad categories of responses. The first, "Gender and the Body," covers *Gender Trouble* and *Bodies that Matter: On the Discursive Limits of "Sex,"* examining them against Butler's lesbian identity and related issues. The second, "Language and the State," looks at *Excitable Speech: A Politics of the Performative* (1997), understanding it within the context of U.S. Supreme Court cases *R.A.V. v. St. Paul* (1992) and *Wisconsin v. Mitchell* (1993).[34] The third part, "Mourning and the Media," examines *Precarious Life: The Powers of Mourning and Violence* (2004) and *Frames of War: When is Life Grievable?* in the context of a post-9/11 world and Israeli discourse about Palestinians. After covering Butler's work from her reception of the Theodor W. Adorno Award in 2012 to her consideration of the Black Lives Matter movement, Rives-East reviews Butler's oeuvre retrospectively as being concerned with who is granted and who is denied subjectivity, and who is worthy of being grieved and who is granted access to a "liveable life." Or, in other words, who is granted the benefits of a democracy and who is not.

Roger Whitson's "Networking the Great Outdoors: Object-Oriented Ontology and the Digital Humanities" completes this anthology with a snapshot of the rise of Object-Oriented Ontology and Digital Humanities taken around November 2008 and a short period immediately following when, he claims, "the character of academia started to change." Whitson establishes as conditions driving this change the rise of the #altac movement, the exposure of the increasing adjunctification of the professoriate, the emergence of open-access scholarship, and the rise of social media use by academics in response to significant social events registering a crisis in democracy, such as the pepper spray incident at U.C. Davis blogged about by Timothy Morton and the Arab Spring in Egypt reported on by Graham Harman from the University of Cairo. Whitson observes how social media and adjunctification created a convergence of pressures that pushed forward the development of both Object-Oriented Ontology and Digital Humanities among a group of scholars concerned with both. These new ways of doing humanities, of reading and of presenting humanities scholarship and artifacts, have come together with the potential to help us "become stewards of the emergent global ecology."

I hope that this collection will shed some light on how our ways of meaning-making have been affected by—perhaps even driven by—a variety of crises in democracy at different points of history so that we can begin to explore the intimacy of the relationship between reading and democracy. I don't think it's a coincidence that chapters 2 and 3 focus on how Hegel and

Marx read history before subsequent chapters discuss direct engagement with texts, or that they are about figures who have deeply influenced textual interpretation in the twentieth century. We are readers of the history occurring around us, conscious or not, before we are readers of any text. This purpose is served as contributors attempt to argue an original thesis about their subjects. I also hoped, however, for this anthology to provide descriptions of the major ideas of each theorist accessible to upper-division undergraduates and to graduate students in the process. This dual purpose required contributors to either focus on one discrete period of an author's production, which narrows a chapter's focus to specific key texts during a certain period, or to take a broader view and divide the author's or theorist's life into key periods engaging different concerns. I think the variety of approaches represented here serves our purposes better than everyone following the same method.

The next question, of course, has to do with our choice of figures studied. Any collection approaching comprehensive coverage of even just major figures in theory would rapidly become encyclopedic in size, and even then the question, "Why this figure and not that one?" would still be asked. My goal was to represent as many different schools of thought as the number of contributors would allow. Beyond that, I was guided only by contributors' interests. I am pleased that unexpected figures surface alongside canonical ones, that post-structuralism, critical theory, and gender studies are represented alongside philosophy, New Criticism, and digital humanities. I believe that one of the key features of this collection is that it engages unexpected figures such as Louise Rosenblatt rather than the more obvious Stanley Fish, and that it engages recent developments in theory and reading such as object-oriented ontology and digital humanities, which have not yet surfaced in many theory readers as of the time of this writing. I hope that as we contributors pursued our disparate and unpredictable interests, our work as a whole contributes a small advancement in our collective understanding of the intersections of reading, history, and democracy.

It occurs to me now that I have failed to define one key term. What is democracy? Democracy is the dream of collective self governance.

## NOTES

1. Søren Kierkegaard, *The Concept of Anxiety: A Simple Psychologically Orienting Deliberation on the Dogmatic Issue of Original Sin*, ed. and trans. Reidar Thomte (Princeton, NJ: Princeton University Press, 1980), 142.

2. Jacques Derrida, *Writing and Difference*, trans. Alan Bass (Chicago: The University of Chicago Press, 1978), 75.

3. Italo Calvino, *If on a winter's night a traveler*, trans. William Weaver (New York: Harcourt Brace Jovanovich, Publishers), 170.

4. Ibid., 170–1.

5. Peter Herman, ed., *Historicizing Theory* (Albany, NY: SUNY Press, 2003).

6. Ibid., 7.

7. Guglielmo Carvallo and Roger Chartier, eds., *A History of Reading in the West*, trans. Lydia G. Cochrane (Amherst: University of Massachusetts Press, 1999), 34.

8. Armando Petrucci, "Reading to Read: A Future for Reading," in *A History of Reading in the West*, eds. Guglielmo Carvallo and Roger Chartier, trans. Lydia G. Cochrane (Amherst: University of Massachusetts Press, 1999), 362–364.

9. "King Me," *Time* vol. 191, no. 23, June 18, 2018, accessed June 17, 2018, http://time.com/5304206/donald-trump-discredit-mueller-investigation/.

10. "Democracy Index 2016," *The Economist*, accessed June 17, 2018, https://www.eiu.com/public/topical_report.aspx?campaignid=DemocracyIndex2016.

11. Martin Gilens and Benjamin I. Page, "Testing Theories of American Politics: Elites, Interest Groups, and Average Citizens," *Perspectives on Politics* vol. 12, issue 3, September 2014, pp. 564–581, doi:https://doi.org/10.1017/S1537592714001595.

12. Meredith Clark, "U.S. More Oligarchy than Democracy, Study Suggests," *MSNBC*, April 19, 2014, accessed June 17, 2018, http://www.msnbc.com/msnbc/the-us-no-longer-democracy#51760.

13. "Nixon: 'I Am Not a Crook,'" *History.com*, accessed June 17, 2018, https://www.history.com/topics/us-presidents/richard-m-nixon/videos/nixon-i-am-not-a-crook.

14. Andrew Cole, *The Birth of Theory* (Chicago: Chicago UP, 2015).

15. Ibid., 71.

16. See James Rovira, "Subverting the Mechanisms of Control: Baudrillard, *The Matrix Trilogy*, and the Future of Religion," *International Journal of Baudrillard Studies* vol. 2, no. 2, July 2005, https://www2.ubishops.ca/baudrillardstudies/vol2_2/rovira.htm.

17. Eric Voegelin, "The Irish Dialogue with Eric Voegelin," *VoegelinView*, lecture transcription, http://voegelinview.com/the-irish-dialogueue-with-eric-voegelin-pt1/.

18. G. W. Trompf, *The Idea of Historical Recurrence in Western Thought: From Antiquity to the Reformation* (Los Angeles: University of California Press, 1979).

19. Ibid., 3.

20. Jacques Derrida, *Of Grammatology* (Chicago: The Johns Hopkins University Press, 1974, 1976), 72. It is hard not to give some credit to Keats at this point.

21. Inflecting our analyses with race, class, and/or gender are different ways of narrowing and specifying historical context.

22. Clayton Roberts, *The Logic of Historical Explanation* (University Park: Pennsylvania State University Press, 1996).

23. Ibid., vi.

24. Ibid., vii.

25. Ibid. Roberts is of course looking back from his vantage point in the mid-1990s, so he cannot take into account developments within the 1990s.

26. Ibid.

27. Henning Trüper, Dipesh Chakrabarty, and Sanjay Subrahmanyam, *Historical Teleologies in the Modern World* (New York: Bloomsbury, 2015).

28. Ibid., 17.

29. Ibid., 12.

30. Ibid., 12.

31. Ibid., 13.

32. See Jerome McGann, *The Romantic Ideology: A Critical Investigation* (Chicago: Chicago UP, 1983). Alain Badiou's concept of the "Event" in *L'Être et l'Événement* (1988) establishes a similar pattern, but I would distinguish the condition/response model here from Badiou's concept of the event by divesting it of any ontological or political content, which I would then describe as kinds of "responses." One model for this approach is James Rovira's *Blake and Kierkegaard: Creation and Anxiety* (London: Continuum, 2010), which theorizes William Blake's late eighteenth-century mythological works using Kierkegaard's mid-nineteenth-century *The Concept of Anxiety* (*Begrebet Angest*, 1844). These authors' religious, economic, and cultural histories are combined with a shared intellectual history in subsequent readings of Blake's and Kierkegaard's works.

33. Derrida, *Of Grammatology*, 99.

34. In *R.A.V. v. St. Paul*, 112 S. Ct. 2538, 120 L. Ed. 2d 305 (1992), a teenager was charged with violating the St. Paul (Minnesota) Bias-Motivated Crime Ordinance for burning a cross in front of a home belonging to an African-American family. The conviction was overturned by the Supreme Court on the grounds that the act was protected by the First Amendment. In *Wisconsin v. Mitchell*, 113 S. Ct. 2194, 14 L. Ed. 2d 436 (1993), the Supreme Court upheld the sentencing of a black man, Todd Mitchell, for beating a white male, Gregory Reddick, after viewing the film *Mississippi Burning* (1988) and supposedly saying to friends, "Do you all feel hyped up to move on some white people?" Mitchell had appealed his conviction, arguing that it was based on the words he said prior to his attack; his sentence had been raised to seven years based on a Wisconsin statute that increased penalties if it could be shown a victim had been singled out for their race, gender, religion, sexual orientation, or national origin. The Court ruled that the conviction was permissible and not a violation of Mitchell's First Amendment rights.

*Chapter One*

# Democracy as Context for Theory

*Plato and Derrida as Readers of Socrates*

## James Rovira

This chapter compares Plato's and Derrida's treatments of philosophical idealism—or the belief that mental objects, not physical objects, are ultimately real—within their respective historical contexts to demonstrate how both authors engaged idealism in response to a dramatic failure of democracy within their lifetimes. Both Plato and Derrida will, in a sense, be approached as readers of Socrates from the points of view of very different historical contexts, but differing historical contexts that shared a crisis in common. Plato's philosophy, to start, will be explained in relationship to a brief suspension of Athenian democracy during his lifetime. I will argue that his intent to shift from literary models of education based on Homer's works to conceptual models based on his idealist philosophy was motivated primarily by his political context, which was an Athenian democracy in crisis following the defeat of Athens by Sparta in the Peloponnesian Wars. While Plato's idealism was driven by his affinity for centralized, authoritarian governmental structures, Derrida's philosophy, driven by a post–World War II and post-Holocaust context, is post-idealist before it is post-structuralist: while Derrida became widely known as a "post-structuralist" for his conference paper "Structure, Sign, and Play in the Discourse of the Human Sciences" (1966), we will see in fact that his engagement with structuralism proceeds from his engagement with idealism. In fact, we will see that in Derrida structuralism is beholden to Platonic idealism, and that his engagement with both was motivated by his childhood experiences as an Algerian Jew under Nazi rule followed by the shock of the Holocaust, so that his disillusionment with idealism was in part motivated by the worst failure of democratic governance in history. I will support this claim by examining Derrida's readings of both

Plato and Husserl starting with his 1953–1954 thesis *The Problem of Genesis in Husserl's Philosophy* and ending with "Plato's Pharmacy," originally published in *Tel Quel* in 1968. I will primarily focus, however, on Derrida's thesis. Setting a chronological limit of 1953–1968 on Derrida's works carries with it the disadvantage of excluding Derrida's most explicit writings about democracy later in his career, but it also allows us to see how deeply political his early works were and what political context motivated them.

Both Derrida and Plato have suffered from similar criticisms: their work is too literary, too non-linear, to be comfortably assimilated to the western analytic tradition. In Plato's case, the literary form of his dialogues raises a recurring question about Plato's relationship to his own works. Plato's works are dialogues among characters that sometimes involve action, even if the action is only Socrates finding a shady tree under which he can discuss writing or, more dramatically, Socrates drinking from a poisoned cup. Plato's conversational philosophy distributes different concepts among different characters and, especially in the early dialogues, often leaves central questions unresolved. This structure makes it difficult to identify any given concept in Plato's dialogues with Plato's own position. Furthermore, this conversational structure embeds the figure/concept dialectic[1] within Plato's works because it establishes characters within a setting ("figure") who are trying to work out concepts.

Kierkegaard provides a useful model for addressing these difficulties in his readings of Plato and of the figure of Socrates, and he comes with the additional benefit of being a significant and very early influence on Derrida. Benoit Peeters, for example, records that Jan Czarnecki introduced Derrida to Kierkegaard's work, saying that Kierkegaard was "one of the philosophers who would fascinate him most, and one to whom he would remain faithful the rest of his life."[2] Kierkegaard suggests that while the dialogues present a range of conceptual options, they also present, intentionally or not, a range of phenomenologies associated with those conceptual structures, so that a dialogue not only articulates ideas but also creates the kinds of characters who would assert them. Kierkegaard based his own pseudonymous authorship on this view of Plato's works, beginning with his reading not just of Plato, but of Plato as a reader of Socrates in his thesis *On the Concept of Irony*, where he attempts to separate the historical Socrates from Plato's presentation of him in the dialogues.

What Plato and Kierkegaard accomplish through dialogues, Derrida accomplishes through aporia, where he points readers toward an unsolvable contradiction within a text's argument or logic. Derrida is again following a Kierkegaardian pattern: the major philosophical works written by Kierkegaard after his thesis create several different pseudonyms, all of them contemplating a range of positions, later works responding to earlier ones.[3] Kierkegaard didn't consider himself the "author" of these pseudonymous works, however, as he explained in his unpaginated appendix to *Concluding Unscientific Postscript*. He thought of himself as the creator of the kinds of characters who would write these works, viewing the works themselves as having been "written by" these characters. "Kierkegaard's" thought advances in the form of a Hegelian dialectic from one pseudonym to the next, previous ideas combining to form new ones with the ultimate goal of crucifying his readers' intellects and moving them toward faith. While Derrida was not concerned with the faith commitments of his readers in that way, his concept of aporia does seem to closely parallel Kierkegaard's crucifixion of the intellect.

Philosophy in literary form, such as Plato's, Derrida's, and Kierkegaard's, not only models an individual's wrestling with difficult concepts, but deliberately guides its readers into these struggles, which because of their subject matter are often personally self-defining. Derrida could be said to have followed a pattern resembling Kierkegaard's pseudonymous authorship most closely in *Glas*, setting his literary and philosophical discourse side by side in two columns without providing direction about how to read them together. In these three authors, therefore, philosophical debates become the stage upon which existential and conceptual struggles occur as they push readers to make self-defining choices within the act of reading. Kierkegaard is therefore a kind of intermediary between Plato and Derrida, influencing in part how Derrida read Plato and what he drew from him.

Why Plato, though? Besides the fact that Derrida was as committed to reading Plato as he was to any other author, Derrida's historical moment resembled Plato's in important ways. Furthermore, approaching Plato's works within their historical contexts can yield useful insights into Plato's relationship to his own works, uncovering the ways in which they were a response to his own historical moment. Kraut's commentary on Plato's relationship to his own works in his introduction to the *Cambridge Companion to Plato* (1992) considers two possibilities: 1. Plato wanted to obscure what he believed to get readers to think for themselves; 2. Plato used the dialogues to express his own beliefs, which are voiced by Socrates or other interlocutors. Kraut's framing of the question can serve as a starting point for a historicized reading of Plato, but he fails to consider a third possibility developed within Plato's Seventh Letter and implied by the dialogues themselves.

Readers of Plato who assume the point of a dialogue is to work out a conceptual problem ignore that in Plato's works acquiring truth is an activity of the soul, not just of the mind. While this claim may seem like another way of stating Kraut's first possibility, for Plato the word "soul" was not merely a metaphor. To understand Plato's relationship to his works and to his own philosophy, we need to take seriously his developmental model, one based upon a composite view of the self that encompasses both affect and cognition. This discussion of the "soul" is necessary even within materialist frame-works, as it reflects the ways in which Plato approached his subject.

The implication of a composite self—one that views the soul as simulta-neously rational, spirited, and appetitive, or oriented toward intellect, toward emotion, and toward the body—is found in a number of Plato's works, some of which provide contradictory pictures of the soul. According to Necip Fikri Alican in *Rethinking Plato* (2012), "The soul of the *Phaedo* is apparently simple, a monadic entity which, being noncomposite, is *ipso facto* indissolu-ble. In contrast, the soul of the *Republic*, *Phaedrus*, and *Timaeus* is explicitly complex, bringing together three essentially different components in organic existence."[4] Stefan Büttner argues in "The Tripartition of the Soul in Plato's *Republic*" (2006) that the soul is monist in nature but tripartite in modes or influences,[5] while Alican elaborates that in *Phaedo* the distinctions "later constituting parts of the soul" surface there as "personality types and charac-ter traits."[6] As I argue elsewhere, this reading of Plato defines the existential edge of Plato's tripartite view of the self found in the Allegory of the Cave in *Republic* Book VII and in the Diotima section of *Symposium*. Different posi-tions within the cave of Plato's allegory represent the soul under different influences: those bound in chains have a primarily appetitive or bodily soul; those whose paths are illuminated by humanly-generated firelight have gained wisdom from social institutions that educated both their minds and feelings; and those living in the full light of the sun represent souls in the Divine light of reason. Diotima of the *Symposium* similarly describes people as seeking after immortality procreatively, through the body; socially, through institutions such as education or government; and spiritually, through philosophy.[7]

This tripartition of the soul in Plato's dialogues has been used to bestow existential significance upon our reading practices, both indirectly in Plato's dialogues and more explicitly in Origen's *On First Principles* (ca. 225), in which literal readings of Scripture are associated with the body, ethical read-ings of Scripture with the soul, and the most complex, allegorical readings with spirit. The tripartition of the soul can also partially explain the literary form of Plato's philosophy. Dialogues in this view prompt philosophical reflection on their subjects, so listeners not only work out conceptual prob-lems but also experience the birth of knowledge. Using Kierkegaard's lan-guage, the dialogue form serves maieutic purposes, bringing to existential birth a self-aware soul, a claim Kierkegaard made for his pseudonymous works. In a similar fashion, as Derrida developed his *concept* of deconstruc-tion, he came to describe it as an *experience* rather than a fixed concept.[8] "What deconstruction is not?" Derrida asks. He then answers, "everything of course! What is deconstruction? nothing of course!"[9] Derrida presents de-construction as both everything and nothing to keep it from being reduced to a series of semantic moves, to a concept in a system, or to a method of literary interpretation. It is not so much a pre-conceptual experience as the experience of being de-conceptualized, or perhaps in Kierkegaard's language, of the intellect being crucified.

In this way of reading of Plato's works, or Socrates's thought within Plato's works, the author's ideas may or may not be represented in any given dialogue. They very likely are, but that question is irrelevant. And because Plato himself may have changed his outlook or opinion while his dialogues remain fixed, his own relationship to the ideas contained in any given dialogue can change over time, just as any author's or reader's relationship to any book can change over time. The question then is not only whether or not Plato agreed with any of the ideas expressed in his dialogues, but also which Plato agreed or disagreed with them: the young Plato who first witnessed the dialogues, a more mature Plato some time during or after writing, or Plato at the end of his life. Any historicized reading of Plato's works will struggle with these questions, and as we struggle with these questions, we will come to see that we are not just engaging concepts, but concepts as a function of a personality embedded in a historical context. We can come to understand ourselves in what we say.

In Plato's specific case, the significance of this struggle becomes apparent with an examination of the conditions surrounding the life of Socrates and the composition of Plato's dialogues. The history of Athenian democracy begins with the overthrow of the tyrant Peisistratos in 510 B.C.E. and ends with Macedonian intervention in 322 B.C.E. At the beginning of this period Athens fought the Persian Wars (499–449 B.C.E.), soon followed by the Peloponnesian Wars (431–404 B.C.E.). The year the Peloponnesian Wars ended, which saw the defeat of Athens by Sparta, the Thirty Tyrants briefly suspended Athenian democracy. They were comprised of an oligarchy sympathetic to Sparta's own. In a mere eight months, up to five percent of the population of Athens were killed. Both Socrates (470–399 B.C.E.) and Aristotle (384–322 B.C.E.) lived their lives under Athenian democracy, but Plato's life (428–347 B.C.E.) began with Athens at war with Sparta, continued through the interruption of Athenian democracy, and then ended in the middle of a relatively stable period of Athenian democracy. Members of Plato's own family were part of the oligarchy that briefly suspended Athenian democracy.

Reliance on democratic governance during times of war can be frightening. When the Athenian city-state expressed a political will or committed to a course of action, it subjected each decision, including every court case, either to the governing body or to a portion of it. Either way, the group had to be convinced of the best decision in any given situation. Oratory skills therefore grew in importance, and with them the importance of language generally. In the case of Socrates, the effectiveness of oratory was literally a matter of life and death, so it's understandable that in this context the Sophists, who were masters of verbal manipulation, would be Socrates's favorite target. In this situation, how might Plato be positioned in relationship to his works? His *Republic*, a later dialogue that many scholars believe employs Socrates as a mouthpiece for Plato's own ideas, advocates for a centralized government in which leaders—who are called "guardians"—are divested of self-interest in their governing. They are not allowed to own land, possess wealth, or even have children or families of their own, as children among the ruling class are communally raised with no clear identification of paternity. Leaders who possess great wealth and a lineage, in Socrates's opinion, resemble statues with purple eyes: purple may well be the most beautiful color, but as an eye color it is grotesque.[10] Plato's Socrates has rejected democracy, but to mediate the negative features of an authoritarian government he divested his leaders of self-interest, so that these new rulers could serve as philosopher-guardians guided by reason in their disinterested pursuit of the good of all. Socrates's goal for his ideal republic is the attainment of the most beautiful form of the state, one in which the whole should be made harmonious and beautiful, so that the state is one rather than divided into rich and poor.

It's not difficult to read Plato's *Republic* against the background of his life. He could be defending the principle of centralized governance while establishing the conditions necessary for it to work, with caveats in *Republic* Book V that such a state could never really exist: "one might doubt whether what is proposed is possible and, even conceding the possibility, one might still be skeptical whether it is best."[11] While *Republic* doesn't emphasize the efficacy or implementation of such a government, it does stress education within Socrates's ideal republic: "neither the uneducated and uninformed of the truth, nor yet those who never make an end of their education, will be able ministers of State."[12] This passage follows the Allegory of the Cave, the primary educational allegory in Plato's corpus, which describes education in terms of different existential orientations, each one creating a different kind of soul. In this light, the Socratic irony of Plato's early dialogues, as well as the pronouncement about Socrates made by the oracle at Delphi, may be implicit critiques of democratic governance and of oratory only to be made explicit by the later dialogues. If Socrates alone is wise because he alone is aware of his ignorance, how can we trust the judgment of a democratic body? Plato's concern for education, therefore, is implicated in his tripartite view of the self, and the two of them together are bound up in his conception of the ideal republic, all of which converge on his desire to ban poets (literature), with democracy, from his ideal republic.[13] All these ideas seem to be heightened in importance in the context of two major wars and the stresses upon Athenian society caused by these wars.

But the place of literature itself in Athens must also be considered and, by extension, the act of reading. The Allegory of the Cave could represent three ways of reading: those who can only read shadows, those who read by direct firelight, and those who read by the divine light of the sun. In more concrete terms, to be educated during Plato's lifetime was to be taught to recite and memorize Homer, who was used as a source text not only for reading instruction, but also for a variety of subjects such as knowledge of good character, of the gods, of government, of war, and of history in ways similar to the use of the *King James Bible* in early America. Socrates's complaints about Homer and the poets in *Republic* focus primarily on the bad behavior of Homer's gods and heroes and on their management of emotions, but to Socrates the worst element of Homer's presentation of the gods is its emphasis on feeling over reason. Socrates's argument in *Republic* therefore criticizes the erotics of literature, represented by shadows on the cave wall in the Allegory, to replace them with the rational instruction provided by philosophy, represented by firelight and then, ultimately, by the true light of the sun. [14] In Plato's thinking, therefore, any shift away from democratic governance required a fundamental change in the *polis* that could only be brought about by a certain kind of education, one that displaced emotion to centralize reason.

The philosopher's progression toward death in *Phaedo* consists of an increasing separation from the body that has been carried out over the course of the philosopher's entire life, while *Crito* effectively rejects public opinion as a valid repository of truth in favor of one's own rational contemplation of the subject, so that between these two dialogues body and soul are rejected in favor of rational spirit as the basis of governance. The tripartite view of the soul, therefore, serves instrumental and political purposes in Plato's works. It identifies differing elements of the individual in order to establish a hierarchy extensible to the organization of a *polis*: body, and then soul (which can be defined as societally conditioned thought and feeling), should be subject to spirit (divine reason), which ultimately points back to our ability to apprehend Plato's ideal forms.

Only philosophy finally disciplines the body and teaches its adherents to live above society, to be guided only by divine light, and it is by means of philosophy that persons attain full individuality, Kierkegaard's "single individual," and perhaps also Derridean "freedom." For that reason, only a community of philosophers who have subjected themselves to continual symbolic deaths in the form of the loss of possessions and the loss of family can be trusted to govern once democracy has been jettisoned for centralized governance: this is the only way that reason can be placed at the head of the *polis*. Plato would therefore also believe an educational system that places philosophy (or cognition, the conceptual, *ideal forms* of every object, including the state) above literature (values, affect, national identity as determined by a historical narrative) can be trusted. Plato privileges the study of concepts, or ideal forms, above literary works that stress the emotional and material con-

texts of Greek life and society, employing literary form to create a phenomenology that suppresses literary works and, by doing so, suppresses affect.

Against this background, *Ion* establishes the fundamental existential oppositions guiding reading practices in Plato. Socrates closely cross-examines
Ion to determine if his recitations of Homer proceed from skill, *techne*, or
only from inspiration. The dialogue sarcastically concludes that Ion does not
know what he is doing, so he must be reciting Homer under a kind of divine
inspiration. Albert Rijksbaron's *Plato. Ion, or: On the* Iliad (2007) suggests
that *Ion* was composed around the same time as *Republic*, that Plato did not
anywhere express the possibility of a *techne* of poetry, and that he believed
pursuing the origins of poetic inspiration was in fact a waste of time: *Ion*
therefore constitutes a demonstration of these assertions.[15] I might add here
Jesper Svenbro's "Archaic and Classical Greece: The Invention of Silent
Reading," which asserts that because of the practice of oral reading, ancient
Greeks believed "the text is not a static object but the name given to a
dynamic relationship between writing and voice and between the person and
the reader."[16] He asserts that early Greeks associated reading aloud with
submission and, by extension, pederasty, the victim of which only retains his
dignity if he does not submit to being an instrument, as Ion apparently did.[17]
Svenbro concludes that this view of reading eventually dissipated with the
rise of the theater and its representations of silent reading.

Havelock, writing much earlier, indirectly reinforces Svenbro's claims,
asserting about Plato's argument in *Republic* that "the only safe and suitable
recipient of political power is the philosopher" is "a novelty."[18] Even more
importantly, Havelock claims Plato was trying to create a new kind of person: "In the *philo-sophos*, meaning a man who is instinctively drawn to
intellectualism and had an aptitude for it, Plato thought he saw a fresh human
type emerging from the society he knew."[19] Plato may have also had the
funeral speech of Pericles in mind, where Athenians are credited with being
able to "intellectualise without sacrifice of manliness."[20] Plato therefore distributed the opposition of manliness/reason with femininity/emotion across
the opposition of philosophy and poetry, and then banished poets from his
ideal republic. These values created a tension between the possibility of a
*techne* as opposed to an erotics of poetry distributed across appetitive and
rational responses to literature. If neither Socrates nor Plato desired to establish a *techne* of poetry, Aristotle's *Poetics* filled that gap, suggesting uses for
the erotics of literature that go beyond mere imitation into the management
of emotions themselves. *Poetics* manages emotions aesthetically, resulting in
catharsis, so that in Aristotle the Greek free man maintains his freedom
through his engagement with literature. Book II of *Rhetoric*, on the other
hand, manages emotions instrumentally, as a tool for functioning effectively
in a democracy. This tool has carried forward to the present across first year
college writing and business communication courses as instruction in *pathos*.

At this point it may be possible to hazard a definition of the theorizing activity itself, especially as it appears in the phrase "literary theory." I would begin by distinguishing theories from laws. Laws attempt to describe observable, regularly occurring sequences of events. A physical law would begin with the observation of an invariably occurring sequence of events, such as the Universal Law of Gravitation or the Second Law of Thermodynamics. A theory, on the other hand, posits a hidden source or cause of currently observable phenomena, such as the Big Bang theory or Freud's theory of the mind. Within literature and rhetoric, verbally oriented cultural products such as speeches and drama are the causes of predictable effects on audiences, effects described in Aristotle's *Rhetoric* and *Poetics*, respectively. These cause/effect relationships resemble laws more than theories in that they explain observable and regularly occurring patterns of audience responses as the effects of a variety of observable and easily manipulated constructions of drama or speeches. On the other hand, Socrates's linking of the sounds of words to their meaning via his concept of ideal forms in *Cratylus*—which in my opinion is a real low point in the dialogues—works more like a theory. It suggests an underlying, hidden cause explaining the observable phenomenon of language. Theory posits an occult origin of language concepts while laws posit a *techne* guiding their uses. Theoretical structures imply a depth psychology, and perhaps even create one: in Plato's case, it would be a depth psychology characterized by ideal psychic forms as its goal, while transition states resemble Id (body) and Superego (society). Laws, on the other hand, need only describe a description of events that regularly occur together: *this kind* of speech regularly prompts *that kind* of emotional response.

Considering the implications of introducing this anthropology into our historical discussion, we might accept that our reading practices as historical events are not machines operating independently of human thought or emotion. While we do not have to accept Plato's tripartite self as an objectively or scientifically valid anthropological model, it has had a profound influence on our reading practices since Plato's day. It is, I would argue, the origin of theory itself and the foundation of the traditional opposition between classicism and Romanticism, in which classicism constitutes a *techne* of language and Romanticism an erotics. Plato's triparition of the soul provides an underlying structure for both Origen's and Aquinas's hermeneutics, both of whom nevertheless rejected the concept of the tripartite self, and it similarly influences Dante's letter to Con Grande della Scala. It surfaces partially in Schiller, which was modified by Kierkegaard (aesthetic, ethical, religious subjectivities), and then it finds a materialist restatement in Freud's Id, Ego, and Superego, which uses it to identify brain structures produced by the brain's interactions with the body, with society, and then by a synthesis of the two. Therefore Plato's tripartition of the soul continues in theory in modified form via Freud, Lacan, and other depth psychologists, and from them in critical theory, which combines the insights of Marxism with psychoanalysis, and then to post-structuralists such as Derrida and Žižek who were influenced by both Freud and Lacan. But most importantly, Plato's tripartition of the soul accounts for the messiness of both history and our reading theories as they originate in differently motivated people reacting in different ways to diverse circumstances. Theory at times synthesizes the erotics and *techne* of reading to take control of our concepts of reading and, in so doing, our responses to the world around us, because whenever we open our eyes with the desire to understand, we begin to read: not passively, but actively, in a way that constitutes the world in which we live.

***

Tensions between democracy and centralization therefore provide historical context for the earliest western theories of reading, theories that were implicated from the beginning in an idealist philosophy. Plato's conscious attention to reading, speaking, and writing strategies originated in shifting iterations of an Athenian democracy under stress of war and in tension with oligarchy. His response was to develop a centralized concept of government that had the structure of an oligarchy but whose members were disinvested from economic and familial interests. The conditions of the United States and Europe following World War II resemble Plato's Greece: two major wars, in succession, both of them representing a significant wound upon the social psyche. Athens's defeat and the rise of the Thirty Tyrants is parallel to, on a much smaller scale, the increasingly horrifying and undeniable revelations about the Holocaust following World War II. In both cases the failure of democracy led to a mass slaughter, and in both cases authors directly affected by this history felt led to engage philosophic idealism.

Of course there are significant differences as well: we might, for example, substitute the word "plutocracy" for "oligarchy" to more precisely reflect conditions under global capitalism after World War II, which we will see serves as background for the major theorists of the 1960s and 1970s even more so than any events in the 1960s themselves. The conditions of democracy in tension with centralization in these two different periods, therefore, saw the rise of theoretical approaches to literature and with them focused attention on the teachings of Socrates, though they are separated by over 2000 years of history. The early works of Jacques Derrida, I will argue below, originates in the twenty-year period immediately following World War II, and given his long-term engagement with Plato, Derrida's writings can serve as an important and relatively recent point of comparison with Plato's works, as similar conditions gave rise to similar responses: a similar focus on Socrates, a similar engagement with philosophic idealism. The latter is especially important, as I will argue here that due to his early engagement with Husserl,

Derrida is best understood as a post-idealist philosopher before he is understood as a post-structuralist.

"Which Derrida?" becomes an important question at this point, similar to "which Plato?" There is, for one, Derrida the (American) literary theorist. This Derrida was created by his own presence at conferences and teaching in the United States, but he was also created by Gayatri Spivak's translation of Derrida's most important text, *Of Grammatology*, and especially by her lengthy introduction to that text. The Derrida of literary theory is an American cultural icon and, for some, a punching bag for "relativism" who is partially to blame for the decline of western humanities. The Derrida created by Spivak's introduction to *Of Grammatology* is the most important point of contact with Derrida for professors teaching literary interpretation at the college level in the United States—and I mean to place a deliberate emphasis on teaching and not scholarship—perhaps even more important than their own reading of Derrida's texts, especially during the 1970s and 1980s.

There are other Derridas, however. The Derrida I am concerned with is a precocious, then genius, Algerian Jew far too young for his accomplishments,[21] but above all else a philosopher, one whose most important work was concerned with western metaphysics. This other, younger Derrida was only secondarily concerned with literary texts, did not have any concept of himself as a "literary theorist," and was very concerned with the ways in which World War II and the Holocaust may have been the legacy of western metaphysics.[22] This Derrida became the subject of attention of professors of philosophy before any literary scholars read him. I will be writing about this Derrida—Derrida as a philosopher whose work engages the idealist tradition within philosophy from Plato to Husserl but who, like Plato, made claims with important ramifications for our understanding of reading and writing.

Because my approach to Derrida will attempt to uncover sociopolitical influences on the shape of his early philosophy, I will limit my discussion of his mentions of Plato to his published writings from 1954 to 1968, most of which will be focused on his 1953–1954 thesis, *The Problem of Genesis in Husserl's Philosophy*. Plato is largely background to his discussions of Husserl and structuralism during this period. Derrida's engagement with Plato begins indirectly with *The Problem of Genesis*, which was then followed up by his introduction to Husserl's "On the Origins of Geometry," published in 1962, and continued through his 1967 books to "Plato's Pharmacy," originally published in *Tel Quel* in 1968 and then collected in his book *Disseminations* in 1972. I don't believe it is coincidental that Derrida's full engagement with Plato occurred in 1968, a significant turning point in Derrida's life, and not only because of the student riots he witnessed in Paris that year. While he gained the attention of an international audience at Johns Hopkins University in 1966 with "Structure, Sign, and Play in the Discourse of the Human Sciences," that was still just a conference paper. He followed up this conference paper the very next year with the near simultaneous publication of three landmark books: *Writing and Difference, Speech and Phenomenon*, and *Of Grammatology*. These publications established Derrida as an international figure, transitioning him from a Parisian scholar and teacher to an international philosophical force. For better or worse, once the reactions to his 1967 books began to surface, he couldn't be ignored. After that point, Derrida had to deal with fame, infamy, invective, and misunderstanding he had not previously experienced in response to his work.

Benoit Peeters lists a number of watershed moments that converged in 1968 in *Derrida: A Biography*, including the death of Derrida's thesis supervisor, Jean Hyppolite. Hyppolite's death marked for Derrida "the end of [a] certain type of membership in the university."[23] While Derrida had already gained the attention of American scholars, after this point he was no longer primarily embedded in the French philosophical scene, which had gone from seeing him as "talented and promising" to being "a real pain" with the publication of his three 1967 books.[24] Derrida was also aware of this year as a kind of watershed for him, asserting in a paper presented at the 1968 conference *Philosophy and Anthropology* in New York that "every philosophical conference has a political significance . . . its very possibility is inseparable from the 'form of democracy.'"[25] The specific events Derrida mentioned at the time included the Vietnam peace talks, the assassination of Dr. Martin Luther King Jr., and the student riots in Paris that May.[26]

During the period of 1954 to 1968, Derrida transitioned from writing and publishing about Husserl while reading and teaching Heidegger in the background[27] to more explicitly engaging Heidegger in his published works. He established central concepts such as différance, deconstruction,[28] the trace, and the supplement through close readings of Husserl and other authors to deploy them in *Of Grammatology*. *Of Grammatology* should be read as the last of his 1967 publications in the sense that its chapters were written after his other works. He can be read as transitioning from a muted or background engagement with politics and democracy early in the period to more explicit discussions of it later, perhaps most importantly in the exergue to *Of Grammatology*. Peeters observes that throughout the period of 1953–1968 Derrida will remain hostile or indifferent to biography. As politics surface more and more in his writing, Derrida becomes less hesitant about biography, especially by the early 1990s and on to the end of his life. And he transitioned from an engagement with Plato primarily as background of the western philosophical tradition to his extended discussion of Plato in "Plato's Pharmacy," which I believe draws a kind of line under his deconstruction of western metaphysics, as if he had substantially completed a work that only needed to be nuanced.

While I feel justified setting up 1968 as a cutoff point,[29] it cannot of course be understood as an influence on writings published that year or before, so that the years leading up to 1968 are of more importance in defining formative interests. During this period, Derrida developed a deep ambivalence toward his homeland and toward democracy. He was born to a Sephardic Jewish family in French Algeria in 1930. He left Algeria at the age of nineteen to study in Paris, but before then experienced conflicts because of his composite French, Algerian, and Jewish identities, both in terms of his status as a French citizen in Algeria and as Jewish in a Nazi-occupied country. Over the course of his early life Algeria transitioned from a French colony in which he and his family could think of themselves as unambiguously French to a Nazi collaborationist state in which his Jewish identity conflicted with his status as a French citizen. It then became an independent and primarily Muslim state that experienced a mass exodus of Jews to France by 1962. The inauguration of an independent democracy in Algeria created a state almost as hostile to Jews as Vichy France,[30] where he witnessed firsthand the Vichy government's collaboration with Nazi occupation and, as a result of that collaboration, experienced being expelled from school at age twelve.

Influences on Derrida commonly asserted in scholarship include philosophy rather than literature as context for writers such as Steven Helmling, who claims that Derrida sweats "bullets confronting a mere [at the time] Foucault" but can be "cocky when stepping into the ring with Hegel."[31] Helmling argues that one's contest in philosophy is with contemporaries rather than, as Bloom asserted about literature, with predecessors. Other influences on Derrida registered in scholarship also extend to his Jewish heritage. He was ambivalent about this background, but it is an influence observed very early on and then developed by later scholarship. Roland Champagne sees in Derrida's "attraction to the works of Edmund Jabés and Emmanuel Levinas . . . a sympathy with the Judaic strains of deconstruction."[32] Geoffrey Bennington, in his section "The Jew" in *Jacques Derrida*, notes stylistic similarities between Derrida and some Talmudic writings. He believes such comparisons lead to conclusions that are "too simplistic," but his discussion of Derrida's engagement of Hegel and of the figure of the Jew in *Glas* makes deconstruction out to be a very Jewish "wandering in the desert" that "never announces the truth."[33]

Arguably, the most important formative influence on Derrida was indirectly related to his Jewish background: World War II and the Holocaust. In this area of scholarship, because Derrida was a contemporary of Foucault's and his student in Paris, historically oriented scholarship on Foucault can contribute to our understanding of Derrida's influences and vice-versa. Evan Carton's "The Holocaust, French Poststructuralism, the American Literary Academy, and Jewish Identity Poetics" establishes the Holocaust as general background for French Poststructuralism and for Derrida in particular. He generally claims for French post-structuralism that

French intellectuals . . . approach (and, arguably, sublimate) the Holocaust: as
the catastrophized product of modernity's politico-philosophical history, a history that mutually implicated France and Germany as it did abstract thought
and realized power, revolution and the state, and, ultimately, humanism and
totalitarianism. In this conceptual frame, moreover, Jews, the primary victims
of modern history, come to be figured as its limit—at once its unassimilable
other and its ineradicable and saving (though unsaved) internal principle of
resistance.[34]

Carton is here writing about French post-structuralism in general, but his
comments proceed from a discussion of the second paragraph of "Violence
and Metaphysics" (1963) in which Derrida claims that "the impossible has
*already* occurred."[35] Carton here explains Derrida's attraction to German
authors such as Hegel, Nietzsche, Husserl, and Heidegger, as they gave him a
way to understand France's "mutually implicated" history with Germany.
The "impossible" alluded to by Derrida is, according to Carton, the Holocaust, the great twentieth-century wound on western thought, feeling, and
philosophy. Carton sees a Holocaust reference in "Ellipsis" as well, another
chapter in *Writing and Difference* in which Derrida asks the question "Where
is the center?" and then answers, "Under ashes." Derrida quotes here the
Jewish-Egyptian poet Edmond Jabès, the subject of a separate chapter in the
same collection.[36] By 1987, Derrida would make explicit connections between the Holocaust and the concept of the trace,[37] but Derrida's earlier
references would have been clear to readers at the time.

   Karen Barber's "Michel Foucault and the Specters of War" establishes
explicit connections between Foucault's thought and the Holocaust that are
applicable to our understanding of Derrida's own background. In it, Barber
describes a telling and probably frustrating interview that Foucault suffered
though as the interviewer attempted to emphasize the 1960s as context for
Foucault's work:

> Undaunted, the interviewer remarks that Foucault tends to dismiss the events
> of May, and suggests that they were more formative to European politics and
> intellectual life than Foucault "would allow, indeed, several questions later, we
> find Trombadori [the interviewer] still inviting discussion on the centrality of
> May '68. The author, however, offers quite a different historical context for his
> work: 'The experience of the war (World War II) had shown us the urgent
> need of a society radically different from the one in which we were living, this
> society that had permitted Nazism, that had lain down in front of it, and that
> had gone over *en masse* to deGaulle.'"[38]

Derrida's work begins in the early 1950s and culminates—the first of several
culminations of his career—in 1967, so formative influences should be identified earlier in this period rather than later. Barber provides additional context for French experiences of the war, including willing collaboration with

the Nazis under Vichy, which led Foucault to accuse the French of lying down before the Nazis. This collaboration is emphasized in Peeter's biography of Derrida. DeGaulle rewrote this history, portraying the French as unwilling, innocent victims. According to deGaulle, France was "humiliated . . . martyrized . . . [but] Liberated by itself, by its own people with the help of the armies of France . . . of the true France."[39] Reference to a "true France" should have resonated with victims of Vichy, who used just that idea to exclude Jews from French identity.[40] The student riots of May 1968 should be understood as independent but similarly motivated responses to the historical milieu that produced Foucauldian order and archeology and Derridean deconstruction, their eruptions in philosophy anticipating eruptions in the streets as France began to confront its own history and complicity with evil. Derrida's philosophy therefore developed against the background of the Holocaust, which touched on his Jewish identity, alongside the background of French complicity with Nazi Germany, which touched on his French identity, leaving him deeply ambivalent about democracy.

The next step in our examination of Derrida is to read his engagement with idealism against the background of the Holocaust and its aftermath, which will involve a discussion of Husserl as the culmination of idealist thought (to Derrida) in western philosophy, Derrida's deconstruction of Husserl, and then his discussion in "Plato's Pharmacy" of Plato's use of the word *pharmakon*. In an article that contextualizes Derrida's work within the anticolonial struggle of northern Africa, John Mowitt asserts that "Derrida's reading [of Husserl] literally zigzags between Merleau-Ponty and Thao, passing back and forth over 'The Origin of Geometry.'"[41] I would like to borrow Mowitt's image of the zigzag to explain Derrida's discussion of idealism from 1954–1968 and make it a bit more concrete: it resembles to me a one-person game of ping pong. Husserl's works are the flat part of the table "over which" the game is being played, Derrida's thought is the ball bouncing back and forth, and Plato's works constitute the upright part of the table against which he plays his game. Throughout this period, Plato's works seem to be a fixed entity against which Derrida leverages his thought, so that when he deconstructs western metaphysics as it had culminated, for him, in Husserl, his next work was to deconstruct its origin—a term now fraught with difficulty after Derrida's early writing about Husserl—in Plato. It is of course a misnomer to say that Derrida deconstructed anything, or that any deconstruction is complete, but as we will see below saying so is later Derrida reflecting on the former Derrida. It is a position arrived at by 1967 that he had just initiated in 1953.

Peeters records that Derrida began his engagement with Husserl in 1953 with Ricœur's French translation of *Ideen 1*.[42] Ricœur was Derrida's way in to phenomenology, which represented a sustained philosophical commitment for him through all of his major writings. Derrida's 1962 Introduction to

Husserl's "Origin of Geometry" takes up 153 pages in the English translation while Husserl's essay itself is only 23 pages long, which gives us a sense of the intensity of Derrida's scrutiny of Husserl's work near the beginning of his academic career. This interest persisted throughout Derrida's career. As late as 1999, Derrida expressed a deep commitment to phenomenology: "There are many places where he [Levinas] says that we have to go phenomenologically beyond phenomenology. That is what I am trying to do, also. I remain and want to remain a rationalist, a phenomenologist."[43] Derrida began with remarkable hopes for his study of Husserl, as illustrated by this passage from his thesis, *The Problem of Genesis in Husserl's Philosophy*:

> Better, we propose to show that it is only from Husserl on, if not explicitly with him, that the great dialectical theme which animates and motivates the most powerful philosophical tradition from Platonism to Hegelianism can be renewed, or if not renewed then at least rounded, authenticated, and completed.[44]

Derrida brackets western philosophy from Plato to Hegel as part of a continuous tradition of philosophy that is both "completed" and "renewed" by Husserlian phenomenology, so that with Husserl western metaphysics can begin again, both fulfilling its past promise and moving forward on new ground.

Husserl's phenomenology—his idealism—broke with the previous tradition of western philosophy by being grounded in individual sense perception and by having a materialist basis. "Origin of Geometry" is a late text of Husserl's that serves as a kind of test case for his mature phenomenology, one that relates to the history of western idealism through Plato's *Meno*. In that dialogue, Socrates attempts to demonstrate that knowledge is recollection by drawing figures on the ground and asking an uneducated slave boy questions about geometry. Socrates argues from the slave boy's success in answering his questions that knowledge is "recollection" in the sense that the slave boy had encountered ideal forms prior to birth, during a period after his last incarnation but before his current life, and that his mind retained a memory of ideal forms that could be prompted through Socrates's conversation with the boy. Ideal forms are located in an externalized heaven in Socrates, and we apprehend them either through recollection or the divine faculty of reason.

Derrida presents Husserl's phenomenology as grounded instead upon the "concrete lived experience of a transcendental subjectivity, constituting [the] source and foundation of essences."[45] Note that while this subjectivity is "transcendental," phenomenology is still based upon "concrete lived experience." I want to emphasize, however, that both Husserl and Derrida distinguish between "psychologism" and "phenomenology." Psychologism is a study of the sensory activity of the human mind, of how it forms sense perception from sense data, and of how that activity constructs human consciousness and its experience of the world. Derrida explains that Husserl started his career with psychologism, but one that from the beginning "had recourse to the a priori idea of an 'object in general.'"[46] In a very important way, Derrida's primary concepts originated in this early engagement with Husserl, for whom the mind deals with representation rather than directly with material reality.

If we were to abstract ideal forms from these sense perceptions in the way that drawings of triangles are abstracted from physical objects, and the concept of a triangle is abstracted from that abstraction, then we would have something of a sense of the *eidos*, or idea, in Husserl's use of the term, and this abstraction is in the end a non-human object. Husserl's *eidos* is fundamentally bound up with perception in a psychological sense, however: it is never separated from it. Husserl calls this process of abstraction the "transcendental" or "phenomenological" reduction. The transcendental subject is constructed from these ideas. These ideal forms don't exist independently of the mind forming them, however, as do Plato's ideal forms, but they are instead innately bound up with the sense perception of the object: "The essences were thus not platonic ideas in the conventional sense of the word; they had no sense nor any foundation 'in itself' independent of intentional acts [of the individual mind] that aimed at them."[47] Developing that concept of the idea was, for Husserl, doing the work of phenomenology.

Because sense perception is always based upon the mind's construction of sensory data, one that involves a miniscule time lag between the existence of the object in the moment and the construction of its image in the mind, Derrida could very famously say in *Of Grammatology* that "there is nothing outside the text."[48] All of consciousness is representation. Consciousness is, therefore, an extended act of reading. The idea that consciousness is a kind of textuality is reinforced by Husserl's idea of protention and retention, which further implicates time in the construction of human consciousness. We do not *only* observe, even in our immediate consciousness, the momentary instant of time defined as the "present." If that were true, we wouldn't be able to listen to music, as all that we would ever perceive is the briefest fragment of a note. Instead, our *immediate* sense perception is made up of our *retention* of immediately past sensory data combined with immediately *anticipatory* sense perception, or protention—the kind of perception, for example, that allows us to catch a ball thrown at us. Both ideas are distinct from what we usually mean by memory and anticipation: memory is recollection in the form of a sense image of a complete object or act from the past, while prediction or anticipation usually refers to a picturing in the future, either near or distant, of a completed action or anticipated object. Protention and retention are versions of memory and anticipation that allow us to constitute our *immediate* sensory environment coherently.

But, in all cases, Derrida observes that we are dealing with forms of representation, and all the more so when Husserl makes recourse to writing as the means of transmitting ideal forms from one generation to the next. Derrida dealt with this topic in Section VII of his Introduction to Husserl's "Origin of Geometry," saying that in Husserl the "possibility of writing will assure the absolute traditionalization of the object, its absolute ideal Objectivity—i.e., the purity of its relation to a universal transcendental subjectivity. Husserl's phenomenology is a way of structuring the forms of representation that make up consciousness."[49] Derrida therefore drew from Husserl, even at this early date, that writing constitutes both human psychology and phenomenology.

While we are used to thinking of Derrida as a post-structuralist because of his engagement with Jean Rousset, Saussure, and Claude Levi-Strauss, from the start Derrida understood Husserl's phenomenology, or his idealism, as a kind of structuralism. In "Force and Signification," Derrida describes idealism as a kind of interior structure: "Thus, the notion of an Idea or 'interior design' as simply anterior to a work which would supposedly be the expression of it, is a prejudice: a prejudice of the traditional criticism called idealist."[50] An "Idea" here is equal to an "interior design" or structure that underlies the external expression of a work of some kind. This way of thinking, we will see, originates in Derrida's early work on Husserl. When Derrida first introduces the problem of the origin in Husserl, he asks, "Without recourse to an already constituted logic, how will the temporality and subjectivity of transcendental lived experience engender and found objective and universal eidetic structures?"[51] Shortly after asking this question, Derrida will define Husserl's *eidos*, or idea, as constituting a structure, a description he will repeat over and over again in his introduction. For this reason Derrida is post-idealist before he is post-structuralist, or better, his post-structuralism is a subset of his post-idealism.

We could add that the simultaneous constructedness of both "lived experience" and the "transcendental I" is at the root of what Derrida sees as the problem of origins in Husserl's geometry, which will lead us to the political implications of Derrida's thought in his discussion of human freedom, which at this point is purely conceptual and internal:

> Lived experience is empirical, constructed by an I, one that is transcendental according to formal categories. It [lived experience] is thus not originary. In the same way, the originary transcendental I is not a piece of lived experience. Effective genesis is thus cut off from all transcendental originality.[52]

Derrida describes his first aporia in this thesis, his first irreconcilable contradiction: the origin cannot be originary. We might say that he has here deconstructed his first text. It is in this first deconstruction that we can observe the germ of political implications for Derrida's work:

> Freedom and absolute subjectivity are thus neither in time nor out of time. The dialectical clash of opposites is absolutely "fundamental" and is situated at the origin of all meaning; thus, it must be reproduced at every level of transcendental activity and of the empirical activity founded thereon. [53]

This originary aporia, this "dialectical class of opposites," is already "at the origin of all meaning" and "reproduced at every level of the transcendental activity and of *the empirical activity founded thereon.*" Anything that encompasses "every level" of the transcendental I and then, by extension, all *empirical* activity must by its nature define all human cognition. Because Derrida defines human cognition as a clash of opposites, and he says it takes this form because of the dual nature of both "freedom and absolute subjectivity," Derrida's early deconstruction of Husserl's idealism—Husserl's structuralism—was carried out to preserve the conditions of human freedom. It did so by first asserting freedom as a fact and then defining the aporias of the structure created by Husserl's idealism as proceeding from the fact of freedom. He was establishing the phenomenology of freedom, of self-governance, or of democracy.

But as we see from the quotation from "Force and Signification" above, Derrida's critique of idealism is not limited to Husserl. It extends back to Plato and forward to French structuralism: "Rousset too runs the risk of conventional Platonism." [54] And, from the beginning, Derrida registered an aporia about the ability of the transcendental reduction to achieve transcendence:

> We run up here against a serious ambiguity in the concept of "world." On the one hand, the world is the antepredicative in its actual "reality." Always already there, in its primitive ontological structure, it is the preconstituted substrate of all meaning. But on the other hand, it is the idea of an infinite totality of possible foundations of every judgment. In it are opposed the actuality of existence as substrate and the infinite possibility of transcendental experiences. [55]

"World" is that which is external to the human subject, so it must include the realm of the political, and it is caught up in its own aporia as it is both what precedes everything we encounter and defines its future possibility. It lies before us and ahead of us, but we are never with it, just between its two realities. Is Derrida only describing an insurmountable contradiction created by terms that are dialectical in nature, or is he also registering an anxiety about the intrusion of world into consciousness via a never too pure idealism? Is the problem that a Husserlian reduction in a post-Holocaust context is never reductive enough? The world intruding upon the Husserlian idea was, for Derrida, the world that produced a Holocaust.

Most of Derrida's references to Plato until 1968 take the form of the quotation about Rousset above: Plato represents a kind of fixed structure that authors either do or do not escape. Rousset does not escape the structure, while Husserl seems to, but only to flounder in newly created aporias. Derrida reserved his first full deconstruction of Plato's works for "Plato's Pharmacy," an article he composed in 1968 focused on Plato's *Phaedrus* originally published across two issues of *Tel Quel*. Much of Derrida's discussion focuses on Plato's use of the Greek word *pharmakon*, which means simultaneously both "cure" and "poison": "Pharmacia (*Pharmakeia*) is also a common noun signifying the administration of the *pharmakon*, the drug: the medicine and/or poison."[56] The fundamental characteristic of *pharmakon* is for Derrida its undecidability, or its introduction of différance to any discourse within which it appears.

Derrida goes on to observe how Socrates uses this word to describe writing: "Only a little further on, Socrates compares the written texts Phaedrus has brought along to a drug (pharmakon)."[57] From that point, Derrida can draw in idealism itself to the concept of *pharmakon*: "The *eidos*, truth, law, the *epistēmē*, dialectics, philosophy—all these are other names for that *pharmakon* that must be opposed to the *pharmakon* of the Sophists and to the bewitching fear of death."[58] Note the appearance of "eidos" in the list. Pharmakon therefore occupies a unique position according to Derrida, serving as a concept in Plato's writings that stands in for writing, then idealism, and then philosophy itself. This dual nature of *pharmakon* and its place in Plato's works gives it a privileged position in western philosophy:

> [*Pharmakon*] is rather the prior medium in which differentiation in general is produced, along with the opposition between the *eidos* and its other; this medium is analogous to the one that will, subsequent to and according to the decision of philosophy, be reserved for transcendental imagination, that "art hidden in the depths of the soul," which belongs neither simply to the sensible nor simply to the intelligible, neither simply to passivity nor simply to activity.[59]

Derrida, true to form, performs quite a bit of work with a single concept: the position that he assigns to *pharmakon* allows it to destabilize western metaphysics at its base. This work involves a chain of significations that implicates writing, idealism, philosophy, and then the "transcendental imagination" itself, the very faculty that creates the self, with an unstable, already deconstructed term, *pharmakon*.

I think that the *pharmakon* here points to the real work that Derrida is doing with his central terms. We might refer back to Spivak briefly: "The movement of 'difference-itself, precariously saved by its resident contradiction,' has many nicknames: trace, difference, reserve, supplement, dissemination, hymen, greffe, pharrnakon, parergon, and so on."[60] We might add "deconstruction" to the list, so that all of these terms invoke the deferral or the delay of meaning—and remember our earlier discussion of time in immediate perception as part of this delay—and thus destabilize the *eidos* itself at the ground of phenomenology. Derrida's work performs a clearing function for the self, one he later terms a *khôra* in his engagement with Plato's *Timaeus* after 1968, a kind of *kenosis* of human subjectivity. Derrida therefore recreates or reconceives of the human self, or at least self-consciousness in the moment, as an unselfconscious emptying of meaning caught forever in the unrest of aporia: a continual process of emptying that keeps the self from stabilizing in any one environment, which would be hostile to human freedom. It is interesting to me that Socrates also says about the scroll that Phaedrus was carrying, which was written by Lysias, as *being* "Lysias himself": "much as I love you I am not altogether inclined to let you practice your oratory on me when Lysias himself is here present. Come now, show it me."[61] Socrates prefers to hear the words of Lysias from the scroll rather than from Phaedrus's own re-presentation of Lysias's arguments, or in other words, he asks Lysias to submit himself to Phaedrus's text by reading it aloud. Writing is both absence and presence, and readers exist in the space between those two terms, in a continual state of aporia. Like Calvino's author, he wishes he were absent so that he could write.

Creating a self that is neither absent nor present, Derrida empties the self of stable content not because he is anti-humanistic or a misanthrope. I believe he does so because the *eidos* is forever impure, infected with the horrors of history, and because his personal history was clouded by the ashes of a Holocaust, and this clearing of the self fulfills the final goal of phenomenology, the reduction. All objects of human consciousness are removed from the immediate, the moment, if only by the slightest instant, and in that instant of removal the self experiences freedom: conceptual, cognitive, personal, political. Persons who do not fix themselves in absolute forms preserve both their own freedom and the freedom of others. Derrida's thought seems to follow the pattern of Romantic irony Kierkegaard describes in *On the Concept of Irony*, in which positions are adopted only to reject previous positions, but then rejected for future positions, so that the self is in a continual process of destabilization. Derrida, however, is not just deconstructing idealism, or structuralism, or the self. Derrida's thought is closer to Kierkegaardian ethical irony, which Kierkegaard identified with Socrates, as through deconstruction he creates an empty space for the possibility of a self that fascism cannot pervert into committing future atrocities. Derrida has a notion of the good, one that is implicit in his 1953–1968 works in their emphasis on freedom. Where Plato embraced his own version of idealism to save the Athenian city-state from the liabilities of democracy and guarantee the success of a centralized government, Derrida deconstructed idealism to save the self from successful centralized governments and their ensuing horrors.

Plato and Derrida therefore represent opposite polarities of idealist thought, a current alternating around the axis of totalitarianism, one shifting toward totalitariasm to serve an ideal form of the state, the other shifting away from it to preserve the democratic, or free, individual. Derrida, late in his career, will finally define democracy as a system of government continually in crisis so that, presumably, the work of deconstruction must continually be carried out.

## NOTES

1. See the Introduction to this anthology for an explanation of the figure/concept dialectic described in Andrew Cole's *The Birth of Theory* (Chicago: University of Chicago Press, 2014).

2. Benoit Peeters, *Derrida: A Biography* (Cambridge, UK: Polity Books, 2016), 33. Despite the very early influence of Kierkegaard on Derrida, Derrida did not extensively engage Kierkegaard until his relatively late book *The Gift of Death* (1996). I can't consider the possible reasons for this decision here, but I will observe that Derrida seems to be following a pattern common to Heidegger, Adorno, Sartre, and other authors.

3. See James Rovira, *Blake and Kierkegaard: Creation and Anxiety* (London: Continuum, 2010) for a development of this idea.

4. Necip Fikri Alican, *Rethinking Plato: A Cartesian Quest for the Real Plato* (New York: Rodopi, 2012); see also Richard Kraut, *The Cambridge Companion to Plato* (Cambridge, UK: Cambridge University Press, 1992).

5. Stefan Büttner, "The Tripartition of the Soul in Plato's *Republic*," in *New Essays on Plato: Language and Thought in Fourth-Century Greek Philosophy*, edited by Fritz-Gregor Hermann (Swansea, UK: The Classical Press of Wales, 2006), pp. 75–94.

6. Alican, 485.

7. Rovira, chapter 3, *Blake and Kierkegaard.*

8. For example, see Steven Gormley: "After outlining the kind of reading that overlooks these aspects of Derrida's work (Section I), I turn to the concept of experience (Section II). Here I try and show that Derrida, from his early through to his later works, is engaged in a project of rearticulating the concept of experience, and this, while overlooked by friends and critics alike, is vital if we are to understand the ethico-political demands of deconstruction" (375). Steven Gormley, "Rearticulating the Concept of Experience, Rethinking the Demands of Deconstruction," in *Research in Phenomenology* vol. 42 (2012): 374–407. Gormley also argues in this article that the concept of experience in Derrida is vital to understanding his discussions of democracy in his later works. See also Peggy Kamuf, "The Experience of Deconstruction," in *Agelaki: Journal of Theoretical Humanities* vol. 4, no. 3 (1999), 3–14.

9. Jacques Derrida, "Letter to a Japanese Friend," *Everything2*, 25 April 2002, accessed 22 June 2018, https://www.everything2.com/title/Letter+to+a+Japanese+Friend+by+Jacques+Derrida. Patterns of capitalization follow the source text.

10. All references to or quotations of Plato's works are taken from the following: Edith Hamilton and Huntington Cairns, eds., *The Collected Dialogues of Plato, Including the Letters*, Bollingen Series LXXI (Princeton: Princeton University Press, 1961), *Republic*, Book IV.

11. Ibid., 689.

12. Ibid., Book VII.

13. Belief in a tripartite self became a minority view within Catholicism no later than the ninth century (see the current *Catechism of the Catholic Church*: Section 2, Chapter 1, Article 1, Paragraph 6.II.362–8), which came to see soul and spirit as two words for the same entity. It continued as a minority position possibly held by Luther, currently held by some groups originating in the dissenting tradition, and certainly held by Kierkegaard, who used it as an organizing principle for *Concept of Anxiety* as he structures his discussion of anxiety around the principles of *soma*, *psyche*, and *pneuma*, not to mention his concepts of the aesthetic, ethical, and religious that permeate his works and the opening pages of *Sickness Unto Death*.

14. See especially Penelope S. Murray, ed., *Plato on Poetry* (New York: Cambridge University Press, 1996).

15. Albert Rijksbaron, *Plato. Ion, or: On the* Iliad (Boston: Brill, 2007).

16. Jesper Svenbro, "Archaic and Classical Greece: The Invention of Silent Reading," in *A History of Reading in the West*, edited by Guglielmo Carvallo and Roger Chartier, trans. Lydia G. Cochrane (Amherst: University of Massachusetts Press, 1999), 45.

17. Ibid., 45.

18. Eric A. Havelock, *Preface to Plato* (Cambridge, MA: The Belknap Press of Harvard University Press, 1963), 13.

19. Ibid., 286.

20. Ibid.

21. Derrida was only 23 when he began writing *The Problem of Genesis in Husserl's Philosophy*. At this age, he would have been, typically, a first year graduate student in the United States.

22. I will be engaging in this chapter McGowan's claim that Derrida's work "is fundamentally the deconstruction of phenomenology, not of metaphysics, and grasping this allows us to accomplish a return to the metaphysical questions that the last two centuries of thought seemed to have put to bed" (96). See Todd McGowan, "The Presence of Phenomenology: Hegel and the Return to Metaphysics," *Mosaic* 46, no. 1 (March 2013), 95–111.

23. Peeters, 230.

24. Ibid., 189.

25. Ibid., 202.

26. Ibid.

27. See Jacques Derrida's notes to his 1964–1965 lectures on Heidegger in Jacques Derrida with Geoffrey Bennington, trans., *The Question of Being and History* (Chicago: The University of Chicago Press, 2016).

28. The process of deconstruction was initially referred to as a "dialectic" and then called "deconstitution" before Derrida settled on the term "deconstruction."

29. See also Peter Helmling, who asserts that he wants "to confront early Derrida with late (or later), which, for my purposes here, means Derrida before 1968 and after" (1). "Historicizing Derrida," *Postmodern Culture* vol. 4, no. 3 (May 1994). Helmling sees 1968 as marking a change from an early Derrida characterized by "'free play' and 'infinite interpretation' [as] projects of liberation" to "steady-state pathos, the 'frozen dialectic' of his mature writing" (3).

30. See especially Lee Morrissey, who asserts that "it is important to note that of an estimated 140,000 Jews in Algeria before the outbreak of the war in 1954, only 10,000 remained by 1962, and by 1970, that number had dropped to 1,000 with only one Talmud Torah in the entire country. And this drop, in most cases, was precipitous as Independence approached: 'whereas in 1961 as many as 22,000 Jews lived in Oran, during the summer of 1962 only 1,000–5,000 remained.'" See "'Nostalgeria' and 'Structure, Sign, and Play in the Discourse of the Human Sciences,'" in *Historicizing Theory*, edited by Peter Herman (New York: SUNY Press, 2004), 105.

31. Helmling, 12.

32. Roland A. Champagne, *Jacques Derrida* (New York: Twayne Publishers, 1995), 56. See also chapter 6 of John Caputo's *Deconstruction in a Nutshell: A Conversation with Jacques Derrida* (New York: Fordham University Press, 1997).

33. Geoffrey Bennington and Jacques Derrida, *Jacques Derrida* (Chicago: The University of Chicago Press, 1997), 297. See also Geoffrey Hartman, *Minor Prophecies: The Literary Essay in the Culture Wars* (Cambridge, MA: Harvard University Press, 1991).

34. Evan Carton, "The Holocaust, French Poststructuralism, the American Literary Academy, and Jewish Identity Poetics," in *Historicizing Theory*, edited by Peter Herman (Albany, NY: SUNY Press, 2003), 23.

35. Jacques Derrida, *Writing and Difference* (Chicago: The University of Chicago Press, 1978), 80.

36. Ibid., 24.

37. Ibid.

38. Karen Barber, "Michel Foucault and the Specters of War," in *Historicizing Theory*, edited by Peter Herman (Albany, NY: SUNY Press, 2003), 51.

39. Ibid., 53.

40. See Peeters, chapters 1 and 2, especially Derrida saying that "Giraud's [who followed Vichy] only plan was to renew and extend the Vichy decrees and ensure that Algerian Jews were still seen as 'native Jews'" (22). It should be noted that Peeters describes an Algerian government even more aggressively anti-Semitic than the French government to which they answered. Derrida identifies this period as the beginning of his ambivalence toward his Jewish background, saying that "On the one hand, I was deeply wounded by anti-Semitism. And this wound has never completely healed. At the same time, paradoxically, I could not tolerate being 'integrated' into this Jewish school, this homogeneous milieu that reproduced and in a certain way countersigned. . . the terrible violence that had been done to it" (20–21).

41. John Mowitt, "Reason thus Unveils Itself," *Mosaic* 40, no. 2 (June 2007), 185.

42. Peeters, 65.

43. Jacques Derrida, qtd. in John Llewelyn, "Approaches to (Quasi) Theology via Appresentation," *Research in Phenomenology* 39 (2009), 226.

44. Jacques Derrida and Martin Hobson, trans., *The Problem of Genesis in Husserl's Philosophy* (Chicago: University of Chicago Press, 2003), xxi.

45. Ibid., 2.

46. Ibid., 1.

47. Ibid., 2.

48. Jacques Derrida and Gayatri Chakravorty Spivak, trans., *Of Grammatology* (Baltimore: Johns Hopkins University Press, 1976), 163.

49. Jacques Derrida and John P. Leavy Jr., trans., *Edmund Husserl's Origin of Geometry: An Introduction* (Lincoln: University of Nebraska Press, 1989), 87.

50. Jacques Derrida and Alan Bass, trans., *Writing and Difference* (Chicago: The University of Chicago Press, 1978), 11.

51. Derrida, *Problem of Genesis*, 2.

52. Ibid., 14.

53. Ibid., 65.

54. Derrida, *Writing and Difference*, 14.

55. Derrida, *Problem of Genesis*, 110.

56. Jacques Derrida and Barbara Johnson, trans., *Disseminations* (London: The Athlone Press, 1981), 70.

57. Ibid.

58. Ibid., 124.

59. Ibid., 126.

60. Derrida, *Of Grammatology*, lxx.

61. Hamilton and Cairns, 477.

## Chapter Two

# Historian, Forgive Us

*Study of the Past as Hegel's Methodology of Faith*

## Aglaia Maretta Venters

Scholarship devoted to analysis of the works of Georg Wilhelm Friedrich Hegel (1770–1831) has raised questions about how his method of reading history related to his sorrow over the grisly failures of the French Revolution. As Rebecca Comay argues, Hegel perceived that the secularism of French leaders during the Reign of Terror became at once a fight against the hold of "superstition" over the people and a tool of blind "fanaticism" as insidious as the religious culture it was intended to defeat.[1] Howard Kainz suggests that Hegel's philosophy of history from the close of the French Revolution to the end of his life allowed Hegel to ascertain fully the philosophic meaning of his faith and the advantages of Protestant morality for society.[2] Glenn Alexander Magee interprets the implications of Hegel's philosophy beyond practical, social concerns and found in them an attempt to globalize the quest for the human actualization of God.[3]

This chapter will investigate the impact of the French Revolution, Protestant doctrine, and Hegel's consideration of the divine in the development of his philosophy of history. It will explore Hegel's eagerness to determine how and why the promise of the French Revolution took its course. It will also examine the significance of the strains that tangible experience of the French Revolution placed upon Hegel's commitment to German Lutheran teachings on the forgiveness of human shortcomings as critical for salvation. This chapter will then demonstrate that Hegel's reading of history subsequently evolved from his understanding of the concept of human striving over time: humanity simultaneously and cyclically advances and fails, perpetually trying to correct the mistakes of past generations while leaving the future to make amends for its own failures. Consequently, Hegel's processing of the violent events in Europe during the last decade of the eighteenth century was the beginning of his quest to forgive humanity and its world, which led him to develop his theory of history throughout the remainder of his life. One of the most important results of his endeavors to accept the human world lay in the evolution of Hegel's theory of history into his methodology for achieving forgiveness beyond religion and its doctrines. Finally, this chapter will argue that knowledge, forgiveness, and reconciliation of opposing sides (faith vs. reason, good vs. evil) became the fulfillment of Hegel's purpose in his study of history.

Students of philosophy, literature, theology, political science, and history find inspiration in their attempts to understand Hegel's methods of reading history. One question for scholars revolves around the role of "dialectic" in Hegel's study of history, for which the philosopher is most often remembered. While J. M. Fritzman reminds us that dialectic was not the total sum of Hegel's work, Charles Taylor emphasizes that Hegel used dialectic in the study of history to gain insight into great philosophical questions that had vexed humanity for millennia.[4] Other recurring themes in scholarship on Hegelian philosophy have involved understanding the connections that Hegel saw between history and morality. Herbert Marcuse, for instance, in the 1930s studied the meaning of Hegel's concept of "Spirit" as a collective force throughout the universe, which included humanity.[5] Alexandre Kojève's work in the first half of the twentieth century explains that Hegel's reading of history allowed him to part with western philosophy's strict insistence on rational structure for all of the world, which allowed the great thinker to see connections between human history and morality.[6]

As the role of morality in Hegel's ideas for the study of history intrigued later scholars, some debated the primacy of the role of religion in the formation of his morality. Howard Kainz, H. S. Harris,[7] and Peter C. Hodgson[8] argue that Hegel's commitment to Protestantism lurked behind his moral code and its role in his study of history, while Rebecca Comay sees the failure of the French Revolution as the catalyst for the philosopher's grand conclusions about human life. Other scholars have contended that Hegel did not separate religion from secular concerns when considering connections between morality and history. Though many have seen Hegel as antagonistic toward the Catholic Church, Andrew Cole found that his philosophies were extensions of long-standing western traditions of thought, many of which were influenced by the polemics of medieval Europe.[9] Some scholars have preferred to regard Hegel's mixture of his moral code and his study of history as having practical implications for human interactions, such as Francis Fukuyama's use of Hegelian dialectic to question ways in which humans pronounce judgment upon each other.[10]

Many scholars also have described Hegel's use of history as a comment on humanity's teleological development into a happy world of freedom and moral justice. The teleological implications of Hegel's study of history have appeared as arguments in the works of scholars such as Glenn Alexander Magee, Will Dudley, Stephen B. Smith, Hans Küng, Daniel Berthold-Bond, Joshua Foa Dienstag, Leon J. Goldstein, Terry Pinkard, Catherine Malabou, and Joachim Ritter.[11] Finally, some scholars (Teshale Tibebu, Joseph McCarney, and Manfred Riedel, for example) have revised the aim of their studies of Hegel's teleological vision of future happiness for humanity to refocus on his place within a western system of thought which continues to prioritize rationality as the basis for human progress.[12]

The conclusions offered by the works of these scholars remain valuable contributions to our understanding of Hegel's philosophy of history. Particularly intriguing is Hegel's suggestion that forgiveness is part of the moral code that he joined to his philosophy of history. Indeed, his ideas about the meaning of forgiveness and about participants and their roles in this process are elements of historical theory that require new discussion for the insights they provide. Squeamishness to adopt the issue of forgiveness (as Hegel had advocated in his philosophy) as a critical reality within the study of history places unfortunate limitations on understanding Hegel. I seek to demonstrate that Hegel's purpose was to assert that maintaining the perspective of forgiveness throughout all phases of reading and studying history opens up possibilities for achieving human self-acceptance and self-actualization. By understanding and applying Hegel's philosophy of history, the living may comprehend that regarding generations past with resentment aggravates the pains of adversarial relationships among people, which in turn impedes the human pursuit of self-knowledge. Reading and analyzing history from a forgiving viewpoint and with an intent to achieve forgiveness has the potential to release historians from adversarial relationships with their subjects, allowing new knowledge to arise through new connections to the past.

During his youth (before his university career began in Jena in 1801), Hegel was preoccupied by the problem of forgiveness of sins until he came to accept that human beings are dependent upon God for redemption.[13] Questions that could not be answered by his knowledge and reasoning gave Hegel the opportunity to find in his philosophy of history a way to address his intellectual discomfort. He knew that humanity was both evil and good, as evidenced by its connection with imperfect (but redeemable) nature, and he came to the conclusion that reconciliation of these opposites through the study of history would help the world to develop.[14] His philosophy served as his plan for realization of Lutheran doctrines of human experience as a struggle through the temporal world, yet reconnecting to God.[15]

As he contemplated European history as it unfolded around him, particularly after the disaster (as he saw it) of the French Revolution, Hegel theorized in his early work (particularly *Phenomenology of Spirit*, published in 1807) that humans never would overcome the evil within themselves, and knowledge of this truth was more beneficial for the world than steadfast insistence on goodness alone. Self-consciousness encompassed the acknowledgment of its antithesis, the "objective reality" in the concrete world; guilt is the result of "seizing one-side of the essence and adopting a negative attitude toward the other, i.e., violating it."[16] Hegel insisted that humanity should not do violence to itself by trying to suppress or hate any side of any contradiction within the world. Instead, he advocated for a resolution of the adversarial relationship between antinomies. Humanity must accept, and forgive, sides of itself considered undesirable (including selfishness), without harsh judgment. In *Phenomenology of Spirit*, Hegel reasons that

> confession is not an abasement, a humiliation, a throwing-away of himself in relation to the other; for this utterance is not a one-sided affair, which would establish his disparity with the other: on the contrary, he gives himself utterance solely on account of his having seen his identity with the other.[17]

Because no side of any paradox in the human world was completely separate from the other, because sameness and difference were not absolute, mutual identification in the process of reconciling these sides was expected. Hegel was able to argue that seeking forgiveness would prove a vehicle for humans to understand themselves from both perspectives. When human beings see themselves from the perspectives of the good and evil within (and the good and evil of others with whom they might be reconciled) and open their minds to self-awareness, the same knowledge allows Spirit to come to know itself.

As he witnessed and then tried to understand the disasters of his time, Hegel was able to conclude that his dialectic, his study of history, and his warning for others to accept all of their contradictions converged into a strategy for working through many of life's conflicts. Hegel saw that survivors of violent historical events could become judge, victim, and abuser at the same time, thereby allowing humans to forgive and to learn much about the individual's guilt in contributing to the world's troubles.[18] Since the goal of history was for Spirit to know itself, Hegel intended for students of history to see themselves. Upon seeing themselves, and reconciling with themselves and others, historians' perpetual self-inflicted violence would cease. Humanity consequently would learn how to stop perpetuating pain.

History, as Hegel came to conceive of it, was the avenue by which humanity could reach self-acceptance. As Spirit and humanity advanced, world growth could occur. Hegel explains in *Phenomenology of Spirit*,

> Just as the realm of the real world passes over into the realm of faith and insight, so does absolute freedom leave its self-destroying reality and pass over into another land of self-conscious Spirit where, in this unreal world, freedom has the value of truth. In the thought of this truth Spirit refreshes itself. . . . There has arisen the new shape of Spirit, that of the *moral* Spirit.[19]

Hegel distinguishes between absolute freedom in a temporal or real sense, which contains within it its demise, and the true freedom that comes with an existence beyond the present-day world yet attainable by humanity. Indeed, he distrusted cries for absolute freedom in the temporal sense because he believed the French Revolution's failure rested in this self-destructive ideal. He uses the French Revolution as an example to admonish the world against absolute freedom in *Lectures on the Philosophy of History*:

> In large empires . . . diverse and conflicting interests are sure to present themselves. . . . In the French Revolution, therefore, the republican constitution never actually became a democracy: tyranny, despotism, raised its voice under the mask of freedom and equality. [20]

Seeing earthly freedom as impossible, Hegel saw ideal freedom for the world as a part of Spirit's transcendence into virtuous existence, which came from self-knowledge. Self-knowledge required humanity to forgive and to be vulnerable enough to be forgiven by self and others. Forgiveness made reconciliation, a choice which united people, possible. Hegel's line of thought became clear: Spirit lurked within and outside of the individual while it chased a dream of transcendent growth, and it was expressed in human thought. Hegel had set humanity the task of gaining self-understanding through the knowledge of Spirit as revealed in history. Spirit, indeed humanity, lived with contradiction, which must be resolved not by choosing sides, but with dialectical historical methods. The purpose of the study of history was to forgive and reconcile human antagonisms, which would allow humanity to gain the critical self-knowledge needed for world advancement.

Developing his philosophy of history allowed Hegel to bring the issue of forgiveness into the realm of thought and to connect it to the idea of freedom. Preoccupation with ideas about freedom arguably became the dominant concern for the European intellectual climate of his time. The French Revolution was a powerful catalyst causing the concept of freedom to captivate European imagination during Hegel's life. He saw the French Revolution as originating in philosophical responses to political corruption,[21] an observation which led him to work so that future advancements in knowledge would be used responsibly and constructively for the benefit of posterity. Entangled inside the intellectual priorities of his time, Hegel turned to history to make sense of everything he saw erupt around him. For Hegel, history was the source of knowledge of freedom: it defined freedom, and it awakened humanity to the possibilities of freedom.[22] As Spirit crept toward its goal of self-knowledge, the human story (world history) had to continue on its quest for freedom.

Progress toward freedom would be a complex responsibility for humanity. Hegel believed that the utopian ideals of freedom propounded during the

French Revolution had failed because the people had neither understood, nor moved past, imperfect society adequately.[23] Ironically, by embracing the idea of unmitigated freedom (which forced the individual to accept enslavement to communal power), the French Revolution inevitably degenerated into the Reign of Terror.[24] Hegel concluded that absolute freedom within the state is impossible.[25] Again, dialectic was vital to gaining the historical knowledge that would guide humanity to freedom. Hegel argues in *Lectures on the Philosophy of History* that "ethical freedom in the state" comes from the unity of human reason and passion.[26] Without human development through self-knowledge, the reconciliation necessary for this unity would be impossible. He therefore discloses not only the urgency of studying history for his own time, but the urgency of a way of reading history. As though compelled to make right the debasement of lofty intentions, and the wrongs subsequently committed, which he saw in the French Revolution, Hegel modified this discourse by insisting upon forgiveness as a vital measure in pursuit of a paradisiacal freedom.

Indeed, Hegel had plans in mind for effecting unity between human reason and passion. For Hegel, bringing together true Christianity (Lutheranism) and the temporal world was central to Spirit's self-knowledge, an important step in the teleological goal of human history.[27] Extremely disappointed by the French Revolution's failure to bring about the virtuous democracy of the Greek *polis*, Hegel envisioned that humanity needed to embrace true faith, expressed in Lutheran Christianity,[28] so that its doctrine of reconciliation could infuse all parts of the modern world.[29] Forgiveness of human frailties was simply too big and too important an issue for religion to address alone. Hegel wanted more than religious exhortations on forgiveness, and a theory of history took over in areas where his religion found its limits. Secularization of forgiveness would become Hegel's strategy to have Lutheran morality overcome all sorts of differences among peoples and seep into all parts of human life.

Hegel's philosophy of history provided the methodology for his process of forgiveness, and by extension, his faith. He writes that the idea of freedom placed "religious imagination into terms of thought."[30] The state's political life throughout history, Hegel warned, was more dependent on its religion than one might suppose. He saw in the development of Christian (Lutheran) society in the European Middle Ages an unfolding of all the modernity in his lifetime and in times to come.[31] Though critical of Catholicism, Hegel saw in the dynamic of possession of power, holiness, truth, and sanctified property, all in the hands of the Church, contradictions (for example, the Eucharist meant that holiness was to be consumed, and therefore objectified and destroyed) to resolve that gave Europe the catalyst to set the modern world on its trajectory.[32] He argues that the revolution in France was doomed by the fact that its society had not embraced the Protestant Reformation, which he viewed as the missing step toward embracing reason, which would have been required before the advent of freedom in the state. [33] This reasoning was based upon his conviction that Lutheranism ultimately resolved the conflict between religion and secular authority by providing moral instruction for the individual and the state. [34] Hegel expressed in *Lectures on the Philosophy of History* that humanity should not relinquish its need for faith and religion: "Religion is the sphere in which a nation gives itself the definition of that which it regards as true. . . . The conception of God, therefore, constitutes the general basis of a people . . . the state is based on religion."[35] Hegel asserts that humanity is dependent on its perception of the divine, which allows him to see another relationship between opposites (the finite and the infinite). He had faith that Lutheran Christianity could reconcile humanity through love between God and humanity, which would unite opposites and contradictions. [36]

However, Hegel came to sense that, by maintaining an image of God primarily as an ethereal entity, religion only lent to humanity limited aid in its evolution toward self-knowledge and its search for the divine. On the other hand, he found within the human capacity for thought a means to outgrow religions limitations, a critical phase for future progress in the search for self-knowledge. Hegel referred to his understanding of the roles of religion and the realm of human reason as stages of self-knowledge in *The Philosophy of Right*:

> The present has discarded its barbarity and wrongful willfulness . . . what thereby becomes objective is their true reconciliation, which unfolds the state as the image and actuality of reason, wherein self-consciousness finds organically developed the actuality of its substantial knowing and willing, just as it finds in religion the feeling and the representation of this truth as an ideal essentiality, and in science the freely conceptualized cognition of this truth as one and the same throughout its mutually self-elaborating manifestations, and the ideal world [i.e., the world of art, religion, and philosophy]. [37]

Religion gave to humanity a portrait of divinity, and science/philosophy led them to reason that it lives around them in their endeavors for self-knowledge. Hegel's goal after the French Revolution was for humanity to acknowledge its dependence on religion, and to apply its capacity for thought, including reading and internalizing historical experiences, as a new step in Spirit's self-knowledge. The leaders of the French Reign of Terror failed to accept this goal, later communicated and endorsed by Hegel, to the extreme detriment of the people. Hegel wrote these conclusions as his contribution to Spirit's future self-knowledge. Almost paradoxically, bearing in mind his idea of history as self-knowledge gained through dialectic, forgiveness, and reconciliation, he concluded that all of humanity must accept that temporal perfection is impossible. This conclusion was reflected in his insistence that absolute freedom must be tempered by the state if humanity is to enjoy any sort of liberty at all. Hegel's work thus allowed him to communicate to his students and readers that falsely trying to make a perfect world is a mistake, especially when humanity has not been reconciled with the world we have. Through this lesson to others, he sought to help the world make amends for the flaws and mistakes that he believed had crushed the promise of the French Revolution. Trying to perfect the world without having forgiven others and self, and subsequently reconciling all divisions, would prove a futile (and possibly dangerous) task for humanity. He did not intend for humanity to build a utopia. The world is too dynamic for perfection; no utopia lasts for long. Hegel clearly knew that humans never undo history; in a dynamic world, only self-knowledge could navigate humanity through new circumstances to avoid the mistakes of the past. Nevertheless, humans could proceed toward self-knowledge to find whatever is most perfect in their world so as to procure happiness for all future environments.

Having emboldened humanity with the chance of self-knowledge, Hegel warned others not to ignore the problem of human powerlessness in the world. He also noted that Spirit creates necessity for humans, which makes the will a force external to the course of world history.[38] Hegel intended to make human powerlessness before external forces in the universe bearable through the study of history.[39] He wanted people to take interest in the world in spite of the pain of inadequacy and mortality. Indeed, he propounded the importance of aesthetics in order to engage people in life and the world.[40] He also reminded his followers that historical study had limits. For example, the Spirit is expressed differently in individuals and peoples in a variety of places and times. Consequently, the human spirit is limited in terms of ideas it can integrate, and incompatible ideas may cause bad outcomes.[41] For example, Hegel had argued that the limits of the spirit of the French at the time of the Revolution (which were still susceptible to the influence of the Catholic Church) had meant that the idea of freedom would not work, and the result was the Reign of Terror. He referred to his observations of this sad conclusion of the French Revolution in *Philosophy of History*:

> Thus liberalism as an abstraction, emanating from France, traversed the Roman world; but because of religious servitude remained chained to political bondage. For its false principle that the fetters which bind right and freedom can be broken without the emancipation of the conscience, that there can be a Revolution without a Reformation.[42]

He also insisted that all conclusions in historical dialectic were also reflections of the spirit of the people of the past with the spirit of the historian.[43] Future historians and philosophers would have to resolve the crises of earlier eras.[44] Hegel did anticipate that the world is dynamic, forever imperfect, and that attaining freedom is a process requiring constant maintenance.[45] In a world that changes, only knowledge can sustain humanity. Hegel introduced eschatological visions for Germany's place in a future characterized by social reform. He was optimistic that German philosophy could discover the possibility for harmony between religion and reason and thereby advance Spirit's journey toward self-knowledge.[46]

Meanwhile, all of humanity should be cognizant that the world progresses regardless of anyone's consent, which means that the past is never repeated completely or identically. The past always has a vast range of consequences, good and ill. Hegel understood that the French Revolution was a complex world-historical event. He found good in the French Revolution as the world-historical event that would convince Europeans to base law upon the principles of freedom.[47] He also believed that modernity began with the French Revolution because it challenged humanity to try to build a new world as an answer to the long unresolved question of the balance of religious and political power.[48] In many ways, the Hegelian philosophy of history depends on polysemy as part of achieving forgiveness and reconciliation. Any individual might draw many conclusions on any issue, especially world-historical events like the French Revolution. The complexities of understanding the issue or event multiply as other individuals join in the discourse, and as the discourse grows, each era will understand historical narratives in their own ways. Understanding and acknowledging polysemy thus brings humanity into a position to gain self-knowledge, to forgive the past and each other, and to find unity. Spirit draws closer to truth.

Hegel's theory of history stemmed from a desire to forgive and reconnect with humanity, the world, and God. Neglecting this aspect of Hegelian theory does the field of history a disservice, because doing so impedes an important part of the self-knowledge Hegel tried to show future generations how to achieve. Without knowledge, forgiveness is impossible. Without forgiveness, there is no reconciliation. Without reconciliation, humanity makes the same mistakes repeatedly. Hegel's philosophy of history also pointed to his hopes for the future. He wrote that societies "are what their deeds are."[49] Action was emphasized in this statement. Yet, he turned the discussion back to the realm of thought by adding that the human spirit can rise above itself to desire better conclusions, thus beginning the evolution of a new spirit, another phase in the growth of the Spirit.[50] Hegel intended for history to maximize the potential of the present and the building of the future.[51] He reasoned that human advancement depends on making sense of the mistakes of the past, so that some truth comes to light. Still, he believed that while humanity could know the ultimate aim of the world, history could not predict how to achieve this end.[52] In some ways, Hegel's philosophy of history allowed humanity to justify earlier events by identifying the positive outcomes arising from these events.[53]

Hegel's tendency to justify the past, indeed his faith in a rational structure of history, are related directly to the teleological and eschatological aspects of his theory. A teleological approach to history allowed Hegel to assert that human life did have meaning,[54] even though he was skeptical of links between events and forces external to the world.[55] In fact, Hegel even acknowledged that odd occurrences in the course of history had significant bearing on humanity's teleological destiny.[56] He also argued that though history may lead the state to its climax, humanity would continue to work on cultural and intellectual achievements.[57] Most importantly, Hegel knew human imperfection would mean that absolute happiness never would be achieved in this world.[58] He did not intend for humanity to rest on a perfectly happy world when history reached its teleological conclusion. Lutheran doctrines on the individual as spiritual and temporal led him to understand human experience as dynamic, constantly changing and proceeding through the unknown.[59] In other words, self-reflection in our reading of history would guide humanity on a course to achieve religion's purpose, living harmoniously with God, throughout all phases of development.

Hegel's theory of history also addressed the role of the mastermind of the universe in which the human world existed. Hegel's God was the "Absolute," dynamic and multi-formed, neither detached nor alone; his will does not force antitheses to remain forever apart from him, but unites all the imperfect (his antitheses) with himself:[60] Hegel exhorted humanity to realize its own responsibility to find God through knowledge in these words from *Lectures on the Philosophy of History*: "On the contrary, we have to be serious about recognizing the ways of Providence, the means it uses, and the historical phenomena in which it manifests itself."[61] Hegel insisted in *Phenomenology of Spirit* that God is "manifested in the midst of those who know themselves in the form of pure knowledge."[62] The study of history led humanity closer to God. Though skeptical of the idea that humanity could understand the world and God, Hegel encouraged humanity to continue making new attempts at self-knowledge.[63] History begins the process of knowledge and thereby allows forgiveness to happen. This is how history propels Spirit; knowledge always begets more knowledge, and forgiveness goes on forever. Forgiveness of others and self allows the Spirit to live with its contradictions, reconciled finally to be at its best. Reconciliation spins into eternity.

If humanity credits God with its redemption, as Hegel suggested, the issue remains of God's accountability. Should humans be so bold as to ask whether God is to be forgiven in the process of reconciliation? Hegel's theory of history addressed the issue of theodicy to answer the questions of God's righteousness in the face of his creation of a flawed universe and hurtful world. He believed history was the linchpin for humanity's discovery of Providence in this passage from *Lectures on the Philosophy of History*:

> Our treatment is, in this aspect, a theodicy—a justification of the ways of
> God . . . so that the ill that is found in the world may be comprehended, and the
> thinking spirit be reconciled with evil. Indeed, nowhere is such a harmonizing
> view more pressingly demanded than in world history.[64]

Hegel's theodicy raised God above the need for human forgiveness. God's intentions exonerated him of all wrongdoing in spite of the pain of the world, an idea that fortified Hegel's hope in the face of the ugliness he saw in his lifetime. He articulated his faith that study of the past could reveal that the course of world history was good by communicating in *Lectures on the Philosophy of History* that "Only insight can reconcile spirit with world history and reality, so that that which has happened and is happening every day, not only is not without God, but is essentially His own work."[65] Again, Hegel intended for the study of history to benefit humanity by bringing it closer to God. Human life had to have failures in order to have meaning. Otherwise, the world would be nothing more than entertainment for God. History would allow humanity to understand as much of this meaning as possible. Hegel seemed to believe that understanding this meaning and being able to trust that it was ultimately good would help humans feel positive about their roles in the universe.

Perhaps there is a way to take Hegel's conclusions further? The Cult of the Supreme Being actually revealed a human inability to forgive God as well as the need for reconciliation of contradictory human qualities (in this case, faith and reason). The drive to reconcile contradictory characteristics within humanity essentially governs all historical action. Hegel saw that an inability to reconcile contradictory qualities leads to human violence. Acceptance of the qualities within humanity proceeding from a study of how these qualities are the source of human action requires forgiveness of the ultimate mastermind. Why did God make humans so flawed and virtuous (simultaneously) in the first place, knowing that we would cause such harm and violence to each other? The very issue of "justification of God" implies that humans suffer some perceived hurt at the hands of Providence and harbor some resentment of the Divine. The case to prove God's innocence before human judgment is history. Hegel's understanding of the study of history is therefore dependent on forgiveness. When taken beyond immediate concerns, it follows that historians' forgiving humanity also means that they will forgive God. This was how Hegel reached further than religion to find spiritual awakening in knowledge of history.

It was difficult for Hegel to maintain a positive view of humanity and the meaning of its existence. He admitted to these feelings in a small lament in *Lectures in the Philosophy of History*: "World history is not the soil of happiness."[66] The history of the world, for Hegel, was the way that human rational capacities could make sense of the presence of evil in the world.[67]

Generations of historians have found Hegel's philosophy of history, especially his dialectic, useful in their studies. His work in world history has also led to controversies. For example, Hegel acknowledged that all ideas of freedom were not always reasonable, and he did not advocate the imposition of "advanced civilization" on people who were "primitive."[68] On the other hand, his views of the future promoted Eurocentric dreams for global progress and justified rule over (and violence against) women, children, lower classes, and all non-European peoples by upper and middle-class white Protestant males.[69] Over time, historians also have questioned Hegel's insistence upon the existence of a rational structure to humanity's story, especially as the twentieth century progressed.[70]

Still, Hegel's legacy appears in the work of historians who stress the importance of approaching history for the purpose of finding self-understanding.[71] Some recent Hegelians (Andrew Cole, for instance) also choose to apply his philosophy of history to encourage historians to avoid supercilious perspectives on past experiences within the human story.[72] Indeed, present day historians may reach further into Hegel's philosophy of history and find that applying the themes of forgiveness and reconciliation within his philosophy of history provides further direction for their studies and a singular, noble sense of purpose that many of their colleagues lack. Also, the Hegelian philosophy of history appears to allow posterity the authority to pass judgment on the actions of states, societies, and individuals,[73] and many historians in the generations since have tried to eschew taking this godlike position in their work. In some ways, refusing to judge in any way actions taken by societies and individuals exonerates historians of the duty to forgive the past that Hegel assigned them. Facing the choice to forgive the past can become uncomfortable for scholars and students. Many historians avoid the guidance Hegelian theory provides to escape from the perturbation caused by admissions of hurt and guilt and unresolved decisions about forgiveness. Some historians have forgotten, at least at times, that Hegel admonished them to embrace their vulnerability as individuals to be corrected and forgiven by future generations. Present day historians who explore Hegel's theme of self-knowledge via reconciliation may find that new dialogues with the past can be opened and all humanity could benefit from what we learn from them.

## NOTES

1. Rebecca Comay, *Mourning Sickness: Hegel and the French Revolution* (Stanford: Stanford University Press, 2011), 60–1.
2. Howard P. Kainz, *G. W. F. Hegel: The Philosophical System* (New York: Twayne Publishers, 1996), 118.

3. Glenn Alexander Magee, "Hegelian Panentheism," in *Models of God and Alternative Ultimate Realities*, edited by Jeanine Diller and Asa Kasher (Dordrecht: Springer, 2013), 422, 430.

4. Charles Taylor, *Hegel and Modern Society* (Cambridge, UK: Cambridge University Press, 1979).

5. Herbert Marcuse, *Hegel's Ontology and the Theory of Historicity*, trans. Seyla Benhabib (Cambridge, MA: The MIT Press, 1987).

6. Alexandre Kojève, *Introduction to the Reading of Hegel: Lectures on the* Phenomenology of Spirit, *Assembled by Raymond Queneau*, edited by Allan Bloom, trans. James H. Nichols, Jr. (Ithaca, NY: Cornell University Press 1980), 252–3.

7. H. S. Harris, *Hegel's Development: Toward the Sunlight, 1770–1801* (Oxford: The Clarendon Press, 1972).

8. Peter C. Hodgson, *Shapes of Freedom: Hegel's Philosophy of World History in Theological Perspective* (Oxford: Oxford University Press, 2012).

9. Andrew Cole, *The Birth of Theory* (Chicago: The University of Chicago Press, 2014).

10. Francis Fukuyama, *The End of History and the Last Man* (New York: Free Press, 2006).

11. Will Dudley, *Hegel, Nietzsche, and Philosophy: Thinking Freedom* (Cambridge: Cambridge University Press, 2002); Steven B. Smith, "Hegel's Discovery of History," in *The Review of Politics* 45, no. 2 (April 1983); Hans Küng, *The Incarnation of God: An Introduction to Hegel's Theological Thought as Prolegomena to a Future Christology* (Edinburgh: T. & T. Clark, 1987); Daniel Berthold-Bond, "Hegel's Eschatological Vision: Does History Have a Future?" *History and Theory* 27, no. 1 (February 1988); Joshua Foa Dienstag, "Building the Temple of Memory: Hegel's Aesthetic Narrative of History," *The Review of Politics* 56, no. 4 (Autumn 1994); Leon J. Goldstein, "The Meaning of 'State' in Hegel's Philosophy of History," *The Philosophical Quarterly (1950–)* 12, no. 46 (January 1962); Terry Pinkard, *Hegel's Dialectic: The Explanation of Possibility* (Philadelphia: Temple University Press, 1988); Catherine Malabou and Lisabeth During, "The Future of Hegel: Plasticity, Temporality, Dialectic," *Hypatia* 15, no. 4 (Autumn 2000); Joachim Ritter, *Hegel and the French Revolution: Essays on the* Philosophy of Right, trans. Richard Dien Winfield (Cambridge, Massachusetts: The MIT Press, 1982).

12. Teshale Tibebu, *Hegel and the Third World: The Making of Eurocentrism in World History* (Syracuse, NY: Syracuse University Press, 2011); Joseph McCarney, *Hegel on History* (London: Routledge, 2000); Manfred Riedel, *Between Tradition and Revolution: The Hegelian Transformation of Political Philosophy* (Cambridge: Cambridge University Press, 1984).

13. H. S. Harris, *Hegel's Development: Toward the Sunlight, 1770–1801* (Oxford: The Clarendon Press, 1972), 227–8, 320, 333.

14. Peter C. Hodgson, *Shapes of Freedom: Hegel's Philosophy of World History in Theological Perspective* (Oxford: Oxford University Press, 2012), 160–1.

15. Philip M. Merklinger, *Philosophy, Theology, and Hegel's Berlin Philosophy of Religion* (Albany: State University of New York Press, 1993), 97–102.

16. Hegel, G. W. F. *Phenomenology of Spirit*, trans. A. V. Miller (Oxford: Oxford University Press, 1977).

17. Ibid., 405.

18. Comay, 151–2.

19. Hegel, *Phenomenology of Spirit*, 363.

20. Hegel, G. W. F. *Lectures on the Philosophy of History*, trans. Ruben Alvarado (Aalten: WordBridge Publishing, 2011).

21. Ibid., 400.

22. Will Dudley, *Hegel, Nietzsche, and Philosophy: Thinking Freedom* (Cambridge: Cambridge University Press, 2002), 113.

23. Comay, 56.

24. Ibid., 68.

25. Dudley, 112.

26. Hegel, *Lectures on the Philosophy of History*, 22.

27. Berthold-Bond, 27.

28. Smith, 181–2.

29. Hodgson, 132.

30. Hegel, *Lectures on the Philosophy of History*, 18.

31. Cole, 71.

32. Ibid., 79, 95–6.

33. Hegel, *Lectures on the Philosophy of History*, 403–6.

34. Howard P. Kainz, *G. W. F. Hegel: The Philosophical System* (New York: Twayne Publishers, 1996), 118.

35. Hegel, *Lectures on the Philosophy of History*, 46.

36. Smith, 182–3.

37. Hegel, *The Philosophy of Right* (Indianapolis: Focus Publishing, 2002), trans. Alan White. Kindle edition.

38. Smith, 187.

39. Ibid., 187.

40. Dienstag, 700–1.

41. Goldstein, 71.

42. Hegel, *Philosophy of History*, 406.

43. George Dennis O'Brien, "Does Hegel Have a Philosophy of History," *History and Theory* 10, no. 3 (1971), 303, 309.

44. Pinkard, 160.

45. Dudley, 112.

46. Comay, 87.

47. Ritter, 51.

48. Comay, 58–9.

49. Hegel, *Lectures on the Philosophy of History*, 68.

50. Ibid., 69–72.

51. Smith, 186–7.

52. Wilkins, Burleigh Taylor. *Hegel's Philosophy of History* (Ithaca and London: Cornell University Press, 1974).

53. Pinkard, *Hegel's Dialectic*, 162.

54. Ibid., 13.

55. Ibid., 103.

56. Catherine Malabou and Lisabeth During, "The Future of Hegel: Plasticity, Temporality, Dialectic," *Hypatia* 15, no. 4 (Autumn 2000), 208.

57. Fritzman, J. M. *Hegel* (Cambridge: Polity Press, 2014).

58. Hodgson, 141.

59. Cyril O'Regan, *The Heterodox Hegel* (Albany: State University of New York Press, 1994), 45.

60. Küng, 433.

61. Hegel, *Lectures on the Philosophy of History*, 13.

62. Hegel, *Phenomenology of Spirit*, 409.

63. Fritzman, 3–6.

64. Hegel, *Lectures on the Philosophy of History*, 14–5.

65. Ibid., 410.

66. Ibid., 25.

67. Wilkins, 51.

68. Goldstein, 72.

69. Tibebu, 330.

70. McCarney, 213.

71. Ibid., 215–6.

72. Cole, 161.

73. Riedel, 187.

*Chapter Three*

# Karl Marx

*The End of the Enlightenment*

Eric Hood

Before he was even in the grave, Karl Marx had lost control of his own theoretical position. By the 1880s, self-proclaimed "Marxists" in Europe were freely mixing the frameworks Marx developed with various other socialist, anarchist, and reformist programs. Friedrich Engels, his longtime friend and collaborator, was no longer participating in Marx's reevaluation of peasant communes or the likelihood of capitalism's economic collapse and was actively reinterpreting Marxism so that it was more in line with the emerging Darwinian consensus in the natural sciences.[1] When the first "Marxist" state appeared in Russia, more than three decades after Marx's death, the desire to present the monolithic image of a paternal sage, "Marx," in place of the man, Karl, only complicated his legacy as a philosopher, activist, writer, and the nineteenth-century founder of the twentieth century's most important political movement. "If anything is certain," Marx himself once quipped, "it is that I myself am not a Marxist."[2]

Working honestly with Marx as a thinker requires more than just stripping away the layers of appropriation. There is also the problem of the man and his work. Marx was notorious for leaving projects unfinished. His corpus is littered with incomplete manuscripts, outlines, and notebooks. We do well to remember, as one Marxist scholar cautioned, that with Marx "there is no doctrine; there are only fragments (and elsewhere, analyses, demonstrations)."[3] Marx spent his life chasing events and working through personal difficulty. Far from being the work of a static prophet with a unified theory of capitalism and its inevitable downfall, Marx's writings are filled with the kind of contradictions that would be expected to develop throughout the lifetime of a serious scholar.

There is no singular Marxism. But with the futures of nations and international movements at stake and the lack of a definitive text from Marx, theorists and activists filled the gaps and straightened the course. The strains of Marxist thought that emerged beyond Marx are just as important as those that come directly from Marx himself—perhaps even more, considering the political antagonisms of the twentieth century. They are, however, beyond the scope of this chapter. Marx has been mystified by the political, social, and philosophical afterlife of his work, and my task is to demystify Marx by first placing the life and work of Karl Marx in its historical context; then, by highlighting the complicated relationship between Marx's interpretive strategies (his reading of history) and the practices of the Scottish Enlightenment and German philosophy (noting along the way what has become problematic and remained valuable in his approach); and finally by examining the development of the theoretical concepts that made Marx's reading of history and capitalist culture possible. By the subtitle, "The End of the Enlightenment," I point to two perhaps contradictory truths regarding Marx. On the one hand, Marx's method of cultural deconstruction undercut the assumptions of objectivity and rationality that were the foundation of the scientifically minded Enlightenment. On the other hand, Marx's commitment to the idea that another world was possible, a world beyond exploitation and ideology, was also the end (or the goal) of the Enlightenment. All Marxisms, I imagine, exist in this interpretive dialectic.

## THE LIFE OF MARX

Karl Marx lived in an age of unprecedented political turmoil. The previous half-century had seen republicanism spread like a contagion. First, the Americans threw off British colonial rule. A few years later, Dutch Patriots forced the ruler of Europe's wealthiest nation into exile. Then, in January 1793, the elected representatives of the French people executed their king and placed his decapitated corpse in an unmarked grave. Armies ten times larger than had ever been seen before on the European continent clashed for more than twenty years. At Leipzig alone, more than 100,000 men were killed or wounded in just four days. Napoleon's *Grande Armée* not only redrew the map of Europe, sundering centuries-old aristocratic claims, it carried with it the ideas of the radical Enlightenment—equality before the law, free speech, meritocracy—infecting the whole of the continent.

Marx was born in 1818, three years after Napoleon's defeat at Waterloo and into the conservative repression that followed. Enlightenment reforms allowed his Prussian father to secure a wealthy, middle-class life as a lawyer, a position he protected by converting from Judaism to the Christian Evangelical Church of Prussia. The young Marx was brought up in a liberal-minded home, influenced by the ideas of Kant and Voltaire, and his early education was placed under the care of head-master Johann Hugo Wyttenbach, a man viewed with suspicion by authorities as a known sympathizer with the most radical and violent phase of the French Revolution.

Marx began studying law at the local university at Bonn, and his father hoped he would pursue a career in civil service. He thought himself a poet, however, and composed small books of unfashionable verse to his childhood friend and future wife, Jenny Westphalen. At eighteen, he transferred to the more cosmopolitan university at Berlin. The change of scene would forever change his path. First, Marx gave up his poetic ambitions. Then, after the death of his father, he felt free to abandon the study of law and pursue philosophy.

At Berlin, Marx became acquainted with the philosophy of G. W. F. Hegel. Hegel was deeply interested in the progress of societies and human thought. Although Hegel had supported the monarchy and was suspicious of the French Revolution, a generation of young scholars centered in Berlin used Hegel's interpretive process to call for the liberalization of the state. Marx joined this circle, known as the Young Hegelians, committed to the hope that philosophical critique, especially the critique of religion, was the best way to achieve the goals of the radical Enlightenment. In Berlin of the late 1830s, philosophy was where the battle between progressive and conservative politics was waged, and Marx sided with the intellectual insurgency against established power.

Among the radical Young Hegelians, Marx remained a reform-minded republican. He worried about the prospects of obtaining a university position during a period of conservative backlash, so, in consultation with his mentors, he attempted to temper his thesis. It made no difference. Aware that he would not be able to find employment in the university, Marx turned to journalism, contributing to and editing a radical newspaper. Again, the young Marx tried to soften the paper's rhetoric in order to build a wider base of support and avoid being silenced by Prussian censors. But when authorities closed the paper, Marx left Germany and moved to Paris in 1843—disillusioned with the compromising path of liberalism.

Paris was teeming with various socialist movements. Louis Blanc sought to bring about a workers' republic. Pierre-Joseph Proudhon advocated the abolition of private property and the state. Babouvists also fought against private property but favored a strong central government. Saint-Simonians did not object to private property but wanted more industrialization and scientific management. Fourierists wanted to end industrialized labor and establish free-love communes. When Marx arrived in Paris, he sought to publish a new journal to build an intellectual alliance between the various forms of French Socialism and radical German philosophy he learned in Berlin, but his efforts failed to find support. In Paris, there was only a passing interest in German philosophy. Unable to launch his own project, he settled in as a contributor to an existing radical German language paper and began to collaborate with Friedrich Engels. Although Marx went largely unnoticed in Parisian socialist circles, he did not escape the attention of the German authorities. In 1845, at the request of the Prussian king, Marx was expelled from France.

Marx, now married to Jenny, hurriedly resettled his young family in Brussels, under an agreement not to write articles that were critical of the Belgian government. The transnational alliance he hoped to foster between radical intellectuals while in Paris had failed to materialize. In its place, Marx now worked to develop and maintain a consensus among a modest circle of relatively like-minded writers and agitators. Although he had been targeted by authorities and held key positions in the Communist Corresponding Society and the Communist League, he continued to work in relative obscurity.

However, this brief period in Cologne, from 1844–1848, was important in terms of developing Marx's distinct theoretical position within the broad socialist movement. During this time, he traveled to England with Engels and was inspired by the popular groundswell of worker's protest, called Chartism, which he believed was the start of a larger proletarian revolt. He worked with Engels to sketch out his differences with his fellow travelers, the Young Hegelians, in *The Holy Family* (1845) and in the unpublished *Economic and Philosophic Manuscripts* and *The German Ideology*. He then turned on the French anarchist, Pierre-Joseph Proudhon in *The Poverty of Philosophy* (1847). In his early twenties, Marx had targeted his conservative enemies, but he now shifted to attacks on other socialists, exposing the weaknesses in their approaches and offering his own alternative vision. Through Engels's maneuverings, the two were commissioned to draft a revision of the program and statement of principles for the newly formed international Communist League. The resulting pamphlet became known as *The Communist Manifesto* (1848), the most influential and widely read of all of Marx's works.

Marx and Engels branded their variant of socialism as thoroughly scientific. Marx argued that other forms of socialism were merely idealist, or "utopian," based on the moral superiority of a particular idea. What would be later known as "Marxism" was to be based on universal economic laws. Where Bruno Bauer, Ludwig Feuerbach, and the other radical Hegelians sought to persuade individuals, Marx believed that material necessity—low wages, poor working conditions, declining rates of profit, and eventual economic collapse—would compel the whole of the working class, the *proletariat*, to overthrow the ownership class, the *bourgeoisie*. Communism, according to Marx, was a grand historical force. It was not an idea. Scientific socialism would not bring about the revolution, but the coming revolution could be explained and guided by science.

Almost simultaneous with the publication of the *Manifesto* in 1848, the European continent was shaken by a series of popular uprisings. Although Marx and his pamphlet had almost no connection to these spontaneous revolts, Belgium officials suspected Marx of seeking to finance an insurrection. Marx and his wife Jenny were arrested. They were cleared of the charges, but Marx thought it best to move his family, first to Paris where he felt he would be protected by a sympathetic revolutionary government, and then back to Cologne to support the revolutions by resuming his writing in the city where he began his career.

Within a year, however, the revolution in France was overturned, and Prussian officials forced Marx out of Cologne. He tried to return to Paris but found the political climate unsafe, and he quickly fled to London in June of 1849. Marx spent the rest of his life in London, most of it in obscurity, poverty, and poor health. Until the outbreak of the American Civil War, Marx steadily contributed colorful analyses of world politics to the left-leaning *New York Daily Tribune*, for which he received a modest but dependable income. But after his relationship with the *Daily Tribune* ended, he was often left scrambling to make ends meet.

Marx spent the last three decades of his life working on a comprehensive analysis of capitalism. Marx's critique of bourgeois political economy was eagerly anticipated within his circle as early as 1844, when he began work on the *Manuscripts*. In 1845, he entered into a contract to write a two-volume *Critique of Politics and Political Economy*, which was later cancelled. He continuously promised to work on the project, but he was easily drawn away to comment on current events or defend his position within the socialist movement. He was also running into difficulty reformulating his approach for a younger generation that thought Hegel's logic out of vogue. In 1857 and 1858, he worked in a series of notebooks that remained unpublished until 1939, which became known as the *Grundrisse*. By 1859, he had at last finished a small book, *A Contribution to the Critique of Political Economy*, but it failed to meet expectations and was largely recycled into the opening chapters of *Capital*.

The first volume of *Capital* did not appear until 1867. Many in Marx's inner-circle hoped Marx would at last detail how capitalism's internal contradictions would inevitably lead to its collapse and replacement by a social system of production in the hands of the workers, but Marx only gestured to this conclusion. For now, that analysis would have to wait. What the first volume of *Capital* revealed, however, with the staggering detail and color of a journalist, was the myriad ways class-struggle played out in England's industrial economy. The classical economists (Adam Smith, Jean-Baptiste Say, David Ricardo) had imagined that the capitalist and the worker met as equals in the labor market and jointly entered into a contract for their mutual benefit. Marx, however, methodically exposed that the capitalist was the only party that benefitted in this so-called free exchange. The wage-system allowed the capitalist to pay the worker just a fraction of the value that had been created through the worker's labor, allowing the capitalist to pocket the rest as profit. Additionally, the capitalist's position was enhanced at every turn by everything from the technologies that increased efficiency, the reduction of skill involved in factory work, continuous unemployment, and the increasing immiseration of workers who were left with nothing to sell but their labor. As a result of this unequal exchange, the capitalist system of production was producing both wealth and poverty on a scale that had never been seen before.

The promised second and third volumes never appeared. When Marx died in 1883, Engels was dismayed to find the manuscripts in disarray, particularly for the third volume that had been tasked with analyzing the capitalist system as a totality and was supposed to show that the declining rate of profit would eventually lead to capitalism's collapse. Recent scholarship has suggested that Marx was beginning to waver on this point in the last decade of his life, noting a number of counter-tendencies that placed the inevitability of collapse in question. If true, this would have been no small shift in perspective, since for many in Marx's circle, including Engels, this was the most important conclusion of Marx's analysis. Nevertheless, Engels dutifully edited and prepared the second volume on the circulation of capital for publication in 1885. The largely unfinished and disjointed third volume was made available in 1894. From 1905 to 1910, Karl Kautsky published another of Marx's unfinished manuscripts from this period on the historical development of theories of surplus-value, or profit, which was intended as the fourth volume to *Capital*.

It was only in the last few years of his life that Marx achieved any degree of popular notoriety or fame. In 1871, another popular revolt erupted in Paris. Marx responded from London with a pamphlet, *The Civil War in France*. Marx tailored his writing for a wide audience and was immediately rewarded with brisk sales. The first volume of *Capital* had sold well in Germany, but *The Civil War in France* made him a known figure across Europe. When the forces of reaction gave undue credit to the International Working Men's Association (IWMA), and especially Dr. Marx as its "chief," it only added to his growing mystique. In the next year *Capital* went to a second German edition along with new editions in French and Russian.

Both feared and celebrated, Marx sat back as control over his legacy slipped away. Tired of maneuvering and infighting, he orchestrated an end to the IWMA. Both of his daughters married prominent socialists with whom he disagreed. He now wrote almost nothing for the public, yet his reputation continued to grow. Wrapping themselves in the glories of the 1871 Commune Marx had celebrated in *The Civil War in France* and the "scientific" socialism that Engels claimed was revealed through *Capital*, socialists and workers parties of all stripes began to refer to themselves as "Marxists."

The man whose name was joined to these movements spent his last years in poor health. First, he lost his beloved wife and then his eldest daughter in 1883. Marx passed away months later in the care of Lenchen, his housekeeper with whom, decades before, he had secretly sired a son.[4] Marx left behind a sprawling, unfinished body of work in philosophy, history, political theory, and economics. Arguably, he brought an end to classical economics and opened the pathway to sociology. His greatest legacy, however, may have been his name, which not only became synonymous with communism but a rhetorical weapon in the service of revolution.

## READING HISTORY: PROGRESS AND REVOLUTION

In popular culture Marx is best known for his interpretation of history, especially his prediction that the *proletariat*, the class of wage-laborers, would soon rise up and overthrow the *bourgeoisie*, the class of capitalist owners. In *The Communist Manifesto*, the whole of the world is presented as caught between these two epoch making forces. The bourgeois capitalist is not only morally unfit to rule, but the pressures inherent in the capitalist system compel him to increase his enemy's numbers and desperation each day. Of course, it is easy to look around today and see that capitalism has not been overthrown. In fact, capitalist systems of production and patterns of consumption continue to spread across the globe. And just as troubling for Marx's prediction in the *Manifesto*: the nations where self-avowed "Marxists" seized control of the state—Russia, China, Korea, Cuba, Vietnam, Afghanistan, Nicaragua, to name only a few—had agrarian economies, not the advanced capitalist economies Marx predicted would breed a communist revolution in 1848.

Although Marx's theory of revolution and historical development are the best-known aspects of his work, they are, today, the least respected. Marx organized history into five distinct stages based on the mode of production that dominated each age. Instead of a history of governments or a history of ideas, Marx looked at how the material needs of society were satisfied at different historical periods. For Marx, this meant looking beyond mechanical technologies (although Marx considered the impacts of technological advancements carefully) and into the system of social relations at the center of production—who worked for whom and under what conditions. Using this interpretive framework Marx determined Europe had already been through the stages of primitive communism, the antique mode of production (exemplified by ancient Rome and Greece), and feudalism. According to Marx, French, American, and British society were now in the fourth stage (the mode of capitalist production) and were about to enter into the final stage (the communist mode of production), which would dissolve class-antagonisms by placing advanced production in the service of all. Much of Asia, according to Marx, had been arrested at a variation of the second stage he called the Asiatic mode of production.

Marx's reading of history is often criticized for its directionality and commitment to progress. In this respect, Marx's interpretive practice is firmly embedded in the eighteenth and nineteenth centuries. Two clear precedents stand out. First, Adam Smith proposed a four-stage theory of historical development, ending with "the Age of Commerce," without progressing to Marx's speculative fifth phase.[5] Smith's theory was organized around modes of subsistence (hunting, shepherding, agriculture, commerce), and, although Smith's history is progressive without being evolutionary, it is a short leap from Smith's focus on subsistence to Marx's focus on production.

The other clear forerunner to Marx's reading of history was Hegel's *Phenomenology of Spirit* (1807). Hegel proposed that history was an evolutionary unfolding of human freedom in stages. Marx conceptualized history through the development of humanity's productive powers, not an unfolding of freedom, but Marx, like Hegel, believed history was moving towards the goal of human emancipation. For Marx, what was most important in Hegel's philosophy was that human nature was not static but developing through history. As Marx stated, Hegel "conceives the self-creation of man as a process . . . he thus grasps the essence of labor and comprehends objective man . . . as the outcome of man's own labor."[6] This recognition that human nature was not fixed, as Adam Smith and the classical economists imagined, but was dependent on human activity—the system of social relations—was the starting point for Marx's radical departures in politics and sociological theory.

Marx is also criticized for his messianic tone when describing the coming revolution, which he sometimes carries off with an apocalyptic flair. Famously, the *Manifesto* ends, "Let the ruling classes tremble at a Communistic revolution. The proletarians have nothing to lose but their chains. They have a world to win. WORKING MEN OF ALL COUNTRIES, UNITE!"[7] Even the otherwise staid *Capital* trumpets the moment of revolutionary rupture:

> Along with the constantly diminishing number of the magnates of capital, who usurp and monopolize all advantages of this process of transformation, grows the mass of misery, oppression, slavery, degradation, exploitation; but with this too grows the revolt of the working class, a class always increasing in numbers, and disciplined, united, organized by the very mechanism of the process of capitalist production itself. The monopoly of capital becomes a fetter upon the mode of production, which has sprung up and flourished along with, and under it. Centralization of the means of production and socialization of labor at last reach a point where they become incompatible with their

capitalist integument. Thus integument is burst asunder. The knell of capitalist private property sounds. The expropriators are expropriated. [8]

The speed and fullness of the predicted break with capitalism is startling. Marx often spoke of a revolution that would sweep all of Europe. In this regard, his politics remained located in the revolutionary potentials of France in 1792 and Europe of 1848. Throughout the 1850s, even as English Chartism fizzled and Paris quieted under the populist conservatism of Louis Napoleon, Marx, like Mikhail Bakunin and so many others who fought and organized in 1848, held on to the hope that the last revolution was still very near. By the time *Capital* was published, Marx's revolutionary vision was dated. If the Russian revolution reopened the possibilities of global revolution in 1917, by the late twentieth century, world-changing revolutions again felt like fantasy to most.

It is important to note, however, that little of the revolutionary fire that animates the *Manifesto* (1848) appears in *Capital* (1867). In the *Manifesto*, bourgeois society was depicted as a short-lived transitional phase that had powerfully swept away the feudal aristocracy within a few decades but lacked its own stability. Now that the productive power of industry had been discovered, it was a short step to forcibly seize that power for the benefit of all. *Capital*, however, presented a very different rise of the bourgeoisie. Shifting his frame of reference from Revolutionary France to Industrial England, Marx charted how the elements of bourgeois society grew over five centuries, taking over one area of production after another, developing new political and economic tools along the way. In *Capital*, bourgeois society was not only adaptive but firmly seated. The ascent of the bourgeoisie was less a revolutionary rupture than a protracted transformation.

Towards the end of *Capital* Marx assures his readers that the transition to communism will not take nearly so long:

> The transformation of scattered private property, arising from individual labor, into capitalist private property is, naturally, a process, incomparably more protracted, violent, and difficult, than the transformation of capitalistic private property, already practically resting on socialized production, into socialized property. In the former case, we had the expropriation of the mass of the people by a few usurpers; in the latter, we have the expropriation of a few usurpers by the mass of the people. [9]

This optimism that the reorganization of bourgeois private-property into "socialized property" will happen much faster than the long history he recounted for the capitalist transformation reads more like a revolutionary hope than an analysis in light of *Capital*'s mass of countervailing evidence. We should notice, however, that the long historiography in *Capital* provides another path for communism's development outside of revolution.

By the late twentieth century, variants of Marxism abandoned Marx's teleological reading of history, the belief that capitalism was guaranteed to collapse and that it would be succeeded by a more equitable system. After the fall of the Soviet Union in 1989, Marx's communist hypothesis was declared dead by some. But without the enforced orthodoxy of the Soviet Empire, new readings of Marx and new Marxist parties arose, particularly in the global south. Moreover, the climate crisis has raised additional questions about the material limits of capitalist production. It may still be too soon to write off progress.

Regardless, we need not accept Marx's historiography to benefit from his materialist interpretation of history. Even if we put aside Marx's statements about historical progress, communism, and the end of history, Marx's detailed analysis of capitalism as a set of practices, structure of social relations, and mode of consciousness led him to develop a sociological framework that linked the limits of thinking to the habits of everyday life—a theory of subjectivity.

## READING EVERYDAY LIFE: ALIENATION, IDEOLOGY, AND THE COMMODITY FETISH

"The wealth of those societies in which the capitalist mode of production prevails, presents itself," Marx writes at the start of *Capital*, "as 'an immense accumulation of commodities.'"[10] Thinking about capitalism as "an immense accumulation of commodities" has become routine. One of the chief benefits of capitalism is its ability to provide an abundance of commodities. During the Cold War, the supermarkets of the West became a symbol of capitalism's generative color and efficiency against the image of gray, Soviet bread lines that stood in for communism. According to eventual U.S. President Nixon during the "kitchen debate" with Soviet Premier Nikita Khrushchev in 1959, it was the supposed inventiveness and freedoms of consumer choice that proved capitalism's superiority. But the phrase "presents itself" is important here. Marx does not say capitalism "is" a mass of commodities. He says it "presents itself" as such. In other words, capitalism appears to be one thing, but Marx will show it is actually something else.

This focus on unmasking appearances is central to Marx's method. Some of the earliest traces can be seen in his appropriation of the concept of "alienation." Among the Young Hegelians, alienation was central to their critique of religion. Ludwig Feuerbach, a radical Hegelian and an important influence on Marx, argued that Christian believers had externalized their own emotions and power as human agents and then worshipped it as "God." Thus, religion separated believers from themselves; it "alienated" the subject by making what was within the believer look as though it was located outside, in the being of God.

For Marx, the rule of the capitalist over the worker was analogous to the rule of God projected from the believer. In preparing the manuscript for *Capital*, he wrote:

> The rule of the capitalist over the worker is therefore the rule of the object over the human, of dead labor over living, of the product over the producer. . . . This is exactly *the same* relation in the sphere of material production, in the real social life process . . . as is represented by *religion* in the ideological sphere: the inversion of the subject into the object and *vice versa*.[11]

Although it may sound complicated, the idea is rather simple. The worker looks to the capitalist as the means by which he survives in the world. The capitalist provides the worker with a job and, therefore, an income—the means of subsistence. Thus, it appears that the capitalist is necessary not only for the well-being of the worker but also for the production of the wealth of commodities within the capitalist system. However, the capital (money, factories, materials used in the production process) that the capitalist possesses is actually the product of previous work by the workers. It is, in Marx's language here, nothing more than "dead labour." In essence, workers make the world of capitalism and the capitalist sells it back to them.

Thus, capitalism appears to be an "immense accumulation of commodities," but it is actually a social relation between the capitalist and the worker. This relationship is unequal in favor of the capitalist and is founded on the basic exploitation of the worker for the capitalist's benefit. But if the workers are the real producers, why don't workers just band together and do without the capitalist? Part of the problem is this exploitative relationship is masked by the workers' everyday experience. Between the worker and the capitalist appear a series of concepts, institutions, and practices that hide their relationship. Systems of wages, rents, credit, property rights, unemployment (to name a few) all stand in the way. All of these aspects of everyday life are historically specific: that is, they have not always been and likely will not always be. But our constant exposure to them naturalizes their existence for nearly everyone so that we become blind to their constructedness. Even the basic concepts which societies understand as foundational are historical, so that while Medieval European society valued "honor" and "loyalty," capitalist societies have come to value ideas such as "freedom" and "equality" more highly. This is no accident. In *The German Ideology*, Marx explains:

> The ideas of the ruling class are in every epoch the ruling ideas; i.e., the class which is the ruling material force of society, is at the same time its ruling intellectual force. . . . The ruling ideas are nothing more than the ideal expres-

sion of the dominant material relationships, the dominant material relationships grasped as ideas.[12]

Marx explains further in the same paragraph that each age has its own ruling
ideas that serve the ruling class. Once "loyalty" served the interests of the
feudal lord by suggesting there was a natural bond between the aristocrat and
the peasant that supposedly protected the interests of both by holding the
peasant to the feudal estate. Today the "freedom" to hire and release workers
as needed and to free labor to relocate to areas where more laborers are
needed (reducing the cost of labor) serves the interests of the capitalist.

Marx had no use for the so-called rights of man or foundational principles
like "freedom," "property," or "equality." In bourgeois society, these high-
minded words were understood in ways that primarily served bourgeois
interests. According to bourgeois economists, workers had the "freedom" to
enter the market and seek the highest wages for their labor. What was never
admitted was how the worker was forced into this freedom by being dispos-
sessed of the means to support himself so that all he had left to sell was his
labor. He was "free" to starve if he could not find a buyer for his labor. In
what we might see today as an Orwellian twist, the meaning of freedom in
bourgeois society was actually compulsion—"freedom" was turned upside
down, made to stand on its head.

This limited, class-based view of the world was what Marx referred to as
ideology. An ideology is not completely false, but it is falsely incomplete.
There are two important points to be made about Marx's conception of
ideology. First, ideology is not simply a hard limit on knowledge or a critique
of rationality. Ideological misunderstandings are historically determined,
changing as the conditions of production change. In fact, at some points,
Marx asserts the end of class rule will bring about the end of ideology.
Second, ideology is not a simple fiction perpetrated by the dominant class on
the rest of society. Ideology springs from the historical social conditions and
affects the whole of society. The capitalists and bourgeois intellectual laborers (or ideologists: the army of politicians, lawyers, teachers, priests, etc.) are
caught, along with workers, within the limits of bourgeois ideology. The
ideologists do not manufacture ideology for the masses but rather intensify
the dominant ideology through their work.

Ideology is a product of alienation, as it is the necessary illusion that
holds class society together by masking the basic conditions of alienation. In
capitalist society, workers are alienated from the products of their labor, as
their power to creatively act on the natural world is reduced to the drudgery
of wage labor. Similarly, while the factory has brought them together with
other workers as collective labor, their essential social being is denied by
capitalism's emphasis on competition. Although workers are responsible for
transforming the world and bringing together the whole of humanity, their

agency in determining the direction of production and association has been externalized and handed over to "the market."

With alienation and ideology in mind we can return now to the commodity. Marx calls the commodity "a mysterious thing," because in the process of commercial exchange the social character of large-scale commodity production acquires the appearance of a relationship between things—between money and the commodity. In other words, the continuous buying and selling of commodities in a market economy produces the collective belief that the value of all useful things can be quantified with a price. The illusion is so encompassing that workers even affix a price to themselves, turning their own bodies into things to be bought and sold. In a capitalist society, Marx writes,

> There is a definite social relation between men that assumes, in their eyes, the fantastic form of a relation between things. In order, therefore, to find an analogy, we must have recourse to the mist-enveloped regions of the religious world. In that world the productions of the human brain appear as independent beings endowed with life, and entering into relation both with one another and the human race. So it is in the world of commodities with the products of men's hands. This I call the Fetishism, which attaches itself to the products of labor, so soon as they are produced as commodities, and which is therefore inseparable from the production of commodities. [13]

Thus, the commodity fetish, which reduces all things, including human labor, to a universal equivalency expressed in a price, not only alienates workers from the products of their own labor, their coworkers, and themselves, it is central to the ideology that naturalizes the ownership of money, commodities, and property.

Marx spent most of his time analyzing capitalist society and had very little to say about how communist societies would function. However, the critiques of alienation, ideology, and the commodity fetish provide insight into what Marx thought it would mean to transcend capitalism. Under communism, the commodity fetish would disappear, as decisions about production and distribution of goods were made according to the needs of society, instead of to maximize profits. The world of appearances, the world of ideology and domination, would give way to a world of human awareness and consciousness. Humanity would achieve its potential as a social being, leaving alienation behind, recognizing its own power as the deliberate maker of its own history.

Marx celebrated capitalism for its productive power, but he thought the single-minded economic development created by the capitalist structure of social relations twisted human thought and behavior. Marx's analysis of alienation, ideology, and the commodity fetish present a gloomy picture of life under capitalism. They are concepts that chart the thoroughness of our domination. But beneath his critique was a profound optimism: to be subject to capital is not the same as being the hopeless subjects of history. "Men make their own history," Marx wrote, "but they do not make it just as they please; they do not make it under circumstances chosen by themselves, but under circumstances directly encountered, given and transmitted from the past."[14] Marx challenges us to not look away from the ways we are subject, all the methods through which we are forced to exist in a world "transmitted from the past." But he also calls on us to "make [our] own history"—not to escape human nature, but to reach our human potential through our own reading of history.

Recovering Marx from all the world's Marxisms is not the task of finding a pure theory, stripped of its layers of accretions and misreadings. As this chapter has attempted to show, Marx himself was full of contradictions. One could make the case that it would have been a better development for the movement of global communism if he had received a university position and spent the rest of his days in a philosopher's armchair working out a system. But, as it was, he spent his life uprooted by exile and poverty, chasing after world political events and grasping at the reins of an inchoate movement. One result was that he finished few of his projects and left no doctrine. The other result, however, was that he was brought into contact with several of the major intellectual currents of his time. Each shifted his position. Each contributed to his working analysis. He used the methods of Hegel and radical German philosophy to discipline the sympathies of Proudhon and other French socialists. Then, with that framework, he undermined the assumptions of Adam Smith and the field of English political economy. He turned the principles of English economics against itself. He redeployed the terms the radical Enlightenment had used against the church and colonized (alienation, fetish) to show that the liberalism of the Enlightenment was, itself, another religion. Yet his most important contribution, not only to cultural theory but to the political movements that used his name, may have been his method: an interpretive strategy that opened the actions and thoughts of daily life to critical reading by recognizing that the ceaseless movements of history make our everyday truths contingent. His was the Enlightenment's critique of the Enlightenment. If Marx had been able to claim himself a Marxist, it might have only meant a radical commitment to a process of reevaluation and dialectical shifts.

## NOTES

1. Although Engels saw a direct connection between Darwin's biological laws and Marx's theory of political and economic development, Marx thought that Darwin's emphasis on competition in the animal world threatened to naturalize struggle within human societies. The classical economists (Thomas Hobbes, Thomas Malthus, Adam Smith) assumed life outside society was, as Hobbes claimed, "solitary, poor, nasty, brutish, and short." Marx, however,

believed the antagonisms that plagued modern society were the result of the alienation caused by private property, capitalist production, and religion. Humans were by nature cooperative, social animals according to Marx.

2. "'Friedrich Engels to Eduard Berstein,' 2–3 November 1882," in *Marx-Engels Collected Works (MECW)* vol. 46 (New York: International Publishers, 1992), 356.

3. Étienne Balibar, *The Philosophy of Marx* (London: Verso, 1995), 117.

4. The paternity of Frederick "Freddy" Demuth is still questioned by some scholars. The Marx family sent Freddy to be raised by a working class family shortly after he was born and encouraged speculation that Freddy was Engels's illegitimate son. The rumor that Marx was the father was dismissed as anti-communist propaganda during the Cold War. However, since the fall of the Soviet Union previously suppressed documents support the claim, and a consensus is building among Marx's biographers (see Wheen, Sperber, and Jones) that Karl Marx was Freddy's father.

5. Adam Smith, *Lectures on Jurisprudence* (1763), edited by R. L. Meek, D. D. Raphael, and Peter Stein (Oxford: Oxford University Press, 1978).

6. Karl Marx, "Critique of the Hegelian Dialectic and Philosophy as a Whole," in *MECW* vol. 3 (New York: International Publishers, 1975), 332–3.

7. Karl Marx, *The Communist Manifesto*, in *MECW* vol. 6 (New York: International Publishers, 1976), 519.

8. Karl Marx, *Capital*, vol. 1, in *MECW* vol. 35 (New York: International Publishers, 1996), 750.

9. Ibid., 751.

10. Ibid., 751.

11. Karl Marx, "Direct Results of the Production Process," in *MECW* vol. 34 (New York: International Publishers, 1994), 398.

12. Karl Marx, *The German Ideology*, in *MECW* vol. 5 (New York: International Publishers, 1976), 59.

13. Karl Marx, *Capital* vol. 1, 83.

14. Karl Marx. "The Eighteenth Brumaire of Louis Bonaparte," in *MECW* vol. 11 (New York: International Publishers, 1979), 103.

*Chapter Four*

# Ludwig Wittgenstein

*Toward a Dialectical Pragmatism*

Steve Wexler

## INTRODUCTION

The irony of a Ludwig Wittgenstein chapter in an anthology designed to historicize theories, theorists, and acts of interpretation will not be lost on those who have some familiarity with the philosopher. Wittgenstein famously dismissed history, philosophical and political, throughout his professional life. He believed that he drew only from the reasonable, obvious, and ordinary to make his claims about what the nineteenth-century Viennese journalist Karl Kraus called the *lifeworld*. In his first and only review, Wittgenstein, aged 24, noted that contemporary logicians knew "no more about Logic" than Aristotle did.[1] Later he would insist that the majority of arguments inherited from the Vienna Circle and other sites of academic philosophy proposed "idle symbolism and pseudo-technical jargon" to put forth "abstract formal conundrums" that lacked "roots in real life."[2] Wittgenstein was against *theory*. He maintained this unpopular position until his death in 1951.

The ostensible clarity and common sense that informed Ludwig Wittgenstein's understanding of his efforts should not suggest an easy affair for the philosopher or for those around him. Wittgenstein's commitment to his work and to his discipline was alienated, alienating, and at times insufferable, a Spartan attempt to reveal, if not synthesize, the varied contradictions that plagued the field. This labor included formulating the main ideas for *Tractatus Logico-Philosophicus*, Wittgenstein's only major philosophical work published during his lifetime, in self-imposed exile in the small village of Skjolden, Norway, and then further refining their exposition on the Russian front as a dedicated and respected soldier for the Austro-Hungarian army during the First World War. So even if at times a solitary figure, Wittgenstein was no philosopher in meditation.[3] Whether he recognized it or not, it is precisely Wittgenstein's relation to history—his role in a developing social consciousness—that permits insight into the philosopher's work and the world in which that work emerged.

With the above sentiment in mind, this chapter argues that Wittgenstein's philosophy is historical in the most profound sense for at least two reasons. First, Wittgenstein's philosophy, both the early and late, is by and large a pragmatism that manifests itself in a dialectic of uncertainty and certainty that begins as far back as the seventeenth century[4] as a contest between humanism and rationalism waged across new disciplines and nation-states. This epistemological contradiction was borne from and reinforced by the material relations of Renaissance Europe and has lasted well beyond Wittgenstein's day. Second, in addition to its role in the long dialectic of uncertainty and certainty, Wittgenstein's pragmatism implicitly suggests dialectics at the moment(s) of meaning-making or, as the later Wittgenstein put it, meaning-use. Wittgensteinian meaning is a normative *and* dialectical event lest there be no *stasis* to the language game, *synthesis* in meaning, and reification in knowledge production (e.g., dictionaries and university curricula). That is, one cannot have "family resemblances," the similarities that connect and make possible Wittgenstein's language games, without relying on some consistency *in* the language game *even if* that game is only realized in the pragmatic event of meaning-use. Wittgenstein makes the case as follows: our expressions are determined by rules for their use, so "without these rules the word has as yet no meaning; and if we change the rules, it now has another meaning (or none), and in that case we may just as well change the word, too."[5] Furthermore, it is the dialectical nature of *inference*—the symmetric, rational contradictions of meaning between individuals in reciprocal relation—that gives *propositional content* its normative status and *pragmatism* its materiality.

In this sense, Wittgenstein lays the groundwork for contemporary pragmatisms that provide the epistemology missing in materialist accounts of meaning. This latter point is especially important to recognize since Wittgenstein's philosophy is too often spurned by Marxists as vulgar or bourgeois antifoundationalism. Understood as a kind of *naturalism*, however, Wittgenstein's pragmatism operates under the historical, material relations in meaning-making and is well within the bounds of a materialist understanding of history. Simply put, how a child comes to learn "cat" or why two individuals disagree over a photograph's likeness to its subject are partly pragmatic moments in meaning-making, a reality inclusive of historical-material relations and therefore amenable to Marx's famous observations that class contradictions drive history and social existence determines men's consciousness. One need only consider the *totality* hinted at in one of Wittgenstein's most famous observations: "What belongs to a language game is a whole culture,"[6] where "whole culture" *includes* rather than *erases* the socioeconomic relations that underwrite materialist accounts of history and subject. What Wittgenstein ultimately reveals through his moment in the dialectic of uncertainty and certainty is that *pragmatism is naturalism shaped by historical relations but not entirely explained by those relations.*

Interpretation—the interpretative event—is an important example of the dialectical-normative relation of meaning. Seen as Wittgensteinian pragmatism, interpretative acts follow *and* realize their rules at the very moments of the acts; that is, a rule *prior* to an interpretation and its reception is inconsequential even as that rule is necessary for what follows. Hence, Wittgenstein says, ". . . any interpretation still hangs in the air with what it interprets, and cannot give it any support. Interpretations by themselves do not determine meaning;"[7] "This was our paradox: no course of action could be determined by a rule, because every course of action could be made out to accord with the rule."[8] These observations recognize that the social reception of interpretation or the extent to which the interpretation already fits within the life form or culture is what matters. This pragmatism is what places the interpretative act beyond any private rule-following (again, since otherwise any "course of action could . . . accord with the rule"). Yet at the same time the rule is *necessary* since the rule or system of rules provides the structure if not content of the interpretative act. The rule gives a specific content normativity but only as—when—the rule is realized in the pragmatic instance of interpretation. Where the early Wittgenstein held that the interpretive act was more important than what could be stated matter-of-factly, the later Wittgenstein redefined interpretation itself.

## THE WITTGENSTEIN TURN

A Wittgensteinian way of reading signals the apex of the linguistic turn in Western philosophy, a paradigmatic shift from Cartesian dualism and rational certainty to the primacy of language in fallibilistic uncertainty. The linguistic turn neither begins nor ends with Wittgenstein but achieves its greatest clarity and cogency in the philosopher's work. The term was coined by Gustav Bergmann in a 1960 review and then made famous by Richard Rorty's 1967 anthology *The Linguistic Turn* as an idea whose implications scholars across disciplines would have to contend with. Those seeking the turn's ultimate source could look to Kant's *Critique of Pure Reason*, which puts logical grammars or propositional content at the points of perception, judgment, and eventual understanding, or Nietzsche's 1873 essay, "On Truth and Lies in a Nonmoral Sense," where his noted observation that truth is a "movable host of metaphors, metonymies, and anthropomorphisms, a sum of human relations"[9] anticipates Foucauldian genealogy, Derridean deconstruction, and the entire poststructuralist canon. Charles Sanders Peirce, Nietzsche's contemporary and father of pragmatism (Peirce's version was pragmaticism), went as far as to suggest a linguistic turn via human-semiotic ontology: "the word or sign that man uses *is* the man himself."[10] W. V. O. Quine's groundbreaking objections to logical positivism, including the analytic/synthetic distinction, rested firmly on a holistic or conjunctive understanding of language: no single sentence stood contentfully independent. In 1956, Wilfred Sellars reanimated Kantian "judgment," Kant's basic unit of meaning, with the "Myth of the Given," and theorized that there is no cognitive state (i.e., a semantic given) without an interdependent "logical space of particulars, universals, and facts."[11] As far back as 1670, Gottfried Leibniz worked toward a *characteristica universalis* or universal language within his larger project of rationalism to bring unity to a devastated and fragmented Europe following the Thirty Years War.[12]

The excellent Wittgenstein historical biographies by Ray Monk and then Allan Janik and Stephen Toulmin demonstrate quite vividly that the role of language as the *sine qua non* of meaning as revealed in the *Tractatus Logico-Philosophicus* and *Philosophical Investigations* is an idea largely indebted to the mathematics, physics, philosophy, art, architecture, and journalism that immediately precede and develop alongside Wittgenstein. There is no early or late Wittgenstein without Heinrich Hertz's innovative *bildliche Darstellung* (pictorial representation) of the then unseen atomistic universe, Ludwig Boltzmann's probabilistic molecular distribution in "logical space" at the heart of entropy,[13] Gottlob Frege's revolution in symbolic logic and analytic philosophy, and Kraus's agonistic aphorisms aimed at German culture and language. The *Wittgenstein turn* parleys these varied influences across pragmatist epistemology and philosophy of language that joins, rather than divides, both Wittgensteins. One finds that regardless of the work or the moment, Wittgenstein and his world were reciprocally transformative.

## A LITTLE NONSENSE NOW AND THEN

The *Tractatus Logico-Philosophicus* borrows its name from Spinoza's *Tractatus Theologico-Politicus* (1670), a major modern philosophical treatise that above all challenges dogmatic readings of scripture and establishes boundaries between secular and nonsecular thought, philosophy, and theology. Wittgenstein's *Tractatus* is no less ambitious and to no small degree a continuation of that project. Wittgenstein believed that he had solved philosophy's problems with his own Spinozian line drawn between things in the world and things beyond. Wittgenstein's division places ethics, aesthetics, *and* philosophy (metaphysics) on the same side, as things which could only be *shown*.

On the other side, separated by an incommensurable No Man's Land, are *a priori* truths, such as $1 + 1 = 2$, logic, and matters of science like the local weather, things that could be *stated*. The self-professed ahistorical Wittgenstein argued that the entire history of philosophy had been a case of erroneously blurring that line and doing so largely through a misunderstanding and misuse of language. And while the instances were vast, the majority of philosophical errors could be reduced to two kinds: (1) claims that would require stepping outside language for their validation, such as mistaking the tautological nature of logical *form* as itself representative and generative, that is, trying to state what the proposition's structure must have in common for it to represent what it depicts ("Propositions can represent the whole reality, but they cannot represent what they must have in common with reality in order to represent it—the logical form;"[14] "The propositions of logic therefore say nothing"[15]), and (2) framing metaphysical pronouncements such as "Man is rational" and "This song is mellifluous" in absolute terms, as matters-of-fact. According to the *Tractatus*, both problems were the result of philosophers trying to say what can only be shown, mistaking nonsense for sense. *But what exactly does that mean?* Wittgenstein's *Tractatus* suggests that the simplest form of meaning is the sentence, not the word. The *Tractatus* makes its case through a *picture theory of meaning* or *bildliche Darstellung* (pictorial representation) comprised of a number of various kinds of declarative statements organized around seven main propositions. Wittgenstein had read about a court case involving a crime scene represented by models and reasoned that propositions were kinds of modeling that yielded a pictorial relation with the fact that it was describing as that fact exists in space. This picture theory shows how language models reality as a thought or proposition with sense. World and proposition shared the same logical structure even if one could not state exactly what it was that made it so, i.e., could not state the *nature* of structure of that relation. Hence, Wittgenstein's reasons, *"The limits of my language* mean the limits of my world."[16] One might consider the relation between world and language, facts and propositions, as laid out below:

a. The world is made up of facts. Facts are made up of states of affairs. States of affairs are the connections of objects.
b. Language is made up of propositions. Propositions are made up of elementary propositions. Elementary propositions are made up of names or basic units of language.
c. World and language parallel each other as follows:

    a. Propositions describe facts.
    b. Elementary propositions describe states of affairs.
    c. Names denote objects.[17]

Hence the arrangement of names in an elementary proposition will be a picture of an arrangement of objects that constitute a state of affairs.

The *Tractatus*'s propositional calculus and *bildliche Darstellung* had been the strategy of Wittgenstein's mentor Bertrand Russell and German physicist Heinrich Hertz. Like Frege, Russell aimed to reduce mathematical truths to a set of axioms by treating propositions as functions rather than Aristotelian subject/predicate connections. Hertz would map mathematical structure onto a language of mechanics that could transcend Ernst Mach's subjective neoempiricism: "the elements of such a structure or model need not be derived from perception" when they are shown by the imposition of that structure on mechanical phenomena.[18]

Returning to the two fundamental philosophical errors, the *Tractatus* states (1) as follows:

> 6.1: The propositions of logic are tautologies.
> 6.11: Therefore the propositions of logic say nothing. (They are the analytic propositions.)
> 6.123: It is clear that the laws of logic cannot themselves obey further logical laws.
> 6.124: The logical propositions describe the scaffolding of the world, or rather they present it. They "treat" of nothing.[19]

Per 6.123, one would have to step outside language to say what exactly made logical form representational, that is, what exactly was it about the form itself that constituted representation. This is why Wittgenstein writes, "4.121 Propositions cannot represent the logical form."[20] Furthermore, propositional logic, according to Wittgenstein, is ultimately tautological since the inferential *relations* between propositions contain nothing new; if one proposition follows another it is only because the first proposition says it already.

As for the second fundamental philosophical error, framing metaphysics as matters-of-fact, as things which can be *stated*, Wittgenstein arguably believed that this was the *Tractatus*'s most important lesson. Here one might interpret the *Tractatus* in at least two ways: that which can only be shown, such as ethics and aesthetics, represents Wittgenstein's penchant for mysticism and makes his book a kind of nonsecular proselytizing. Wittgenstein had, after all, clung to and referenced Tolstoy's *Gospels in Brief* during his military service and held Dostoevsky's *Brothers Karamazov* depiction of the Christian ideal above all others. Yet the far more compelling view is to see "showing" as something necessarily demonstrative and pragmatic for individuals and *between* individuals. And here one finds the crucial link between Wittgenstein's early and later work. When Wittgenstein writes in 1929 that "[t]he good is outside the space of facts,"[21] Wittgenstein stands between nonsense and use.

The *Tractatus* suggests two kinds of showing: reflexive and demonstrative. Reflexive showing is when logical form reveals itself, e.g., with tautology. Demonstrative showing is the response to and use of the aesthetic and ethical:

> SAYING: Propositions, facts
> SHOWING (REFLEXIVE): Logical form
> (DEMONSTRATIVE): Ethical and aesthetic

*It is the demonstrative case of showing that is pragmatic and common to both the early and later work.* Martin Pulido's example of a knock-knock joke is helpful. There is nothing intrinsically funny about a knock-knock joke; that is, one doesn't find "funny" as part of the text itself. Rather, "funny" is in the joke's effect, the laugh. [22] Or one might consider the statement, "The portrait of John is excellent." Whether or not "excellent" here means the portrait's likeness to its subject (i.e., an immediacy), use of light, or something else, it is a quality that exists not in the painting but with the observer's experience of the painting. As Pulido puts it, "Language and pictures cannot say what their structures have in common, they can only show them, because any language or picture relies on the logical form that is mirrored in them." [23] Hence, this demonstrative case of showing in which the aesthetic response or experience is something that cannot be stated as matter-of-fact; it can only be shown. This demonstrative case holds for the ethical, too. "Man is good" is for Wittgenstein a kind of nonsense since the very qualities that the statement depends on do not exist in the world as do a temperature reading or simple math equation.

While the Vienna Circle would hold Wittgenstein and his first work in the highest regard, as a text that realized their greatest ambitions—logical positivism and the reductive project of the new analytic philosophy—Wittgenstein believed that it was what couldn't be stated that truly mattered: the aesthetic and ethical. This is one reason why Wittgenstein felt that Russell had fundamentally misunderstood the *Tractatus* (Russell wrote the book's introduction) and why Wittgenstein chose to read poetry to the Circle after accepting their invitation to discuss his work!

To summarize: The *Tractatus* held that the proposition was in a pictorial relation with the fact that it was describing. World and proposition shared the same logical structure even if one couldn't state exactly what it was that made it so, i.e., the *nature* of that relation. That move would require stepping outside of language. Hence, Wittgenstein's powerful observation, "*The limits of my language* mean the limits of my world." [24] For the early Wittgenstein, philosophy (i.e., metaphysics) was *nonsensical* since philosophy, particularly aesthetics and ethics, had been trying to state in absolute terms what could only be shown, that is, demonstratively. The "ladder" used to reach the

*Tractatus*'s most significant claims would have to be thrown away since here too was a case of stating something that could only be shown. Wittgenstein's "cheating" had the profound effect of clarifying the limits to positivistic certainty and reductionism as well as revealing what mattered most: the ethical and aesthetic. Wittgenstein concludes, "Whereof one cannot speak, thereof one must be silent."[25] The problems of philosophy had been solved, and Wittgenstein would move on.

Frank Ramsey,[26] the equally brilliant Cambridge standout, reviewed the *Tractatus* positively but not without pointing to its fundamental flaw: the "atomic proposition" is only contingently true or false; "logical relations . . . hold not between the things or the facts of the world, but rather between propositions."[27] Ramsey's observation is seen as the main impetus to Wittgenstein's return to Cambridge and to philosophy, with Ramsey as Wittgenstein's supervisor.[28]

The later Wittgenstein would abandon the *Tractatus*'s reductive pretensions to universality in logical form and posit instead a pragmatic rendering of meaning, one rooted in *"Volkerpsychologie,"* the idea that "language is a social phenomenon."[29] Throughout the *Philosophical Investigations*, Wittgenstein echoes Viennese journalist-philosopher Fritz Mauthner's contention that "language is not the possession of the solitary individual, because it only exists between men."[30] Rather than meaning-as-representation (via language or perception), Wittgenstein argues instead for *meaning-use*, where meaning is realized—externalized—in the pragmatic moment, through the communicative act that included language as the primary medium. The posthumous *Philosophical Investigations* stated that there is no private language, to the extent that something as clearly palpable and personal as one's own pain could be cast in doubt since one could only confirm pain through language, which is always already social—that is to say, if one could *not* doubt one's pain, one could not be sure that it was pain one was experiencing. The atomization of language, logic, and world gave way to a number of logics and family resemblances that served specific language games: "To imagine a language means to imagine a form of life."[31] In this sense, Wittgenstein's later pragmatism merely restates the anthropology and materiality in "meaning-use," a *naturalism* recently affirmed by philosopher Hans Sluga.[32]

Perhaps the most noted example of this Wittgensteinian revolution is Wittgenstein's "Beetle in a Box" thought experiment.[33] Wittgenstein asks readers to imagine a group of individuals each holding a box containing a beetle and not being permitted to look inside another's box. How does one know that a beetle is contained in another's box? *How does one know one has a* beetle *in one's box?* The only thing one can be certain of is what comes from the communicative act itself, the language-game "This is a beetle." And in such a game the very thing referenced—the beetle—is unimportant: "if we construe the grammar of the expression of sensation on the model of 'object and designation' the object drops out of consideration as irrelevant."[34] Wittgenstein's "beetle in the box" demonstrates that there can be no private language and that meaning is not something inside one's head. Where the *Tractatus* had revealed metaphysics as nonsensical, *Philosophical Investigations* leveled psychology. Psychoanalysis, in particular, was hit hard, as Wittgenstein had reduced Freudian science to myth. Yet in doing so, Wittgenstein would likely say that he gave Freud the empirical dimension he never had.

## THE RISE OF UNCERTAINTY

As Stephen Toulmin describes it, rationalism was a lofty plan urged on by Rene Descartes, Blaise Pascal, and Gottfried Leibniz, facilitated by Gutenberg's movable type and necessitated by Europe's Thirty Years' War to unite "ideas of rationality, necessity, and certainty into a single mathematical package."[35] Erasmus, Montaigne, and Rabelais, humanists who embraced all aspects of daily life, high and how, were deemed profligate in a time of dire rebuilding. The quest for certainty was a dream for some and a nightmare for others. As Wordsworth lamented, "Our meddling intellect / Mis-shapes the beauteous forms of things:— / We murder to dissect."[36] And if rationalism would enjoy the spoils, as it clearly did throughout the following three hundred years of industrialization, imperialism, and technological innovation, it was not without a fight: like Wordsworth and other Romantics, Wittgenstein would resist rationalist hegemony.

The *Tractatus Logico-Philosophicus* could be seen as a brash and ascetic young philosopher's attempt to set limits to the logic underlying the emergent positivism and expanding scientism taking hold on the academy and, really, much of European and Anglo-American intellectual thought, an extension of the quest for certainty. *Positivism*, the idea that reality is knowable through scientific method and that every rational assertion is scientifically verifiable, and *scientism*, the privileging of scientific activity above all others, were purposely, self-consciously reductionist. As Jürgen Habermas notes, for the positivists, "Any epistemology that transcends the framework of methodology . . . now succumbs to the same sentence of extravagance and meaninglessness that is once passed on metaphysics."[37] Positivism's "pseudo-scientific propagation of the cognitive monopoly of science"[38] replaced the "knowing subject's reflection upon itself"[39] with the "phenomenon of scientific-technical progress"[40] to the extent that the "history of the species [was] the history of the realization of the positive spirit."[41] To what degree this reductionism was demanded by a crisis in democracy or the new, robust industrial capitalism and its requisite bureaucratic rationalisms should be explored, but it is epistemology that most certainly begins with Frege's masterworks *Begriffsschrift* (*Concept-Script*) (1879) and *Grundgesetze der*

*Arithmetik (Fundamental Laws of Arithmetic)* (1884). The *Begriffsschrift* and *Grundgesetze* each contribute to modern thought in profound ways. Aristotelean syllogistic logic had held sway until Frege demonstrated its inability to reduce the complexity of mathematics to analytic, symbolic form, the *Begriffsschrift*'s central aim. Frege presents a *logicism* or language of symbolic logic that provides an axiomatic system that makes definite and explicit logical relations and inferences. In doing so, Frege invents modern logic. Frege's *Grundgesetze* attempts to define exactly what a number is. In paragraph 62, Frege introduces his "Context Principle" that distinguishes sense from reference or denotation. Frege asks, "How, then, shall a number be given to us, when we cannot have any representations or intuitions of it?"[42] Frege surmises that "only in a complete sentence do words really have meaning [*Bedeutung*]."[43] Since a number has no objective or subjective meaning on its own, one must look to the number's context for meaning. Hence, where the *Begriffsschrift* introduces predicate logic, the *Grundgesetze* permits the reduction of mathematics to symbolic logic. Frege formalizes the linguistic turn.

One could also look to enormous shifts in math and physics represented in the work of Ernst Mach (1838–1916) and Ludwig Boltzmann (1844–1906). These two prodigious figures along with Frege provide a better understanding of Wittgenstein's part in the dialectic of uncertainty and certainty. Michael Stöltzner calls the nineteenth-century moment of Mach and Boltzmann "Vienna Indeterminism," when physicists defined "determinism and causality within a Kantian framework" that refused "*a priori* categories as a criterion for empirical reality."[44] Where Mach held that scientific laws served our sensations rather than objective reality and that determinism was "empirically unprovable" but "still an unavoidable regulative principle, Boltzmann admitted the existence of genuinely statistical laws."[45] This was a constructivist mathematics that paved the way for Wittgenstein's pragmatic and naturalistic language games. Almost in direct line with Frege et al., Wittgenstein reveals the fundamental error in "seeing mathematics and logic 'as being about a body of truths which exist in their own right independently of whether anyone believes them or knows about them.'"[46]

## INTERPRETATION: MEANING: EVENT

We should at this point recognize that Wittgenstein's position in the dialectic of uncertainty and certainty as well as the dialectics at the heart of his pragmatism resist rather than affirm the hegemony of epistemic antifoundationalism.[47] Consider the *naturalism* in his reasoning: "I can think of no better expression to characterize these similarities than 'family resemblances': for the various resemblances between members of a family: build, features, colour of eyes, gait, temperament, etc. etc. overlap and criss-cross in the same way. —And I shall say: 'games' form a family."[48] According to Susan B. Brill, Wittgensteinian criticism offers "a *method* that is both dynamic and responsive in its actual applications, comprehensive in its applicability towards a wide range of texts, and expansive in its potential results."[49] Yet, for Wittgenstein, a theory represents a fundamental misunderstanding of the language game of interpretation and hence is "without value."[50] The main issue is that theory suggests a static, preconceived framework to which "a reality *must* correspond."[51] Instead, one should see "interpretation as a process of theorizing."[52] Meaning and interpretation will vary according to use, context, and individuals. This position reaches back to Wittgenstein's understanding that an object does not contain a word's meaning, what the word names, but rather that meaning is through use alone. Recall how Wittgenstein's beetle became inconsequential in the language game and moment of meaning-making. The beetle's status is more or less what comes of the text itself, a position, by the way, that would appear to fly in the face of the Affective Fallacy,[53] since all that counts *is* the effect—emotional, intellectual—created through the reading, interpretation, and so on. The later Wittgenstein's emphasis on ordinary language and use would render language classification and theory itself a misunderstanding of the language-game, a *misuse* of language. So if interlocutors find their meanings through the use and context of their speech acts, then it would stand to reason that the interpretative act exists somewhere between individual and text—novel, painting, essay, photograph, and so on. Wittgenstein's meaning-use anticipates the more recent reader-response criticism that places meaning between individual and text; that is, meaning neither begins nor ends with reader, writer, or text. With Wittgenstein's understanding of the *language game* as a whole culture and *language* as a form of life—the common features shared among language games—we might suggest that any one interpretation of a text already belongs to a community of interpreters even if interpretations do not bring meaning.

I want to conclude by returning to the second account of dialectics in Wittgenstein's thought. As suggested above, Wittgensteinian pragmatism provides a narrow epistemology missing in materialist accounts of meaning, or better gives contemporary pragmatisms their role in historical materialism only insofar as the pragmatism places dialectics at the moments of meaning-making. Simply put, while Marx's *historical materialism* does not attempt to explain in any final, comprehensive sense how and why one *reasons*, Marx's *materialism* permits a pragmatist account of the matter, a pragmatism that neither erases nor occludes Marxist orthodoxy and is well within the bounds of Marx's understanding of history. It is the pragmatists who omit these material relations from their antifoundational analytics. A specific example of such pragmatism will help clarify my point.

Genealogy, according to Robert Brandom, "seeks to dispel the *illusion* of reason"[54] that was the Enlightenment's answer to the obedience model of authority. As Brandom puts it, this was nineteenth-century naturalism's "revenge" on eighteenth-century rationalism.[55] Genealogy depends on counterfactual logic that unmasks reasons as causes or products of contingencies (e.g., geographical, biographical) "that are not evidence for the truth of what is believed."[56] Had these contingencies been otherwise, then so, too, the reasons, for example, "If Mary had caught the train to Manchester on time, Mary would have come to believe *P* instead of *Q*." The genealogy project presents a problem for epistemology: the genealogist potentially ignores his *own* blind faith in reason, that is, in the very capacity to connect contingencies in objective and final terms beyond the genealogist's situatedness.

Brandom addresses this problem quite remarkably in "Reason, Genealogy, and the Hermeneutics of Magnanimity" by redefining genealogy as an Hegelian retrospective rational reconstruction of meaning. The genealogist, through diachronic reciprocal recognition, *retrospectively* gives the original contingencies that shaped the attitudes at the heart of objective reasoning their normative status. For Brandom, Hegel's reciprocal "symmetric normative construal of the relations of authority and responsibility between universals and particulars"[57] provides the social dimension to Kant's asymmetric division of semantic and epistemic labor. Kant's rational, autonomous individual already has on hand (i.e., spontaneously) semantic or propositional contents (universals) when she goes off to make epistemic commitments or judgments (particulars) as an authority unto herself. Kantian conceptual content remains unaffected by its application in judgment. This cleaving of semantic and epistemic labor ignores that "judgments shape our concepts no less than our concepts shape our judgments."[58] Kant's own semantic naiveté, like the genealogist's that abandons reason altogether (that is, abandons since reason itself is only inferentially and hence contextually realized), takes for granted the conceptual content (universals) influencing attitudes.

Hegelian retrospective rational reconstruction, however, is reciprocal, inferential, and social in nature. Its counterfactual logic already allows for the mutual influence of concepts and judgments and therefore illuminates *the vast productive relations in meaning-making* (again, since Kant's construal of reason, while normative, ignores the other's—and hence socioeconomic—influence in recognition and realization). The counterfactual logic underwriting the genealogy project and Brandom's reading of Hegel that would rescue that project (the better reason itself) by making reason diachronically and reciprocally formed (to borrow from jurisprudence: formed via the backward glance—*adjudication*—that then gives contingencies—*precedents*—their normative status) defines knowledge, meaning, and disciplinarity in complex causal, material, and social terms, and avoids what Jennifer Cotter et al.

rightly dismiss as "singularities of 'events' rather than a totality of relations, or materially grounded connections."[59]

More to the point and why this brief excursion into reconstructive genealogy in the first place: Brandom's Hegelian pragmatic inferentialism (the activity *and* rules governing an individual's giving and asking for reasons) should be seen as a Wittgensteinian *dialectical event*, that is, a language-game involving material, historical contradictions. Georg Lukács, for one, reminds us that "the most vital interaction" is "*the dialectical relation between subject and object in the historical process.*"[60] For Lukács, "even the category of interaction requires inspection. . . It must go further in its relation to the whole: for this relation determines the objective form of every object of cognition."[61] Vittorio Hösle has similarly stated that recognizing the dialectics in inferentialism would help "overcome the contingency and relativism that threatens . . . anti-empiricist accounts of concepts."[62] On the one hand, *historical materialism* cannot entirely explain how we use a language or why we respond differently to the same text. These examples are partly pragmatic moments in meaning-making. On the other hand, a pragmatism or inferentialism that does not make explicit the material relations and material facts surrounding the inferential act (e.g., social class and labor theory of value) is incomplete since *reason* then hangs in the air, to borrow from Wittgenstein. The dialectical nature of inference—the normative practice of giving and asking for reasons—gives pragmatism its materiality and materialism its epistemology. Without dialectical pragmatism, Hegelian reconstructive genealogy, too, like Enlightenment rationalism, "retains a spark of divinity in the form of the faculty of reason."[63]

## NOTES

1. Ludwig Wittgenstein, "Review: P. Coffey, *The Science of Logic*," *The Cambridge Review* 34, no. 853 (March 6, 1913), 351.
2. Allan Janik and Stephen Toulmin, *Wittgenstein's Vienna* (Chicago: Elephant, 1996), 260.
3. I have in mind here Rembrandt's famous painting (1632) and its implied Cartesianism.
4. Stephen Toulmin, *Cosmopolis: The Hidden Agenda of Modernity* (Chicago: University of Chicago Press, 1990), 35.
5. Ludwig Wittgenstein, *Philosophical Grammar* (Oxford: Blackwell, 1974), 133.
6. Ludwig Wittgenstein, *Lectures and Conversations on Aesthetics, Psychology, and Religious Belief,* edited by Cyril Barrett (Oxford: Basil Blackwell, 1966), 8.
7. Ludwig Wittgenstein, *Philosophical Investigations*, trans. G. E. M. Anscombe (New York: Macmillan, 1953), 80e.
8. Ibid., 81e.
9. Friedrich Nietzsche, "On Truth and Lies in a Nonmoral Sense," *The Nietzsche Reader*, edited by Keith Ansell Pearson and Duncan Large (Malden, MA: Blackwell, 2006), 117.
10. Charles S. Peirce, *Selected Writings: Values in a Universe of Chance*, edited by Philip P. Wiener (New York: Dover, 1958), 71.
11. According to John McDowell, "Sellars's dictum implies that it is a form of the Myth to think sensibility by itself, without any involvement of capacities that belong to our rationality,

can make things available for our cognition. That coincides with a basic doctrine of Kant." John McDowell, "Avoiding the Myth of the Given," September 2010, https://voices.uchicago.edu/germanphilosophy/files/2010/09/mcdowell-Avoiding-the-Myth-of-the-Given1.pdf, 2.

12. Stephen Toulmin, *Cosmopolis: The Hidden Agenda of Modernity* (Chicago: University of Chicago Press, 1990), 100–103.

13. Allan Janik and Stephen Toulmin, *Wittgenstein's Vienna* (Chicago: Elephant, 1996), 185.

14. Ludwig Wittgenstein, *Tractatus Logico-Philosophicus*, trans. C. K. Ogden (New York: Barnes & Noble, 2003), 53.

15. Ibid., 123.

16. Ibid., 117.

17. One might see the *Tractatus*'s opening lines as a continuation of Plato's distinction of form and matter and Kant's noumena and phenomena.

18. Allan Janik and Stephen Toulmin, *Wittgenstein's Vienna* (Chicago: Elephant, 1996), 142.

19. Ludwig Wittgenstein, *Tractatus Logico-Philosophicus*, trans. C. K. Ogden (New York: Barnes & Noble, 2003), 123, 131.

20. Ibid., 53.

21. Ludwig Wittgenstein, *Culture and Value*, trans. Peter Winch (Chicago: University of Chicago Press, 1980), 3e.

22. Martin Pulido, "The Place of Saying and Showing in Wittgenstein's *Tractatus* and Some Later Works," *Aporia* 19, vol. 2 (2009), 14.

23. Ibid., 17.

24. Ludwig Wittgenstein, *Tractatus Logico-Philosophicus*, trans. C. K. Ogden (New York: Barnes & Noble, 2003), 117.

25. Ibid., 155.

26. Ramsey's accomplishments include groundbreaking work in mathematics, philosophy, and economics, and prior to that earning the title "Senior Wrangler" as Cambridge's top undergraduate mathematics student, what D. O. Forfar calls "the greatest intellectual achievement attainable in Britain." These feats are perhaps all the more remarkable given Ramsey's early death at 26. Wittgenstein's belated acquiescence to Ramsey's insightful comments on the *Tractatus* was a rare thing indeed, and the catalyst behind the more radical *Philosophical Investigations*.

27. Ray Monk, "One of the Great Intellects of His Time," *The New York Review of Books*, December 22, 2016, http://www.nybooks.com/articles/2016/12/22/frank-ramsey-great-intellects/.

28. Ibid.

29. Allan Janik and Stephen Toulmin, *Wittgenstein's Vienna* (Chicago: Elephant, 1996), 127.

30. Ibid., 128.

31. Ludwig Wittgenstein, *Philosophical Investigations*, trans. G. E. M. Anscombe (New York: Macmillan, 1953), 19.

32. Hans Sluga, "Hans Sluga on the Life and Work of Wittgenstein," *Entitled Opinions (about Life and Literature)*, Stanford University Radio, October 7, 2015, accessed September 23, 2016, http://french-italian.stanford.edu/opinions.

33. Ludwig Wittgenstein, *Philosophical Investigations*, trans. G. E. M. Anscombe (New York: Macmillan, 1953), 100e.

34. Ibid., 100e.

35. Stephen Toulmin, *Return to Reason* (Cambridge, MA: Harvard University Press, 2001), 13.

36. William Wordsworth, "The Tables Turned," *The Poetry Foundation*, August 13, 2017, https://www.poetryfoundation.org/poems/45557/the-tables-turned.

37. Jürgen Habermas, *Knowledge and Human Interests*, trans. Jeremy J. Shapiro (Boston: Beacon Press, 1971), 67.

38. Ibid., 71.

39. Ibid., 71.

40. Ibid., 71.

41. Ibid., 72.

42. Michael Losonsky, *Linguistic Turns in Modern Philosophy* (Cambridge: Cambridge University Press, 2006), 163.

43. Ibid.

44. Michael Stöltzner, "Vienna Indeterminism: Mach, Boltzmann, Exner," *Synthese* 119, no. 1/2 (1999), 85–111. http://www.jstor.org/stable/20118164 , 85.

45. Ibid., 86.

46. Hugo Meynell, "Doubts about Wittgenstein's Influence," *Philosophy* 57, no. 220 (Apr. 1982), 253.

47. Cornel West, "Theory, Pragmatisms, and Politics," *Consequences of Theory*, edited by Jonathan Arac and Barbara Johnson (Baltimore: Johns Hopkins University Press, 1991), 24.

48. Ludwig Wittgenstein, *Philosophical Investigations*, trans. G. E. M. Anscombe (New York: Macmillan, 1953), 32e

49. Susan B. Brill, *Wittgenstein and Critical Theory: Beyond Postmodern Criticism and Toward Descriptive Investigations* (Athens: University of Ohio Press, 1995), 30–31.

50. Ibid., 9.

51. Ludwig Wittgenstein, *Philosophical Investigations*, trans. G. E. M. Anscombe (New York: Macmillan, 1953), 131e.

52. Susan B. Brill, *Wittgenstein and Critical Theory: Beyond Postmodern Criticism and Toward Descriptive Investigations* (Athens: University of Ohio Press, 1995), 10.

53. Stanley E. Fish, "Literature in the Reader: Affective Stylistics," *Reader-Response Criticism: From Formalism to Post-Structuralism*, edited by Jane P. Tompkins (Baltimore: Johns Hopkins University Press, 1980), 70.

54. Robert Brandom, "Reason, Genealogy, and the Hermeneutics of Magnanimity," November 21, 2012, http://www.pitt.edu/~brandom/downloads/RGHM%20%2012-11-21%20a.docx, 4.

55. Ibid., 4.

56. Ibid., 4.

57. Ibid., 12.

58. Ibid., 3.

59. Jennifer Cotter et al., *Human, All Too (Post)Human: The Humanities after Humanism* (Lanham, MD: Lexington Books), 223.

60. Georg Lukács, *History and Class Consciousness*, trans. Rodney Livingstone (London: Merlin Press, 1971), 3.

61. Ibid., 13.

62. Michael Morris, "A Review of *The Dimensions of Hegel's Dialectic*," *Notre Dame Philosophical Reviews: An Electronic Journal*, September 21, 2010, http://ndpr.nd.edu/news/the-dimensions-of-hegel-s-dialectic/.

63. Robert Brandom, "Reason, Genealogy, and the Hermeneutics of Magnanimity," November 21, 2012, http://www.pitt.edu/~brandom/downloads/RGHM%20%2012-11-21%20a.docx, 5.

## Chapter Five

# Robert Penn Warren

*Poetry, Racism, and the Burden of History*

## Cassandra Falke

In 1985, Robert Penn Warren was America's "most eminent man of letters."[1] He had been a Rhodes Scholar, a National Book Award Winner, twice a Guggenheim Fellowship holder, the first US Poet Laureate, a MacArthur fellow, and the only person to win the Pulitzer Prize in both poetry and fiction. He won for poetry twice. He had authored ten novels, sixteen poetry collections, over one hundred critical essays, a biography, books of scholarship on Melville and Dreiser, a biography of John Brown, an assessment of the legacy of the Civil War, and two books on race relations. It is difficult to know how to assess the contribution to scholarship made by someone so prolific, someone looked up to as a voice for literature for half a century. In 1994, he was still considered "one of the most gifted writers who had ever lived."[2] But the complexity and force of Warren's legacy as a critic are not always recognized. The number of works published about him per year has fallen, since 2010, to about a third of what it was in this century's first decade.[3] And there is only one book-length study of his contributions as a critic.[4] As Charles H. Boehner has noted, his versatility—working in poetry, fiction, drama, and literary and social criticism—"has cost Warren some of the critical attention" given to his contemporaries.[5]

Just as his versatility in multiple genres has diluted some of the attention that might have been given him, his versatility within literary criticism has left him outside of many accounts of critical and theoretical history. In the *Norton Anthology of Theory and Criticism*, his name appears as a friend to John Crowe Ransom and a footnote to Cleanth Brooks, signaling his association with New Criticism, but also his peripheral position in relation to its main ideas.[6] As the least dogmatic of the scholars associated with New

Criticism, he is the most subtle, but not the most exemplary, and consequently his criticism is less often reprinted today. Nevertheless, his legacy as a critic is still discernable in classrooms all over America. *Understanding Poetry*, the textbook he published together with Brooks in 1938, "transformed the way in which literature was analyzed and appreciated around the country" for several decades, remaining in print until 1976.[7] The companion volume, *Understanding Fiction*, had a similarly long print run (1943–1979). Their still-used format of an introduction of a literary technique, followed by some exemplifying works, followed by questions and editorial commentary reflects their success in shifting the focus of literary instruction away from the world that gives rise to a literary work and toward interpretive possibilities.

In light of his peripheral position in relation to New Criticism, or any other "school" of criticism, it would not be unreasonable to question why Robert Penn Warren should be included in a book like this. He rejects the label of "literary theorist" and in spite of his productivity claims not to have been a critic in a serious way. He writes of Cleanth Brooks and I. A. Richards that "they develop a system." That system becomes their "main interest." In characterizing himself, however, Warren says his interest is in "this poem or that poem." He is "not interested in trying to create a system" as much as a new "kind of understanding."[8] But Warren very much deserves a place in a collection that approaches interpretive practices, theory, and history in a unified way. He returns again and again to questions of an individual's relationship to history and to some new "kind of understanding" that, once achieved through literature, can enable interventions in concrete struggles for social justice. The diversity of his work reflects his relentlessness in addressing these questions. Literature, he says, is "an antidote, a sovereign antidote for passivity."[9] When we, in a "deep sense, open the imagination to it, it provides the freshness and immediacy of experience that returns us to ourselves, and, as Nietzsche puts it, provides us with that 'vision,' that 'enchantment,' which is, for man, the 'completion of his state' and an affirmation of his sense of life."[10]

I begin the remainder of my essay by trying to clarify Warren's own vision for himself as a critic, focusing on two of his most famous critical essays, "Pure and Impure Poetry" and "A Poem of Pure Imagination." I then position his work in relation to a broader history of criticism. Often, Warren is associated too completely with New Criticism, an association that obscures his subtle attention to readers' responsibility, not just to the text but also to the historical moment in which they read it. Finally, I comment on Warren's personal history and the weight that he felt that history to have. A grandson of a Confederate soldier and one-time Southern Agrarian, he was also a pioneering civil rights documentarian. Warren sensed that his skills as a literary critic could be effectively repurposed for social critique. I end by offering a re-evaluation of his critical legacy that includes the late works of social criticism, notably *Segregation* and *Who Speaks for the Negro*?

## WARREN'S CENTRAL IDEAS

The closest Warren comes to articulating a system of criticism is in a pair of essays he wrote for *The Kenyon Review* in 1943 and 1946. The first of these, "Pure and Impure Poetry" begins with the pronouncement that "The critic who vaingloriously trusts his method to account for the poem, to exhaust the poem . . . is doomed to failure."[11] In keeping with this belief, Warren offers no one way to approach all works of literature, but he does stake out several key theoretical positions. In the later essay, "A Poem of Pure Imagination: An Experiment in Reading," Warren writes an extended analysis of Coleridge's "The Rime of the Ancient Mariner," and in contrasting his practice with regard to the poem with the practices of other critics, articulates his theoretical premises even more clearly. The paragraphs that follow draw primarily on these two essays and his later book, *Democracy and Poetry*. Warren points out that criticism focusing on elements "intrinsic" to a work is essential for clarifying what a work does to a reader and how, but that intrinsic features only become meaningful when combined with "extrinsic" concerns.[12] Warren's division of intrinsic and extrinsic elements of critical practice provides a useful structure for investigating his main ideas.

Warren believed that poetry's "intrinsic" themes are elaborated through formal devices such as language, imagery, and character construction. He typically wrote about the specific techniques of a theme's presentation and especially the interrelationship of these themes.[13] He shared the New Critical interest in "the drama" of a work's structure and the ways that "the fires of irony" refine an author's theme by creating tension.[14] His analyses of works' formal elements are rigorous and range across multiple levels of textual detail. Although he claimed that rhythm, "not mere meter, but all the pulse of movement, density, and shadings of intensity of feeling—is the most compelling factor revealing to us the nature of the 'made thing,'" he tended to discuss works in terms of their structure, more than their temporal unfolding.[15] This is because for him the "'made thing'—the poem, the work of art—stands as a 'model' of the organized self."[16] Describing the relationality of elements within that model is, therefore, one of the critic's most important tasks.

The focus on relationality and structure characterizes his criticism at the level of individual words as well as larger "shadings of intensity of feeling." For example, he notes single words in Robert Frost's "After Apple Picking," when those words push against the lexical register established in the lines around them. Analyzing the predominance of moonlight in Coleridge's "Ancient Mariner," he includes analysis at the level of the line, but mostly works with the poem's architecture more broadly. The Mariner, he observes, receives a curse from his fellow sailors by the light of the moon, blesses the sea snakes under the moon, and finally relies on the moon for guidance back into society. Warren suggests that the moon is associated with the generative imagination. He then considers the interaction of this theme of the imagination with the poem's other major theme of "sacramental" life—life in which original sin connects an individual with divine powers of expiation and restitution. Moonlight-fed imagination, he suggests, facilitates that restitution by revealing to the Mariner his connectedness to other life. Having performed a close analysis of individual word clusters and more distanced analyses of the recurring images' revelation of the poem's major themes, he backs up further to comment on the interaction of these themes and then their interaction with Coleridge's larger poetic project. Warren rejects the New Critical tendency to isolate works and instead sees each of an author's works as existing in relation to one another. That does not mean he lapses into what W. K. Wimsatt and Monroe Beardsley would call "the intentional fallacy." He maintains that "even if the poet himself should rise to contradict" an interpretation consistent with the poem as a whole, he would "reply that the words of the poem speak louder than his actions."[17] But for all that, Warren accepts that the actions of the author outside of a single text do have something to say.

Already, in the proposition that the structure of an artwork relates to the structure of the self, Warren's intrinsic criticism has begun to spill into extrinsic concerns. Some questions extrinsic to a literary text that interest Warren relate to the author-text relationship and some the reader-text relationship. At the end of "A Poem of Pure Imagination," he lists four areas extrinsic to a work where a critic must look to assure that his or her interpretation is reasonable. Any interpretation should be consistent with: (1) "the intellectual, the spiritual climate of the age" in which the piece was composed, (2) "the over-all pattern of other artistic work by the author," (3) "the thought of the author from other artistic sources," and (4) "the facts of the author's life." Each of these elements should be treated "as factors of control in interpretation"—interpretative boundary setters—and not be used to produce "crude historicism" or "crude psychologism."[18] An assertion Warren makes about "Ancient Mariner" reveals the theoretical assumption underlying his conviction that an author's works should be read as a whole and as arising within a specific historical "climate." He writes that in the act of creating art, "the moral concern and the aesthetic concern are aspects of the same activity, the creative activity."[19] That activity responds to the particular vicissitudes of history; Warren expresses elsewhere that "we cannot discuss. . . poetry as existing outside of history."[20]

Warren conceives the act of reading, like the act of writing, to be creative, to reflect the historical moment in which it occurs, and to involve moral and aesthetic concern. Already in 1943, Warren pointed out that "a good poem involves the participation of a reader."[21] The reader's importance extends to genres other than poetry as well, as Warren demonstrates in his writing about plays and novels. A work of literature is the "light by which the reader may view and review all the areas of experience with which he is acquainted." In this sense, "the reader does not interpret the poem but the poem interprets the reader." The event of reading a work of literature will unfold differently for the same reader at different times of his or her life as the reader's "history and nature" evolve. The reading event also varies based on a reader's "perspective of interest. We may look at [a work] as a document in the history of a language, in the history of literary form, in the history of political ideas, or in a thousand other different perspectives, and in each of them discover a different kind of meaning."[22]

Warren does not identify one of these perspectives as preferable over the others, and hints that none of them should be excluded. Rather than approaching a work of literature with a specific set of questions in mind, a reader should be open to the questions invited by the work itself.[23] In Warren's reading of "The Rime of the Ancient Mariner," he takes as central the question of the imagination's role in reconciling us to our own capacity for violence or grace and therefore lets the relationship between poetry reading, writing, and imagination inspire the theoretical issues relevant for that essay. He comes to reading as one comes to a conversation, with theoretical positions intact, but lets the event of the reading determine which of those positions it might be relevant to explore on the particular occasion. And, like a good conversationalist, Warren is open as a reader to being changed. Reading facilitates change because, as Warren says in a 1978 interview, the self "is not something you go find under a leaf. The self is what you *do*."[24]

The ultimate burden of a work of literature, according to Warren, is to wake readers up to our own lives.[25] He quotes Henri Bergson's claim that a novelist can bring us "back into our own presence" by representing the associative and conflicting presence of feelings, ideas, and occurrences that form the experience of selfhood in time.[26] This is done through the portrayal of lives lived concretely. The author suggests meaning "immediately, through the sensuous renderings of passionate experience" rather than defining "meanings in abstraction, as didacticism or moralizing."[27] Meaning communicated with the immediacy and complexity literature offers facilitates self-reflection, but it also works on a reader in ways he or she may not recognize. It serves a "therapeutic role."[28] Literature is uniquely able to do this because, for Warren, the self develops in ways that one cannot control and can only incompletely, belatedly, recognize. Writing in the twentieth-century's middle decades, Warren anticipates questions of the self's constitution that would come to the fore in literary theory forty years later. For him, the self develops in time, is made possible by the presence of community, and gains a moral identity through the exercise of responsibility.[29] The individual is always in a position of responsibility to a person present with him, to the community within which he acts, and to the self he has been and wants to become. The proliferation of competing definitions of selfhood propagated in a technocratic society that prioritizes material gain leads to the proliferation of "roles" and the incapacitation of responsible selfhood.[30] Literature can "affirm and reinforce the notion of the self" in the midst of the "disintegrative forces of society" that block self-awareness and the recognition of responsibility.[31]

## WARREN IN THE HISTORY OF CRITICISM

The "school" of criticism that Warren is most closely associated with, personally, is that of New Criticism.[32] The turn to New Criticism was, as Richard Forster has claimed, "the most extraordinarily successful of all conscientiously waged literary revolutions."[33] Although Warren's criticism turns toward history and philosophizing more often than stricter New Critics like Ransom could quite approve (Warren is only mentioned in Ransom's overview of New Criticism as the co-author of *Understanding Poetry*), his affiliation with the "literary revolution" Forster identifies has extended the interest his criticism would probably have merited on its own. But it should be remembered that Warren rejected "New Criticism" as a label and distanced his critical practice from the practice of the men most closely associated with the term, John Crowe Ransom and Cleanth Brooks, while still maintaining friendships with both of them.[34]

New Critical interest in how a work of literature manifests meaning through its form can be discerned in all of his critical work, but Warren constantly transgresses the boundaries of individual works to look at more of an author's oeuvre, to ask what a literary work does for its readers and how, or to contemplate a philosophical question that a particular work bids readers to ask. He explicitly re-engages the historical processes that Ransom claimed New Criticism must exclude. In the frequently anthologized "Criticism, Inc.," Ransom pictures himself at the head of a vanguard of English professors "tilt[ing] against historians" as Don Quixote "tilts" against windmills.[35] He admits that "language and history are aids" to literary criticism and confesses even that they are essential to studying older literatures because "Out of our actual contemporary mind we have to cancel a great deal that has come there under modern conditions but was not in the earlier mind at all."[36] And yet, in attempting to define what literary criticism is, Ransom enumerates six things it is not, and one of these is history. For Ransom, it is not only possible, but necessary to separate literary criticism from history in order to advance criticism as a "science" in its own right. Warren, on the other hand, never has great confidence in a critic's ability to escape history. When Ransom writes of the need to forget what contemporary life has taught us in order to understand authors of the past, he ironically re-inscribes authors within their own periods as though their work could not illuminate realities of our present world that the authors themselves never foresaw. Warren cannot bring himself to doubt that the contemporary relevance of past literature exceeds what its author could have known. Warren does not always address history in his literary criticism, but he distinguishes himself from other New Critics in that he never writes as though history were something we could step out of to see clearly.

Warren's resistance to dogma of all sorts, not just New Critical dogma, makes him difficult to locate in any history of criticism that defines "schools" of theory by the strength of their disagreement with what came before them. His approach is best appreciated for the way it takes up various practices advocated by theorists of his time and demonstrates their ability to yield insights about particular works and authors. The two essays mentioned earlier, "Pure and Impure Poetry" and "A Poem of Pure Imagination," put into practice ideas that were being theorized by others. And however resistant to theoretical system-making he may have been, Warren was immersed in early conversations about theory through his friendship with Allen Tate. Tate and Warren had become close friends and roommates at Vanderbilt in the early twenties. Warren's biographer, Joseph Blotner, refers to Tate as an "older brother" to Warren and one much beloved.[37] Their friendship continued throughout their lives. When Tate moved to Kenyon College in Gambier, Ohio, he worked diligently to establish *The Kenyon Review* and the Kenyon School of English. Thomas Daniel Young declared that "These two developments brought together more distinguished and soon-to-be distinguished poets, critics, and writers of fiction than almost any other of this century."[38] It would be *The Kenyon Review* that published Warren's essays on pure and impure poetry, and it would publish several groundbreaking essays by important mid-century theorists within five years. To take one year as an example, in 1951, *The Kenyon* published Northrop Frye's *The Archetypes of Literature*, Douglas Bush's *The Humanist Critic*, Cleanth Brooks's *The Formalist Critic*, Stephen Spender's *The Function of Criticism*, and Austin Warren's *The Teacher as Critic*.

What is remarkable about this selection is not only its representative quality—the dominant and emerging theoretical positions of mid-century are represented quite thoroughly—but also the diversity of perspectives. Around a shared table, these gentlemen would have disagreed with one another about any number of things. Brooks's formalist restrictions do not combine well with Bush's concern for literature's humanist function. Frye's archetypes conflict with Spender's view of "different worlds of poetic experience" emerging incomparably from different authors' work.[39] Still, it is not hard to tell that these theorists were reading Penn Warren and that he was reading them. His practice of "backing up" from reading at the level of the word or line to the level of interlocking themes and structures anticipates Frye's structuralist practices in *The Anatomy of Criticism*. He has clearly benefitted from the rigors of formalism practiced by his former colleague and collaborator Brooks, even if he rejects the restrictiveness of New Criticism. He would agree with Bush's statement that "It is only through historical scrutiny that we can distinguish, in both ideas and technique, between the commonplace and the original, between historical and permanent significance."[40] Although he probably would not have been as bold as Bush in saying that "literature is ethical," he does repeatedly assert its relevance for ethical reflection.

Warren's critical writing also manifests affinities with critics who wrote after him, or whose works have only come to prominence after his own positions were defined. His emphasis on the reader's role anticipates Stanley Fish in its recognition that reading within different communities of critical practice gives rise to very different experiences of a text. His focus on literature's ability to defamiliarize the world resonates with Victor Shklovsky's 1917 "Art as Technique," which was translated into English in 1965. His emphasis on the self's development in time resonates with phenomenological and existential investigations of selfhood, investigations that would become important to literary criticism through the work of Paul Ricœur. Moving into even more recent work, his conviction expressed in *Democracy and Poetry* that literature can help restore readers to the "massive relations of recognition and reverence" that constitute human beings' right relationships to one another resonates with contemporary theoretical work in global, comparative literature.[41]

Forster made his claim for New Criticism's dominance in 1962. Humanist, structuralist, Marxist, psychoanalytical, and phenomenological criticism were all afoot by then, but none of them competed with formalism for dominance—not in terms of how literature was taught and not in terms of how widely they were practiced. But of course another revolution was coming, one wherein "a critical universe for which literature is the center and where the attempt to generate models to understand its functioning" has been replaced by "another universe where the questions about literature are no longer pressing and where, without shared questions of this sort, analysts address a multiplicity of topics, hoping that some general methodological questions will bring them into dialogue."[42] In this new "universe," Warren's criticism may seem relevant for critics now only as a matter of literary history. Warren had no interest in the post-structuralist practices that were, by the time of his retirement from Yale in December of 1972, overturning so many assumptions about literary theory and criticism. Of the three "boa-deconstructors," as Geoffrey Hartman charmingly calls Derrida, de Man, and Hillis Miller, de Man and Hillis Miller were already at Yale by this time.[43] Derrida began his lectures there in 1975. While these men were investigating the linguistic and cultural processes on which literary and critical practice depend, Warren was teaching his Yale students that "you go back to the thing itself, and you encounter it on its own terms, and you pray to be relieved of the bondage of preexisting expectations or interpretations."[44] Now that the excitement of deconstruction's integration into English-language literary theory has settled, it is easier to appreciate Warren's attention to a work's ability to overthrow a reader's expectations.

Just as he emphasized experiencing a work on its own terms, Warren emphasized approaching people on their own terms when he moved into social critique. Warren was a pioneer cultural critic, particularly with regard to racial divides in the south, and it is only very recently that scholars have begun to recognize the importance of his work as a cultural critic. Because of his early alignment with "the Fugitive" group at Vanderbilt, the progressive-ness of Warren's work in *Segregation* and *Who Speaks for the Negro?* have sometimes been overlooked. The title of this second work makes contemporary readers cringe, but as Benji de la Piedra puts it, *Who Speaks for the Negro?* is "a precious artifact of America's recent past. It is a snapshot of certain ways in which people intelligently advocated against white supremacy and legalized segregation in 1964, before certain customs, laws, and words changed."[45] By consolidating multiple perspectives from the Civil Rights Era, Warren's book highlights the rich variety of approaches to overcoming discrimination already devised by the some of the period's most important thinkers. By putting the voices of his interviewees first, contextualizing them attentively and sympathetically, and reflecting critically on the inevitable limitedness of his own perspectival horizon with regard to the experiences of discrimination, Warren offers a model of practices of oral historiography that are still being thought through.

## PERSONAL AND SOCIAL HISTORY

Warren's positions as a critic arise out of his practice as a poet and novelist negotiating the pressures of personal history and those of a particular historical moment. Personally, Warren had a great deal of history to reckon with. He was born in Guthrie, Kentucky, in 1905. Kentucky had been a neutral border state at the commencement of the Civil War, but by 1862 had competing governments and soldiers fighting for the Union and the Confederacy. After the Union invasion of Virginia in May of 1861, Warren's grandfather Gabriel Thomas Penn, born south of the state border in Tennessee, had joined thousands of others in volunteering for the Confederate army. "He was opposed to slavery," Warren reported to a shocked Dick Cavett in 1978, and opposed to secession, "but when the time came, he was on horseback. . . . He said you go with your people."[46] Gabriel Penn died when Warren was 15, but several of his childhood summers had been spent on his grandfather's farm, and the memory of the old man became a kind of talisman that the poet carried all his life. Warren "felt," in the words of a late poem, that all reality "had been cupboarded in that high head."[47]

A Southerner, a gentleman, Gabriel Penn was a picture of the region's conflicts in the post-war era. Warren describes his grandfather's "blue gaze, so fixed and far" as "Aimed lethally past the horizon's fact."[48] The latent violence of that gaze and its aim beyond the bounds of factual history charac- terize much of Warren's writing. Although the violence is made most explicit in his fiction, his criticism, too, recognizes what he calls "the mystery of the corruption of the will."[49] As Allen Tate observes, any Southerner's attempt to "unlock the Southern mind is . . . bloody and perilous. . . . The South has had reverses that permit her people to imagine what they might have been. (And only thus can people discover what they *are*.)"[50] Warren—always keeping his Kentucky lilt, returning almost obsessively to southern history and the problems it bequeathed to the region—imagines again and again what the south might have been by critiquing what it had become.

In a late essay, Warren describes the relationship between history and self-becoming:

> [M]an's fate is double, an outer and an inner fate, the world the self is in, and the self that is a world. And more and more we see, painfully, that the two worlds are indissolubly linked and interpenetrating—mirror facing mirror, as it were—and more and more we see that one of the errors of the past, an error from which we must learn, has been to treat them as though each were in isolation.[51]

In his writings about the self in *Democracy and Poetry*, Warren expresses the beliefs that led him to feel responsible for the plight of people suffering from economic and racial discrimination. In this passage, Warren expresses a re- lated premise in historical terms. The individual's self-becoming is shaped by his or her historical circumstances. The responsibility toward another person then extends to include the alteration of public policy that handicaps another individual's self-development. At the end of his 1956 book *Segrega- tion*, Warren included an interview with himself in which he says that "Re- sponsibility is a seamless garment. And the northern boundary of that gar- ment is not the Ohio River. . . . We all live with a thousand unsolved problems all the time. We don't even recognize a lot of them. We have to deal only with those which the moment proposes to us."[52] As a southerner living outside of Fairfield, Connecticut, he felt responsible for doing what he could, as a writer and social critic, to combat segregation. It was the problem that the moment of Civil Rights had proposed to him through his family's history, his intimate knowledge of southern ways of thinking, and his connections in publishing and his eloquence.

During the nineteen months between the Supreme Court's landmark *Brown vs. the Board of Education* decision (May 1954) and Warren's trip south to perform the interviews that would become *Segregation* (January 1956), race-related violence had intensified across the South. Fourteen-year-old Emmet Till had been beaten to death and his body dumped in Mississippi's Tallahatchie River in August of 1955. The white jury acquitted the killers after less than an hour of deliberation.[53] In December of that year, Martin Luther King Jr. had begun the bus boycott in Montgomery, Alabama. These events made international news, but there were other events that did not. According to one report from 1960,[54] there were 530 separate instances of racial violence and intimidation in the southern states between January of 1955 and January of 1959. These cases do not include police brutality, juvenile delinquency, or cases communicated to the authors personally. They are all instances reacting directly to the desegregation mandate, and they are all gleaned from press reports. Many of the incidents reveal the operation of organized intimidation and violence. In addition to a "revivified but disjointed" Ku Klux Klan, "Citizen's Councils" had sprung up.[55] "Councils" worked through economic and social intimidation and lobbying to maintain segregation, whereas the Klan favored physical intimidation. Some events are clearly independent of any organization, and in the anonymity of criminals and victim lies part of their terror: "Selma, Ala.: A white couple poured gasoline on a Negro woman's home and set it ablaze. (September 23, 1955)."[56] The same report finds that some communities' reactions to desegregation were characterized by "patience, responsibility, courage and good will by both Negroes and whites," but the extent of racially motivated violence in these years was appalling, and Warren felt responsible to use the talent and position he had to address the problem.[57]

Warren's goal in conducting interviews in Kentucky, Tennessee, Arkansas, Mississippi, and Louisiana in 1956 was to represent the complex combination of differing reactions within single communities and even within single individuals. Talking with Ralph Ellison the following year, he says that "The problem is to permit the fullest range of life into racial awareness."[58] The division between one person and another is important, he says, but "not as important in the long run as the division within the individual."[59] So, he interviews a newspaperman, a white, Southern integrationist, who nevertheless fumes, "Well, by God, it's just a fact, it's not in them [the Northern media] not to load the dice in a news story!"[60] Elsewhere, a black schoolteacher responds to his question about resentment: "'Some of us try to teach love,' she says, 'as well as we can. But some of us teach hate. I guess we can't help it.'"[61]

Sometimes the contradictions people feel are expressed directly, as with these two, but sometimes the conflicting pressures become clear through Warren's description of the setting or situation. For example, he documents a televised interview with "a tall, well-set-up, jut-nosed, good-looking dark brown man in a blue suit," who is supposed to say to the cameraman what he said to the white journalist the night before in private, that this "separate but equal stuff" is "a lot of hogwash." He says to the camera that he wants an "interracial discussion of the 'how' of desegregation—but with the back-ground understanding that the Court decision is law." One senses at the end of the interview that he has not "La[id] it on the line" in quite the way the interviewer wanted. The dark brown man replies, "you are all going back to New York City. But we stay here" before making a joke about which one of them will hire him to drive that nice Cadillac he sees out front.[62] By documenting just the right details from the interview, Warren communicates to the reader that behind his recording of what is being said about desegregation, there is so much that would never be said, but must be lived in to understand. One of Warren's interviewees tells him that a man from New Haven had come down and asked him to describe the race problem: "Mister, I can't tell you a thing about that. There is nothing I could tell you. If you want to find out, you better just move down here and live for a while."[63] *Segregation* achieves its aims through documenting the extent to which individual actors react to pressures that cannot be clearly grasped, much less documented.

Warren's later book on race, *Who Speaks for the Negro?*, uses some of the same techniques as *Segregation*. Warren conducts interviews across the South, this time with black leaders at the community, state, and national level. He recognizes, although the language for the problem has not yet been provided, that he is trying to give subaltern voices a way to speak. He knows that his presence alters the conversations, that the conversations will be fil-tered through his beliefs, and that the publication format dictates, in obscure ways, what will and will not make it into the book's final draft. He tries to minimize his influence on the project as a moral or rhetorical filter by having interviewees respond to what other interviewees have said or to quotations from the writings of interviewees such as James Baldwin and Ralph Ellison. The themes include double-consciousness, the resort to violence, and media representations of black cultures. Students provide their opinions alongside leaders like Malcolm X and Martin Luther King Jr. He puts first a voice that never would have been heard nationally if not for this book: the voice of Reverend Joe Carter of West Feliciana Parish, Louisiana. Reverend Carter's story of being the first black in his parish to register to vote emphasizes the need for a work like *Who Speaks for the Negro?* by underlining the persisting barriers between blacks in the South and free political self-expression.

## CONCLUSION

Warren's whole range of critical and creative practices seems to be guided by three principles: responsibility toward others (including toward authors and readers); a willingness to reckon with complexities without reconciling them; and a striving for awareness of the way one's own interest and attention shape a critical project. In an interview in 1966, just after *Who Speaks?* had come out, an interviewer in Schenectady, New York, is pressing Warren about the problem of prejudice. Warren asks,

> remember that wonderful book *Let Us Now Praise Famous Men*, with pictures by Walker Evans and James Agee's text? Everybody's heart bled for those poor people—the white sharecroppers of Alabama. Now those who then were doing the weeping go down to Tuscaloosa or to the march on Montgomery and see those same people and they become the hounds of hell in the public eye. They're no worse and no better than they ever were, but you change the question and you get a different perspective.[64]

Warren changes his questions all the time, but his tendency to do so does not reflect an absence of a critical theoretical stance. His stance is that one *must* change the questions—according to the reading invited by a particular text and according to the questions plaguing the critic's or the author's historical moment. Warren was concerned that "hyperaesthetical criticism" was "flourish[ing] in the very citadels of academic respectability," threatening to cut readers off from the experience of reading literature as meaningful for them as historically responsible individuals.[65] He rebelled against "hyperaesthetical criticism" in its New Critical and deconstructive forms. He rejected the temptations to align his critical practice with a single, recurring approach, and maybe his reputation as a critic has suffered for these refusals, but literary and cultural theory today is ready for his ideas in a way that it was not in the last decades of his life.

## NOTES

1. Harold Bloom, *Poets and Poems* (New York: Chelsea House, 2005), 323.
2. Mark D. Miller, "Faith in Good Works: The Salvation of Robert Penn Warren," in *Mississippi Quarterly* 48, no. 1 (Winter 94/95), 57.
3. The MLA database shows an average of 21 titles per year 2000–2009, 7.7 per year 2010–2016.
4. Charlotte Beck, *Robert Penn Warren: Critic* (Knoxville: University of Tennessee Press, 2006).
5. Charles Boehner, *Robert Penn Warren* (New Haven: Twayne Publishers, 1964), 17.
6. Vincent Leitch et al., eds., *The Norton Anthology of Theory and Criticism* (New York: Norton, 2010), 969, 1228.
7. David Eldridge, *American Culture in the 1930s* (Edinburgh: Edinburgh University Press, 2008), 31–32.

8. Floyd Watkins, John T. Heirs, and Mary Louise Weaks, eds., *Talking with Robert Penn Warren* (Athens: University of Georgia Press, 1990), 257

9. Robert Penn Warren, *Democracy and Poetry* (Cambridge: Harvard University Press, 1975), 89.

10. Ibid., 72.

11. Robert Penn Warren, *Selected Essays* (New York: Random House, 1958), 3.

12. Ibid., 213.

13. Ibid., 213.

14. Ibid., 29.

15. *Democracy and Poetry*, 74.

16. Ibid., 69.

17. *Selected Essays*, 269.

18. Ibid., 270.

19. Ibid., 253.

20. *Democracy and Poetry*, xiv.

21. *Selected Essays*, 27.

22. Ibid., 212. All of the quotations in the paragraph are from this page.

23. Ibid., 213.

24. *Talking with Robert Penn Warren*, 269.

25. *Democracy and Poetry*, 71.

26. Ibid. Henri Bergson, *Time and Freedom: An Essay on the Immediate Data of Consciousness*, translated by F. L. Pogson (London: George Allen and Unwin, 1910), 134.

27. *Selected Essays*, 57.

28. *Democracy and Poetry*, 3.

29. Ibid., xiii, 25, and xiii.

30. Ibid., 59.

31. Ibid., 42.

32. In his advocacy for the literary criticism practiced before the 1970s, Colin Campbell says that "New Criticism was the most powerful force in literary studies at the time, and the presence at Yale of distinguished New Critics such as Robert Penn Warren, Cleanth Brooks and W. K. Wimsatt testified to the school's eminence." "The Tyranny of the Yale Critics" *New York Times Magazine* (February 9, 1986), Np.

33. Richard Forster, *The New Romantics* (Bloomington, IN: Indiana University Press, 1962), 22.

34. *Talking with Robert Penn Warren*, 283.

35. John Crowe Ransom, "Criticism, Inc.," *Virginia Quarterly Review* (Autumn 1937), https://www.vqronline.org.

36. Ibid.

37. Ibid., 50.

38. Thomas Daniel Young, *Gentleman in a Dustcoat: John Crowe Ransom* (Baton Rouge: Louisiana State Press, 1976), 287–291.

39. Stephen Spender, "On the Function of Criticism," *The Kenyon Review* 13, no. 2 (Spring 1951), http://www.kenyonreview.org.

40. Douglas Bush, "The Humanist Critic," *The Kenyon Review* 13, no. 1 (Winter 1951), http://www.kenyonreview.org.

41. See, for example, work on the concept of recognition by Nancy Fraser, Shu-Mei Shih, and Vincent van Bever Donker. Nancy Fraser, "Rethinking Recognition," *New Left Review* 3 (2000), 107–20. Shu-Mei Shih, "Global Literature and the Technologies of Recognition," *PMLA* 119, no. 1 (2004), 16–30. Vincent van Bever Donker, *Recognition and Ethics in World Literature: Religion, Violence, and the Human* (Stuttgart: Verlag, 2016).

42. Jonathan Culler, "New Literary History and European Theory," *New Literary History* 25, no. 4 (1994), 876. doi:10.2307/469379.

43. Geoffrey Hartman, "Preface" to *Deconstruction and Criticism*, edited by Harold Bloom, Paul de Man, Jacques Derrida, Geoffrey Hartman, and J. Hillis Miller (New York: Continuum, 1979), vii–ix.

44. Nathaniel Lewis, "David Milch at Yale: An Interview," in *Dirty Words in Deadwood: Literature and the Postwestern*, edited by Melody Graulich and Nicolas S. Witschi (Lincoln: University of Nebraska Press, 2013), 15.

45. Benji de la Piedra, "Fifty Years Later: Robert Penn Warren's *Who Speaks for the Negro?*" *Oral History Review* 42, no. 2 (2015), 374–379. doi:10.1093/ohr/ohv060.

46. *Talking with Robert Penn Warren*, 281–282.

47. Robert Penn Warren, "When Life Begins," *The Collected Poems of Robert Penn Warren*, edited by John Burt (Baton Rouge: Louisiana State University Press, 1998), 383–384, line 19.

48. "When Life Begins," lines 21–22.

49. *Selected Essays*, 227.

50. Allen Tate, "The Profession of Letters in the South," in *On the Limits of Poetry*, edited by Allen Tate (New York: Morrow Press, 1948), 265–281.

51. Robert Penn Warren, "The Uses of the Past," *New and Selected Essays* (New York: Random House, 1989).

52. Robert Penn Warren, *Segregation: The Inner Conflict in the South* (Athens, GA: University of Georgia Press, 1994), 64–65.

53. Devery S. Anderson, *Emmett Till: The Murder that Shocked the World and Propelled the Civil Rights Movement* (Jackson, MS: University Press of Mississippi, 2015).

54. Southern Regional Council, the American Friends Service Committee, and the Churches of Christ, *Intimidation, Reprisal and Violence in the South's Racial Crisis* (Atlanta: Southern Regional Council, 1960).

55. *Intimidation, Reprisal and Violence*, 1.

56. *Intimidation, Reprisal and Violence*, 16.

57. *Intimidation, Reprisal and Violence*, 1.

58. *Talking with Robert Penn Warren*, 48. The interview occurred in 1957, in Ellison's apartment in Rome, and was published in abbreviated form in *The Paris Review*. Eugene Walter also takes part.

59. Warren, *Segregation*, 53.

60. Ibid., 15.

61. Ibid., 61.

62. Ibid., 36–37.

63. Ibid., 15.

64. *Talking with Robert Penn Warren*, 82–83.

65. *Selected Essays*, 200.

*Chapter Six*

# Louise Rosenblatt

*The Reader, Democracy, and the Ethics of Reading*

## Meredith N. Sinclair

Louise Rosenblatt (1904–2005) occupies a curious place in the pantheon of literary theorists. As Wayne Booth notes in his introduction to the fifth edition of Rosenblatt's *Literature as Exploration,* perhaps no other literary critic of the twentiethth century "has enjoyed and suffered as sharp a contrast of powerful influence and absurd neglect as Louise Rosenblatt."[1] Although Rosenblatt's transactional theory of reading[2] has been foundational to the teaching of literature at the secondary level since the publication of *Literature as Exploration* in 1938 (and thus has influenced how generations have learned to encounter texts), her work has been largely overlooked by her fellow literary theorists. Perhaps they mistakenly have misread Rosenblatt as having only importance to those interested in pedagogy; after all, *Literature as Exploration* is explicitly addressed to teachers. But to dismiss Rosenblatt's work as merely pedagogical, or to overlook the importance of understanding reading pedagogy to understanding literary theory, shows a lack of imagination about why we care about literature in the first place.

I first encountered Rosenblatt's work during my PhD studies while working through my own theories about the role of literacy—and more specifically reading—in the intellectual and social lives of adolescents. Even though I had previously spent five years as a high school teacher and (in hindsight) owed much of my pedagogy to Rosenblatt's ideas about reading, I had not encountered her theoretical work. What struck me most was Rosenblatt's clear commitment to the idea that reading is a lived experience and therefore a powerful means to engage the world. The process of reading literature and engaging one's social and emotional world in constructing meaning through transacting with that text develops readers who are then able to apply this frame of thinking to their engagement in other social spaces. Rosenblatt's work was groundbreaking in that it sought to give agency and interpretative authority to all readers and in turn democratize the study of literature. Through considering pedagogy—the process of teaching literature—Rosenblatt developed her insights into how reading works and why interpretative authority should rest with all readers. Ultimately, her work upended the notion that interpretation was an activity accessible only to an elite few and laid the groundwork for the growth of multiple branches of literary criticism (including reader response theory, reception history, feminist theory, postcolonial theory, cultural studies, and queer theory) that invite multiple perspectives into interpretative practice.

This chapter focuses on Rosenblatt's *Literature as Exploration*, first published in 1938 (now in its fifth edition),[3] and the historical moment around its writing and publication. While the ideas developed there were refined over the years (most notably with the publication of *The Reader, The Text, The Poem: The Transactional Theory of the Literary Work* in 1978) as Rosenblatt continued to work and write until her death in 2005, *Literature as Exploration* introduced the core tenets of Rosenblatt's work: the importance of literary study to the healthy functioning of a democracy and the transactive nature of reading. *Literature as Exploration* advanced the idea that "the experience of literature, far from being a passive process of absorption, is a form of intense personal activity."[4] Rosenblatt was clear that the text matters but also sought to recognize the agency of the reader: "anything we call a literary experience gains its significance and force from the way in which the stimuli present in the literary work interact with the mind and emotions of a particular reader."[5] Close attention to the text in conjunction with the reader's emotional, social, and cultural contexts results in meaning-making. Over her career, Rosenblatt's writing continued to push back against both theories of reading that positioned meaning solely in the text (or that called for "ideal" readers) and those that allowed a reader's response to exist at the expense of the text.

While Rosenblatt's work does much to help us understand the relationship between reader and text, it also has implications for how we understand the value of texts and the role of reading in the world. Rosenblatt confronted the politics and ethics of education and challenged the idea that reading is only a neutral activity. By engaging in a transactive relationship with texts, readers in turn can become more engaged in their communities and the world beyond. Rosenblatt notes the "capacity of literature to nourish the imaginative flexibility that is essential to really social beings": through literature we gain the ability to understand the implications of our actions in the world and presumably become better actors and neighbors.[6]

These ideals spoke directly to the historical moment in which Rosenblatt was writing, a moment of shifting ideas about education broadly and the study of literature more specifically, a time when American society was working to figure out a new social order in the aftermath of the Great Depression and in sight of the growing clouds of fascism in Europe. American isolationism had been forced to an end by WWI and global interconnectedness was intensifying in the years leading up to WWII. Compulsory education had become the norm, more and more students achieved a high school diploma, and university education was expanding beyond society's most elite. Schools struggled to define their function as either a site for the development of "good citizens" and a future workforce (the practical reality of most schools supported by policy) or a space for intellectual development (a purpose espoused by progressive educators). Access to texts through increased literacy rates, greater numbers of publications, less expensive books, and the increasing ubiquity of the radio and motion pictures meant information and ideas were widely broadcast. Making sense of these texts and an increasingly complex world called for a different understanding of the activity of reading and a new literacy pedagogy, one that was intentional in placing responsibility for interpretation with all readers.

## SCHOOLING AND EDUCATION: COMPETING NARRATIVES AROUND THE PURPOSE OF READING

*Literature as Exploration* does not shy away from being a book about pedagogy nor does it hide a sincere interest in the power and possibility of individual readers. Rosenblatt's interest in the reader, particularly the adolescent reader, and the reader's social and emotional world in constructing meaning put her at odds with the traditional conception of the discipline. The object of concern in the English literature classroom had been the text; readers merely showed up to bask in the meaning already there. Or worse, even meaning was sidelined in favor of understanding the text merely in terms of its place in a literary lineage. Several factors in Rosenblatt's own experience contributed to the way she came to understand literature and the importance of pedagogy. As she recounts while reflecting on her career, she benefitted from an undergraduate education at Barnard College that encouraged her to explore her own interests instead of conforming to a pre-defined program of study. She also saw herself as an interdisciplinary scholar; her literary study was informed directly by philosophy, particularly pragmatist philosophers including John Dewey and Charles Sanders Peirce, and anthropology, an interest she continued to pursue through formal study even after earning her doctorate in literature at the Sorbonne.[7] Rosenblatt's cross-disciplinary expertise earned her an advisory role on the Commission on Human Relations, a project administered by the Progressive Education Association that aimed to publish a series of books for adolescents on various social science issues.

This work exposed her formally to the discourse of education, curriculum, and pedagogy and caused her to consider the value of discussions about human relations that arose from discussions of literature in her classes; surely these were equally as valuable as the more scientific but less personal accounts of human relations that were the subject of the book series. [8]

*Literature as Exploration* was first published by the Commission on Human Relations, and it certainly owes something to the work of that group. But to fully appreciate the scope and importance of Rosenblatt's work, one must consider more broadly the competing narratives around the role of literacy, and in turn education, in American society. [9] The notion that education is fundamental to American society has been a part of the landscape of schooling since the founding of the colonies. But there have always been (and continue to be) competing narratives about why this is so. One is that "schooling" frames schools as sites to prepare students for readiness to contribute to the capitalist economic system while instilling a common set of cultural values. The other is that "education" imagines schools as spaces to nurture students as the free thinkers and compassionate neighbors that are needed for a democratic society.

In the nineteenth century, the common school movement drove the expansion of public schooling and compulsory education for all. Reformers such as Horace Mann argued for a uniform, basic education in literacy and numeracy that would improve the economic prospects of students and produce a citizenry prepared to participate in American democracy. The 1890s ushered in the progressive era in education with its greater interest in pedagogy and teacher training. Progressive educators such as John Dewey were interested in curriculum reform, so situated education in experience; learning should be intimately connected to the social and emotional lives of students. A second set of reformers saw a need for increased efficiency in the form of administrative changes and uniform curriculum and instruction. [10] The former group envisioned schools that were responsive to and shaped by the individual needs of students and the social lives of communities; the latter imagined the institution of school as shaping students and their communities.

In 1935, the year Rosenblatt was appointed as an advisor to the Commission on Human Relations, 40 percent of American youth earned a high school diploma. A generation earlier in 1910, that figure had been only 9 percent. [11] This rapid rise in secondary school attendance was a response to societal and economic changes; new technologies and increasing industrialization demanded a differentiated workforce while continued immigration and increased migration to urban centers meant greater diversity within communities. The modern concept of "adolescence" as a time of unsettled personal growth was itself born in this era; suddenly society found itself with an entire generation of young people working to navigate changes in both self and society. [12]

Both "schoolers" and "educators" wanted to help youth navigate this new terrain, but their disparate beliefs about the role of schools led to competing ideas about how those schools should look and the sort of learning they should produce. Schooling generally meant uniform instruction and passive learning. Education placed learning in experience and gave agency to all learners and not just society's elite. As Rosenblatt notes in her reflections on her long career, the efforts of these two reform groups and their impact on shaping education are often conflated: "Unfortunately, this anti-intellectualistic effort to prepare pupils to serve, to 'adjust' to the needs of the status quo, was confused with the progressives' concern for meeting the needs of students. The progressives sought rather to help them to develop their capacities to the full, a view of education assuming a democratically mobile society."[13] A careful review of education history shows this division persists even to our current moment.

From a structural standpoint, the "schoolers" were more directly responsible for the growth of the high school and the inclusion of more students in secondary education. Education bureaucracy (including school administration and teacher training models) made for easy expansion as programs that "worked" could be quickly replicated. Communities were also swayed to invest in high schools by the economic argument that a high school education would make graduates more employable and more competitive on the economic market.[14] But the emotional heart of the expansion was the territory of the curriculum reformers who saw possibility and promise in an era of change; offering equitable educational opportunity to all would benefit both students and their communities and make good on the promise of American democracy.

Rosenblatt aligns the need for a new understanding of reading and the tasks of education with the needs of a changing world. She argued that schools are challenged

1. To supply youth with the tools and knowledge necessary for a scientifically objective, critical appraisal of accepted opinion . . .
2. To help such emancipated youth create new emotional drives strong enough to counteract outmoded automatic responses . . . [15]

A parallel argument can be made about the value of literacy and the purposes of study of literature. Where we place interpretative authority and why we value texts speaks to our larger values about the function of education and the relation of individuals to a democratic society. Literary study that allows for only one "correct" reading cedes interpretative authority to a small cadre of specially trained experts and narrowly defines literature as those texts that model a shared cultural ideal—reading literature through "schooling." A theory of reading that values the experience of the individual reader provides space for liberation through interpretation and sees literature as a landscape of cultural possibilities—reading literature as "education." James Gee describes the tension around these possibilities for interpretative authority as "Plato's dilemma": because literacy can function both as a means for personal liberation and an authoritative means for social engineering, literacy "always comes with a perspective on interpretation that is ultimately political."[16] Likewise, the aims of education are inexorably entangled in politics.

Although Rosenblatt does not use the language of "literacy" in describing reading literature, *Literature as Exploration* responds to the question of interpretative authority and argues for the liberatory possibility of reading. Gee suggests that there is no real solution to Plato's dilemma, no escaping the political implications of interpretative authority. However, he offers that being explicit about the political implications of literacy instruction moves in the right direction: "Much follows, however, from what comes with literacy and schooling, what literacy and schooling come wrapped up in, namely the attitudes, values, norms, and beliefs (at once social, cultural, and political) that always accompany literacy and schooling."[17] Ultimately, it is not the ability to read (or having received an education) that matters; rather the political philosophy that shapes the aims of that instruction has the greater impact.

Rosenblatt understood that in order for literature to live up to its liberatory promise, scholarship needed to attend to pedagogy and the political implications of how literature is framed. Interpretive authority is at the center: "If the school, for example, is based on the principle of unquestioning obedience to authority . . . we cannot reasonably expect the development of people capable of functioning intelligently in a democracy."[18] By extension, if we tell students what a text means, how can we possibly claim that we are empowering them to think freely and responsibly elsewhere in their lives?

Rosenblatt returned to her alma mater, Barnard College, as professor of literature in 1927. Despite feeling a fair amount of latitude in how she conducted her courses, she grew increasingly frustrated with the disconnect between the traditional literature curriculum and pedagogy and the lived experiences of students, a disconnect caused by "faulty assumptions about the nature of reading and the aesthetics of literature" that limited the democratic possibilities of literature study.[19] Like many teachers, Rosenblatt instinctively turned away from rote lecture and towards class discussion; *Literature as Exploration* includes informal analysis of some of her students' responses to texts. But she also felt that to realize its full potential, literature pedagogy needed grounding in theory.[20] The reader alone is not responsible for meaning; rather it is produced through a back and forth between reader and text.

Rosenblatt was not alone in wanting to reform literature pedagogy. Cleanth Brooks and Robert Penn Warren's *Understanding Poetry,* published the same year as *Literature as Exploration,* also worked to engage a broader audience in literary study. Ultimately both are interested in rescuing the discipline from simply being the study of literary history, biography, or language and returning aesthetic appreciation to the forefront. While both emphasized close reading of the text (just as education reformers emphasized the importance of schools), their paths diverged in how they positioned the reader (as reformers differed in their positioning of the student). Brooks and Warren (and other New Critics who followed) foregrounded text and method; in a sense, the reader became secondary to the authority of method. In the spirit of those who believed in the liberatory potential of education as fundamental to democracy, Rosenblatt positioned the reader as an equal partner in meaning-making with the text. Her interest in *how* those readers made meaning brought her to pedagogy; pedagogy, in turn, informed her understanding of the process.

## LITERATURE AS LIVED EXPERIENCE: AN ETHIC OF READING

Rosenblatt's interest in pedagogy played another pivotal role in the development of her theory of reading. It led her to understand meaning-making as an ethical act that functioned as a proxy for interactions in the world. Citing Charles Sanders Peirce, she argued for schools as "institutions for learning" rather than "institutions for teaching":

> The student should go to school and college, not for the purpose of being taught ready-made formulas and fixed attitudes, but in order that he may develop the will to learn. He must acquire command of techniques that make possible a constantly closer approximation to the truth, and he must develop *the flexibility of mind and temperament necessary for the translation of that critical sense of truth into actual behavior.* . . . Instead of drifting blindly with the stream of circumstance, he will be able to set up more rational personal and social goals and to understand better the conditions under which they can be achieved.[21]

Here Rosenblatt fully embraces the political nature of education and literacy. We can either create institutions and practices that reify "ready-made formulas and fixed attitudes" or we create institutions that nurture "flexibility of mind and temperament." In doing the latter, we embrace the ethical dimension of learning. Because reading is "lived experience"—that is, meaning-making draws on the social and emotional experience and knowledge of the reader and is constantly being negotiated and adapted based on the feedback loop between text and reader—Rosenblatt reasoned that the experience of reading would nurture habits of thinking that translated into behaviors in the social world.

The dynamic social world of the 1930s offered domestic challenges brought on by increasing diversity and displacement from community as well as an increasing existential threat to democracy in the form of European fascism and the rise of the Nazis. Rosenblatt critiqued those who called for a steely-eyed reason or a "defensive attitude of callousness" when faced with uncomfortable events at home or abroad. She wrote, "The way the youth in fascist countries has lent itself to a philosophy of force and brutal sadism is ample proof of the great social dangers inherent in that kind of disillusioned cynicism and flight from altruistic feeling."[22] Simply put, Rosenblatt held fast to the notion that reading literature makes us better, a point emphasized by her closing to *Literature as Exploration*: "Literary experiences will then be a potent force in the educational process of developing of critically minded, emotionally liberated individuals who possess the energy and the will to create a happier way of life for themselves and for others."[23]

This does not happen because of some vague notion about how literature and art make us feel or think. Rather Rosenblatt saw a direct parallel between the thinking required to negotiate meaning with literature and that required to read and reevaluate the world. Because readers "interpret the book or poem in terms of our fund of past experiences, it is equally possible and necessary that we come to reinterpret our old sense of things in the light of this new literary experience, in the light of the new ways of thinking and feeling offered by the work of art."[24] More than simply aesthetic experience (although the aesthetic experience is important), encountering literature is also about changing patterns of thinking and interaction in the world when faced with new knowledge and new situations.

Rosenblatt emphasized that this was not a process that young readers would do well without some guidance. The teacher's task, then, was to draw attention to the process, to challenge students to return to their initial responses in light of the text and to revise them. This was the spirit of the progressive educators like Dewey who felt children learn best by doing, in particular by doing what matters to them. By acknowledging the reader's emotional response and by using it as a springboard for further analysis, Rosenblatt brought "what mattered" to students into the classroom. This ownership of the intellectual process came with an obligation to take responsibility for the consequences of one's reading, including a willingness to acknowledge missteps in understanding. While some saw the growing high school population as in need of indoctrination to American cultural values through the study of seminal texts, Rosenblatt saw an opportunity to engage students in a plurality of opinion. Studying literature functioned as a corrective to "schooling" by teaching how instead of what to think.

Rosenblatt acknowledged that situating responses to literature in personal experience opens the door to biased readings. Instead of viewing this as a liability, she saw this as an opening for growth. As communities diversified and communication advanced, students were increasingly in the presence of those who thought differently than they did. Dogmatic adherence to one's beliefs often led to misunderstanding in such encounters. The sort of flexible thinking students could learn through having their assumptions challenged by texts could be used to learn a recognition of bias in order to move past bias. Simply acknowledging that human beings have human emotions also improves social relations: "The emotional character of the student's response to literature offers an opportunity for helping him to develop the ability *to think rationally within an emotionally colored context.*"[25] By inviting emotional responses into the study of literature, Rosenblatt created space for readers to recognize the effects of those emotions in and out of textual spaces.

In her preface to the fifth edition of *Literature as Exploration*, Rosenblatt wrote:

> Democracy implies a society of people who, no matter how much they differ from one another, recognize their common interests, their common goals, and their dependence on mutually honored freedoms and responsibilities. For this they need the ability to imagine the human consequences of political and economic alternatives and to think rationally about emotionally charged issues. Such strengths should be fostered by all the agencies that shape the individual, but the educational system, through all its disciplines, has a crucial role. The belief that the teaching of literature could especially contribute to such democratic education generated this book.[26]

Rosenblatt was critical of the American impulse to independence at the expense of others, an impulse that underlies a capitalist economy, saying that the "individualistic emphasis of our society builds up a frequent reluctance to see the implications for others of our own actions, or to understand the validity of the needs that motivate other people's actions. The fact that the success of the individual must so often be at the expense of others places a premium on this kind of blindness to the needs and feelings of others."[27] To emerge from the Great Depression, Americans had to embrace "their dependence on mutually honored freedoms and responsibilities." To reject individualism in favor of communitarianism required empathy; empathy requires the ability to imagine the experiences of others. For Rosenblatt, the power of literature lay in its function as a space for developing this social imagination, not simply by exposing readers to other ideas but by inviting them to consider, challenge, and negotiate meanings.

## ECHOES

*Literature as Exploration* is explicitly addressed to teachers of diverse student bodies, not simply those who will instruct future literature scholars.

Rosenblatt held that her pedagogy necessarily should be undertaken by all teachers of reading in order to fulfill the promise of progressive education and the liberatory power of literacy. In the years that followed its publication, *Literature as Exploration* became a foundational text for secondary teachers (either directly or because of its influence on the profession) even as it was neglected by departments of English embracing New Criticism. In 1948, Rosenblatt accepted a position at New York University's School of Education; she would spend her career largely devoted to the teaching of English, solidifying her belief that understanding how to teach texts was key to understanding how texts worked.

In a 1999 interview, Rosenblatt affirmed her career-long commitment to engaging all as readers and all readers in critical literary study:

> Ultimately, if I have been concerned about methods of teaching literature, about ensuring that it should indeed be personally experienced, it is because, as Shelley said, it helps readers develop the imaginative capacity to put themselves in the place of others—a capacity essential in a democracy, where we need to rise above the narrow self-interest and envision the broader human consequences of political decisions. If I have been involved with the development of the ability to read critically across the whole intellectual spectrum, it is because such abilities are particularly important for citizens in a democracy.[28]

Our current historical and political moment parallels in many ways that of Rosenblatt's early career, giving new resonance to her insistence on reader agency in meaning-making. Rosenblatt's work speaks directly to two challenges in our current political, social, and cultural context. First, reading pedagogy is being increasingly driven at the K–12 level by neoliberal education reforms, including the implementation of the Common Core State Standards, which frequently frame reading as a process of passive information reception and collection. Higher education and literary scholarship are not immune to the effects of this shift; universities are increasingly tasked with producing workers instead of thinkers. While literary scholarship continues to pursue exciting new avenues and lines of inquiry, that intellectual discovery has small impact if it does not engage readers broadly. Secondly, while texts are more available than ever, our rapid-fire information age often results in superficial engagement with texts instead of a careful reading process. The rise of "fake news," the sway of social media, and increasing pervasiveness of anti-intellectualism are all symptoms of passive reading. Rosenblatt's transactional theory of reading, and perhaps more importantly her deliberate claim to literary study as a place for democratic possibility, offer contemporary literary theorists and educators a way to reframe why texts and reading matter.

## NOTES

1. Wayne Booth, foreword to *Literature as Exploration*, 5th edition (New York: MLA, 1995), vii.

2. Rosenblatt adopted the language of "transaction" beginning with the second edition of *Literature as Exploration* in 1968. In the preface to the fifth edition she writes, "*Interaction*, the term generally used, suggests two distinct entities acting on each other, like two billiard balls. *Transaction* lacks such mechanistic overtones and permits emphasis on the to-and-fro, spiraling, nonlinear, continuously reciprocal influence of reader and text in the making of meaning. The meaning—the poem—'happens' during the transaction between readers and the signs on the page" (xvii, original emphasis). For an exploration of the language changes between the first subsequent editions of *Literature as Exploration*, see Mark Dressman and Joan Parker Webster, "Retracing Rosenblatt: A Textual Archaeology," *Research in the Teaching of English* 36, no. 1 (2001).

3. Given the aim of placing Rosenblatt's work in the historical moment in which it was written, I will be citing the first edition unless otherwise noted.

4. Louise Rosenblatt, *Literature as Exploration*, first edition (New York: Appleton-Century-Crofts, 1938), vi.

5. Ibid., 35.

6. Ibid., 221.

7. Rosenblatt, "Retrospect and Prospect"; Nicholas Karolides and Louise Rosenblatt, "Theory and Practice: An Interview with Louise M. Rosenblatt," *Language Arts* 77, no. 2.

8. Ibid.

9. This conversation is not unique to American society, of course. One can trace similar arguments about the purpose of education and literacy at least as far back as the writings of Plato.

10. John Rury, *Education and Social Change: Themes in the History of American Schooling*, 2nd edition (Mahwah, New Jersey: Lawrence Erlbaum, 2005).

11. Claudia Goldin and Lawrence F. Katz, "Human Capital and Social Capital: The Rise of Secondary Schooling in America, 1910–1940." *The Journal of Interdisciplinary History* 29, no. 4, 1999.

12. Nancy Lesko, *Act Your Age: A Cultural Construction of Adolescence*, 2nd edition (New York: Taylor & Francis, 2012).

13. Rosenblatt, "Retrospect and Prospect," 289.

14. Goldin and Katz, "Human Capital and Social Capital."

15. Rosenblatt, *Literature as Exploration*, 212.

16. James Gee, *Social Linguistics and Literacies: Ideology in Discourses*, 4th edition (New York: Routledge, 2012), 64.

17. Ibid., 65.

18. Rosenblatt, *Literature as Exploration*, 212.

19. Rosenblatt, *Literature as Exploration*, 5th edition, xvi.

20. Rosenblatt, "Retrospect and Prospect"; Karolides and Rosenblatt, "Theory and Practice."

21. Rosenblatt, *Literature as Experience*, 155, original emphasis.

22. Ibid., 220.

23. Ibid., 328.

24. Ibid., 126.

25. Ibid., 269, original emphasis.

26. Rosenblatt, *Literature as Exploration*, fifth edition, xv.

27. Rosenblatt, *Literature as Exploration*, 108.

28. Karolides and Rosenblatt, "Theory and Practice," 169.

*Chapter Seven*

# Aesthetic Theory

*From Adorno to Cultural History*[1]

## Philip Goldstein

While literary theory has undergone a decline since the 1990s, the aesthetics of Theodor Adorno has experienced a revival.[2] As the MLA bibliography indicates, from 1999 to the present there have been nearly 299 articles on Adorno's aesthetics, whereas from 1958–1998 there were only 127 articles.[3] Critics commend Adorno's aesthetics because it resists capitalist commodity production and, unlike critical theory, justifies formal, textual analyses and aesthetic autonomy and negativity even as it engages in substantial socio-historical critique.[4] Heidegger too claims that art preserves its autonomy and uncovers hidden or forgotten truths, although Heidegger maintains that such uncovering or unconcealment reveals Being. These parallels suggest that Adorno's aesthetics is open to the critique which Derrida makes of the autonomous art defended by Martin Heidegger. Derrida shows that, just as the Kantian analytic of judgment is a theoretical framework, not a form of autonomy, so is the aesthetic autonomy of Heidegger. This critique implies that what explains the opposition of aesthetics and commodity production is not Adorno's realism but his Kantian framework. This critique implies, in addition, that the historical methods of Michel Foucault, who opposes the instrumental reason of Adorno as well as the onto-theological tradition of Heidegger and Derrida, can bring together literary or textual interpretation of texts, films, or the media and the socio-historical analysis of the practices of readers, viewers, audiences, or fans.

## THE AESTHETICS OF THEODOR ADORNO

Adorno was a longtime member of the Institute for Social Research, later known as the Frankfurt School, an independent research institute directed by Max Horkheimer, Adorno's close friend and collaborator. In his youth Adorno studied music, but after he joined the institute he developed the critical social theory which displaced the School's initial Marxist orientation and which addressed broad social issues, not the specialized perspectives of academic disciplines. After the Institute was reestablished in the United States, where in the 1930s Jewish members of the Frankfurt School had immigrated to escape German fascism, Adorno and Horkheimer wrote the *Dialectic of Enlightenment*, in which they argue that, by reducing "mass" art or culture to mere amusement with no real pleasure, insight, truth, autonomy, or individuality, the culture industry turns readers, viewers, and audiences into supporters of the status quo. He makes a similar argument in *Aesthetic Theory*, which was published in 1970, after he and Horkheimer successfully re-established the Frankfurt School in post-WWII Germany. In that work, he complains not only that the "fetish character of commodities" destroys art's autonomy but also that the "psychologism" of art caters to the consumer: "Today the consumer is allowed to project his impulses and mimetic residues onto anything he pleases, including art, whereas in the past the individual was expected to forget himself, to lose himself in art in the process of viewing, listening, and reading."[5] Repudiating the reader's responses, Adorno complains that, its autonomy lost, art now frees the consumer to interpret "anything he pleases, including art," instead of losing himself in it.

Adorno attributes the reification and the psychologism destroying art's autonomy to Enlightenment reason, which Adorno and Horkheimer say opposes mythological outlooks at the same time that it imposes an equally mythological faith in modern science. Their account of Enlightenment reason derives from Georg Lukács, who revises and extends Karl Marx's critique of commodity production.[6] Marx shows that the commodity fetishism imposed by capitalist production governs the social and the economic institutions of bourgeois society.[7] Lukács grants that this fetishism governs those institutions, but he rejects Marx's materialism and favors a totalizing Hegelian theory. As a consequence, he maintains that once economic institutions gain their independence, capitalism imposes the commodity fetishism on all realms, including the intellectual. The sciences, the humanities, and the other disciplines functioning within this context examine the internal relations of their disciplines and ignore their social relations. Like commodities, these "reified" disciplines consider themselves autonomous and ignore their underlying social conditions.

Similarly, Adorno and Horkheimer maintain that commodity fetishism dominates capitalist life and that an instrumental rationality dominates bourgeois social life. They argue, however, that this instrumental rationality begins with the classical Greeks, not the capitalist system. In *The Dialectic of Enlightenment*, they claim, for example, that Homer's *Odysseus* shows Ulysses resisting the sirens in order to underline the Greek mastery of nature: "Measures like those taken on Odysseus's ship in face of the Sirens are a prescient allegory of the dialectic of Enlightenment."[8] The mastery of nature, along with opposition to mythology, characterizes the propositional logic and conceptual discourse of both the Greeks and the modern enlightenment. The empirical science of the Enlightenment era sought to dismiss primitive mythology and superstition and to control nature but produced, instead, its own scientific mythology. Unlike the great artwork, which retains the absolute totality and spiritual aura of the old, primitive myth, scientific mythology denigrated nature, reified logic, aesthetics, information, and the status quo, and ensured, thereby, the conformity and the repression of the masses.

Lukács, by contrast, examines the historical opposition of art and society, not the broad, sociological opposition of art and society. For example, in *The Theory of the Novel* (1920), he shows that what novels reveal is an alienating tension of ideal values and inadequate circumstances. However, after WWI, when the Hungarian and the Soviet revolutions moved him to defend the scientific humanism of Karl Marx, he adopts a realist view of fiction. The conventions of realists like Balzac and other nineteenth-century novelists include typical characters, an intention or totality articulating the structure of a transindividual subject, and a plot which shows an objectively valid insight into social conflict. Moreover, he condemns modernist art, whose subjective modes of narration divorces art and society. As Peter Uwe Hohendahl says, in Lukács' view the "disappearance of the old fashioned omniscient narrator of the nineteenth-century novel is equated with the destruction of objective representation, which in turn is equated with misunderstanding objective reality."[9] By contrast, Adorno and Horkheimer defend high modernist art. They argue that, unlike popular culture, which remains trivial, lacks depth and originality, makes false promises, frustrates or crudely gratifies desire, and, in general, ensures ideological conformity and capitalist domination, high art resists its character as a commodity and reveals social reality.[10] To do so, it foregrounds what Hohendahl calls "the subjective moments . . . interiorization becomes the hallmark of the modern novel."[11]

In addition to the status of modernist art, Lukács and Adorno dispute the character of Hegelian theory. That is, to explain the historical insight of realist art, Lukács defends the Hegelian unity of part and whole or structure and function. Adorno claims, by contrast, that this Hegelian reconciliation of part and whole itself represents the domination of Enlightenment reason. Purely conceptual, this reconciliation imposes an abstract identity which denies the subject's concrete particularity. While the Marxist Lukács maintains that in reconciling subject and object realist art shows the historical development which culminates in communism, Adorno argues that the non-identity of subject and object liberates art, preserving its autonomy by dividing form and content and allowing many different totalities. As he says of Hegel, "Nowhere does he define the experience of the non-identical as the *telos* of the aesthetic subject or as its emancipation."[12]

In addition to his Marxist realism, Lukács defends the revolutionary potential of the working class. In the influential essay "Reification and the Consciousness of the Proletariat," he maintains that the practical activity of the working class can overcome the divisions and the conflicts of social life and establish the unity of subject and object in communism. In 1921, when the Soviet revolution was still flowering and even western revolutions looked possible, an optimistic Lukács moved to the USSR and supported the oppressive Stalinist regime, which he believed would evolve into something better. Frankfurt School theorists also considered Stalinist communism dogmatic and oppressive, but they claimed that the whole modern world is equally oppressive because they consider Enlightenment reason totalitarian. After the Holocaust and WWII, with fascism recently defeated, the Stalinist dictatorship securely in power, the Cold War underway, and American capitalism booming, Adorno and Horkheimer argue that instrumental rationality assimilates all opposition, including the working class and the communists, whose parties and governments impose the oppressive domination of Enlightenment rationality.

## ADORNO AND HEIDEGGER

Although Adorno's view of instrumental reason derives from Lukács, Adorno rejects his faith in the working class, communism, historical development, and Hegelian theory, which did not accord with the post-WWII era. Adorno also rejects Heidegger's views, especially his notion of *Dasein* or Being, which he considers a "jargon of authenticity" that emerges out of fascism and which affirms the religious notions that Heidegger, along with other existentialists, mean to reject. As Peter Gordon says, the jargon "was clearly a species of secularized religion. It carried an unmistakable odor of piety that granted its practitioners the sham dignity of this-worldly priests."[13] Nonetheless, Adorno's view of instrumental reason approximates Heideggger's view of equipmental reason. Heidegger also says that since the classical Greek era equipmental or technological modes of understanding, which are those concerned with propositional truth or with the uses of things, have dominated.[14] Speaking in phenomenological and not in Marxist terms he maintains, however, that they produce the presence of beings but not the truth or the unconcealedness of Being, what he terms "*aletheia*." In addition, both Adorno and Heidegger fault the reification of things, but Heidegger argues that by demonstrating their ontological origin things can be construed positively as soul or spirit.[15] As Gordon says, "Heidegger suggests that any critique of reification cannot leave unexamined the deeper ontological status of the subject in question."[16] Adorno takes Heidegger's critique of reification to obscure its social and historical contexts. In addition, as Deborah Cook points out, since he adopts the Hegelian dialectical method in which opposites both oppose each other and come together, his views are not compatible with Heidegger's;[17] they both maintain, however, that an equipmental or instrumental rationality has dominated society since ancient times.

Moreover, they both critique the conceptual truth of rationalist and / or Hegelian theory. Adorno grants that art represents Spirit, as Hegel says, but like Heidegger's "happening," it is a "surplus" or "animating breath," not the reconciliation of subject and object sought by Hegelian theory.[18] Moreover, faced with what he aptly termed "life after Auschwitz," Adorno defends the non-identity of subject and object because their non-identity divides form and content and, as a result, preserves art's autonomy and historical particularity. The non-identity of subject and object limits theory, whose classifications, types, and conceptual constructs fail to grasp the concrete text.[19]

Heidegger's *Poetry, Language, Thought* does not limit theory in this way, but it does deny that a text constructs a totality which cancels and preserves partial methods or unifies form and content, as Hegel and Lukács claim. By debunking conventional views, including the "workly" character of the work, the "thingly" character of the thing, or the "equipmental" character of equipment, Heidegger shows instead that art enables Being or truth to reveal itself. More precisely, art brings "what is" "into the Open," but it does so as a "happening," revelation, or "unconcealment."[20] As Barbara Bolt points out, this "unconcealment" depends, in turn, on the "strife" between "earth," or the substance of art, and world, or the "values, practices, attitudes, and institutions" which "structure how we operate."[21] Heidegger claims, then, that art uncovers hidden or forgotten truths and that such uncovering or unconcealment, not the interpreter's sensibility or experience, reveals Being. More precisely, the artistic text overcomes its technological "enframing" and reveals and conceals Being, disclosing and hiding truth.[22] As Bolt says, Heidegger maintains that "in truth there is always untruth."[23] Adorno, in contrast, defends Kant's claim that art is purposeful purposelessness. That is, instead of conveying a message, providing pleasure, or accomplishing a purpose, art preserves its autonomy. At the same time, figuration enables art to reveal social conflicts and divisions. As he says, "Real partisanship . . . dwells deep down, where social antinomies turn into the dialectic of forms. Artists articulate these antinomies in the language of the art work."[24]

Heidegger and Adorno both defend the aesthetic autonomy of art; however, instead of preserving aesthetic disinterestedness or a purely formal text, Heidegger maintains that art reveals and conceals Being, disclosing and hiding truth. Similarly, despite his criticism of Hegelian theory, Adorno accepts the Hegelian realism whereby the concrete formal or textual object implicitly overcomes the reification imposed by instrumental reason and reveals the historical truths mediating between it and society. As he says, "exposing the irrationality and absurdity of the status quo" (*Aesthetic* 78), art resists its reified character and discloses the objective truths of a divided society.[25]

## THE HISTORICAL METHODS OF MICHEL FOUCAULT

Foucault also develops a Heideggerian account of cultural practices, but he establishes their positive historical influence, rather than their formal autonomy, critical force, or objective truth. In the 1950s, as a student at the École Normale Supérieure and the University of Paris, Foucault, who studied with Louis Althusser, a Marxist, and Gaston Bachelard and Georges Canguilhem, philosophers of science, adopted their belief that changing paradigms, not universal norms, explain the historical evolution of science. Foucault assumes, however, that distinct configurations of power and knowledge regulate the body, institutions, and even society. As a result, in keeping with the "human sciences," Foucault examines impersonal regularities dispersed across societies, institutions, and individual bodies. Moreover Foucault, who late in his life said, "My entire philosophical development was determined by my reading of Heidegger,"[26] reads Heidegger through Nietzsche: the will to power explains the ability of language to bring what is into the open, or into the clearing where it becomes visible even as it recedes into darkness.[27] As a consequence, in *The Order of Things*, he grants that equipmental or technological reason constitutes the subject, as Heidegger says, but shows that changing historical conditions, not what Kant called the transcendental forms of human understanding, explain the changing modes of discourse.

Heidegger also rejects the Kantian distinction between transcendental reason and empirical sensibility and, as Michael Schwartz says, adopts the historical belief that the conventions and norms or "being" of an epoch explain its changing discourses.[28] Heidegger argues, however, that, since the classical Greek era, western society has "darkened," losing, he believes, the capacity to experience the poetic "shining of truth." Propositional and equipmental or technological modes of understanding dominate, making things important and producing the presence of beings but not of Being itself. Foucault, by contrast, emphasizes the Nietzschean notion that discourse does not uncover a pre-existent object; discourse constitutes the objects, including the human "object," which it purports to uncover. Neither these discourses nor the "will-to-power" of Nietzsche show, however, that Being has been forgotten and that the contemplation of truth or Being is justified, as Heidegger says;

rather, positively organizing and reorganizing social life, these technologies constitute the "normal" individual or social subject.

For example, in *Madness and Civilization: A History of Insanity in the Age of Reason* (1961) and in *The Order of Things* (1966), Foucault maintains that evolving paradigms explain the historical development of a discourse or science. In positive histories, he shows that the Renaissance, the classical era, and the modern era constitute a historical ontology or "episteme" establishing the disciplines which subsequently undermine it. In *The History of Madness*, Foucault argues that institutional changes, not scientific enlightenment, explain the modern treatment of the insane. Medical historians discover in ancient treatises examples of pathologies, neuroses, paranoias, or hallucinations as though these forms of madness were eternal and unchanging, whereas the changed, institutional arrangements of the eighteenth and nineteenth centuries actually allowed these scientific forms of madness to emerge.

In Foucault's early, Nietzschean mode, he favors an existential resistance in which the disciplines' silent and repressed other transgresses their ethical and social norms. In his later works, he examines the socio-political import of disciplinary discourses, whose power to constitute a subject extends to the individual as well as the "social" subject but does not preclude their freedom to resist. More importantly, he distinguishes between an archaeology, which explains the broad episteme underlying and justifying the norms and procedures of established discourses, and a genealogy, which, unlike a totalizing episteme, reveals the local institutional contexts in which a discourse has evolved and acquired legitimacy. His archaeologies of madness, punishment, and sexuality examine the positive historical paradigms explaining how the treatment of the mad, prisoners, or sexual perversity have changed over several centuries. His genealogies examine the ruptured evolution of the technology by which various institutions or discourses constitute or regulate the subject. Since a genealogy recounts the discontinuous or fragmented history of a particular discourse, it describes a discourse's internal divisions, conflicts, or politics rather than its coherent field. As strategies with dispositions and techniques, these discourses form a complex which Foucault terms governmentality and which organize or regulate diverse institutions in equally diverse or discontinuous ways.

In *Discipline and Punish* (1975) Foucault shows, for example, that, as disciplinary knowledge, these strategies of power have a constitutive or "subjectivizing" force enabling the subject to act. Emerging in the eighteenth and nineteenth centuries, with the decline of the monarchy's power to punish or kill, disciplinary power constituted the individual subject in prisons, asylums, schools, and factories. Foucault's most forceful example is Bentham's panopticon, which allowed prison guards to observe everyone. As Marcello Hoffman points out, Foucault considers the panopticon the "perfect expression of disciplinary power": "By inducing *in* inmates an awareness of their own constant visibility, the Panopticon compels them to structure their own behaviour in accordance with its power mechanism."[29]

Similarly, in *The History of Sexuality*, volume 1, Foucault argues that sexuality was not repressed in the eighteenth and nineteenth centuries and freed in the twentieth century, as scholars say. Sexuality, like punishment, was governed by disciplinary power, which engaged in "the policing of sex" or "regulating sex through useful and public discourses."[30] Concerned about population, the government intervenes in premarital and marital as well as extra-marital sex. Schools examine children's sexuality. Masturbation was also regulated. Initially considered sodomy, homosexuality became a perversion and was extensively regulated. As Foucault says, "Four key figures emerged from this preoccupation with sex, which mounted during the nineteenth century . . . the hysterical woman, the masturbating child, the Malthusian couple, and the perverse adult."[31] Moreover, science made confessions of sexual activity an important way of interpreting sexual or revealing perversions. At the state level, what Foucault terms "biopower" regulated sexual activity to ensure population growth and capitalist development.

In *Genealogy as Critique*, Colin Koopman argues that a genealogy and an archaeology are not opposed; rather, the genealogy is implicit in the archaeology.[32] I have suggested, however, that they differ substantially: the archaeologies depict the broad historical context of a discourse while, much narrower, the genealogies indicate that the specific discourses of modern technologies impose their forms of presence in a positive or enabling manner. I have also suggested that Foucault's work is Heideggerian.[33] As Stuart Elden points out, while Foucault interprets Kant's account of the Enlightenment in historical terms, Foucault's view of genealogy parallels Heidegger's account of ontological knowledge.[34] That is, they both reject the universal subject of modern humanism: Heidegger examines the history of being and its relation to truth, and Foucault, disciplinary power and its regulation of the body. Michael Schwartz suggests, for example, that the epistemes described in *Les Mots et Les Choses* differ from but still parallel the dominant worldviews depicted in Heidegger's *The Question of Technology*.[35] Foucault also accepts Heidegger's claim that equipmental or technological reason constitutes the subject and imposes dominant notions of consumption and the modern world. As Leslie Thiele suggests, both "Heidegger and Foucault insist that our self-made jails are . . . sites of the extensive and intensive pursuit of heightened productivity and consumption."[36]

## JACQUES DERRIDA

Jacques Derrida critiques the historical studies of Foucault as well as the aesthetic autonomy defended by Heidegger and Adorno. Derrida was born in

Algeria, but because of its anti-Semitism, moved to France, where he studied with Foucault and criticized his work even though he acknowledges that Foucault was his professor. As he says, "I retain the consciousness of an admiring and grateful disciple."[37] In his critique of Foucault's *Madness and Civilization* (1963), he suggests that Foucault could not examine madness itself or show that madness excludes reason in the eighteenth century because Foucault's account itself remains within reason. Foucault argues, however, that he examines the historicity or the historical forms of reason. Derrida also argues that in the *Meditations* Descartes does not exclude madness as Foucault's account of reason and madness maintains; rather, Descartes takes both madness and dreaming to enable him to preserve his meditative self. In other words, madness is included within reason or the *Cogito*. Foucault objects that Derrida misunderstands the nature of a mediation and, as a result, reduces it to a textual matter.[38] As Pierre Macherey explains,

> Foucault argues that, "by reinstating madness within the field of meditation by means of dreams," Derrida brings "Descartes' discourse back to the level of the enunciative regime of demonstrative theoretical argumentation, without taking into account the . . . practical regime of enunciation through which the subject of truth effectively constitutes itself."[39]

In addition to these disputes with Foucault, which ended their friendship, Derrida disputes Heidegger's belief that, as a "happening, revelation," or "unconcealment," art brings "what is" "into the Open."[40] In the influential essay "Differance," Derrida argues that for truth to "occur" or "happen" this disclosure must subvert the reader's conventional modes of understanding. What Derrida objects to is not this subversion of the reader's understanding but the ensuing revelation of "being." Speaking of writing in general, Derrida says that, instead of manifesting it, writing generates it as a discursive effect or defers it indefinitely. While traditional phenomenology treats speech as the expression of consciousness and writing as a mere supplement of speech, both Heidegger and Derrida deny that language serves the ends of thought; however, Derrida goes on to deny that writing supplements and corrupts speech, that phonemes articulate the concept, and that the visible represents the intelligible. Heidegger preserves the privileges of consciousness, including its status as "self-presence" (what Heidegger calls the "onto-theological determination of being"), but Derrida undermines those privileges, for he claims that writing, which lies outside being, generates effects which Heidegger (mis)construes as the venerable presence of "being." As Derrida says, "presence is a determination and effect within a system which is no longer that of presence but that of difference."[41]

More importantly, in *Truth in Painting*, Derrida faults Heidegger's claim that an account of art's origin requires an explanation of art's essence, which means determining what is internal or intrinsic to art and what is external or extrinsic. This explanation draws, Derrida says, on Kant's belief that a judgment of taste is pure or disinterested rather than a form of pleasure or utility. What makes such judgments possible is the autonomous work which as an object in itself has an interior, intrinsic value independent of its exterior contexts or extrinsic uses or purposes. Derrida maintains that the frame of the work or parergon allows such pure judgments of taste by making works autonomous, but the frame itself is not inside or outside the work.[42] As Simone Heller-Andrist explains, in Derrida's account the parergon "is neither part of something else, nor does it stand entirely on its own." Heller-Andrist adds that, paradoxically, "[t]his means that it is always also part of something else."[43]

Derrida shows that the parergon distinguishes the autonomous work from the utilitarian, or the intrinsic, interior space from the extrinsic historical or social context. The parergon is not part of the work or external to it; rather, the frame or parergon is a construct imposed by Kant's analytic of judgment which establishes what is intrinsic and extrinsic to a work or where its border or framework lies: "It is the analytic which *determines* the frame as *parergon*."[44] As David Carroll says, Derrida indicates that

> [i]n placing a frame around the aesthetic . . . Kant, at the same time, reveals its problematical status . . . how the frame itself—even as it delineates an inside and an outside for each art work—permits, and even encourages, a complicated movement or passage across it both from inside out and outside-in.[45]

Such framing undermines Heidegger's distinction between art's intrinsic and extrinsic features. Derrida also shows that, although Heidegger accepts Kant's belief that this enframing establishes the aesthetic autonomy of art, he inconsistently maintains that art truthfully depicts the world. He claims, for example, that the shoes depicted by a Van Gogh painting are peasant shoes. Derrida maintains, by contrast, that the shoes, if they are a pair, may not belong to anyone, and that in this way Heidegger depicts the shoes as a "presentative reality" outside his discourse on truth in painting.[46]

The aesthetics of Adorno shows a similar inconsistency. He accepts the Kantian notion that the disinterested nature of aesthetic judgment establishes the autonomy whereby art resists the world rather than providing pleasure or accomplishing a purpose, but he construes this notion of autonomy as the reified state which consumer culture imposes on art and which sets art against society. Even though art is autonomous, Adorno claims that it can, by virtue of its unresolved oppositions, reveal the true divisions and conflicts characterizing social life. As I have indicated, Derrida's account of Kant's aesthetics does not simply undermine such realism; in addition, his account suggests that the frames provided by Kantian as well as other theoretical frameworks create the intrinsic textual context of art, which is, as a result, incompatible with Adorno's and Heidegger's realism. Derrida assumes, however, that this "deconstruction" of Heidegger's and Kant's aesthetics justifies the notion of writing which he derives from Heidegger's onto-theology and which shows writing generates being as a discursive effect or *"defers"* it indefinitely.

Moved by the difficulties which in the 1980s and 1990s communism and its demise posed for Marxist and cultural theory,[47] poststructuralist Marxists or post-Marxists suggest, by contrast, that interpretation is not a purely textual or discursive matter. In the 1940s, after the Holocaust and WWII, with the Stalinist dictatorship securely in power, the Cold War underway, and American capitalism booming, Frankfurt School theorists claimed that the whole modern world is oppressive because instrumental rationality assimilates all opposition, including the working class and the communists. However, in the 1970s and 1980s, when poststructuralist Marxism or post-Marxism develops, the Soviet Union is close to its demise, the western working class remains conservative, and the independent movements of feminists, blacks, trade unionists, environmentalists, postcolonialists, and others have developed. John Frow, Ernesto Laclau, Chantal Mouffe, Tony Bennett, and others who represent post-Marxism address many traditions and methods and do not form a movement or a school. However, they all restate and revise the poststructuralist Marxism of Louis Althusser and/or the historical theory of Michel Foucault and, unlike traditional Marxism, which emphasizes the priority of class struggle and the common humanity of oppressed groups, these scholars all reveal social life's sexual, racial, class, and ethnic divisions and progressive import. Stuart Sim says that "the decline in importance, both socially and politically, of the working class . . . has obvious implications for the growth of a post-Marxist consciousness, given the critical role that classical Marxism allotted the working class as the 'gravediggers of capitalism.'"[48] Sim is right, but an equally important social development is the independent African American, feminist, gay, ethnic, or postcolonial movements because their emergence shows that the interests and policies of oppositional groups involve much more than class context or struggle.

Initiating post-Marxism, Althusser's account of Marx undermines the humanist and the totalitarian views of Marxism. In a Foucauldian manner he maintains that a particular science or discourse resists the ideological commitments which form part of its history.[49] In keeping with the conventions, norms, and ideals which make up its context or "problematic," each science elaborates its own theoretical concepts. Economics, history, philosophy, mathematics, and other scientific disciplines and practices do not develop a general opposition of ideology and science; in accord with their distinct problematics, they establish their own "inward" criteria of validity and produce their own legitimate objects and discourses.

John Frow elaborates the post-Marxist theory of Althusser but, addressing cultural issues, he construes literary realism as the effect of established conventions, not the imitation of an independent reality, and literary texts as intertextual practices, not ideological forms. Frow goes on to show that the interpretive practices of readers explain a text's import and, more generally, literature's history. Drawing on Foucault's genealogies, John Frow suggests, in addition, that interpretation is not a purely textual matter; rather, it is a product of what he terms a literary regime, which makes value the result of "specific (and changing, changeable) social relations and mechanisms of signification."[50] This approach assumes that a text is fragmented by contrary or differing interpretations because contrary aesthetic norms regulating the reader's activity are established in educational or cultural institutions. Frow claims, as a result, that criticism does not refute wrong interpretations; rather, it illuminates the intertextual literary system or "regime of reading" governing a reader's interpretations. Moreover, citing Paul de Man, Frow claims that a regime can be constructed only a posteriori, from established interpretations. That is, Frow grants the Foucauldian assumption that a regime of reading constitutes a text's meanings, framings, or interpretations. As he says, "Textuality and its conditions of possibility are mutually constitutive and can be reconstructed only from each other in a kind of hermeneutic bootstrapping."[51] This "hermeneutic bootstrapping" means that neither texts and readers nor readers and regimes have an independent status or character; rather, their status and character depend on the regime of reading which constructs their relationship. Scholars argue, however, that the literary import of Foucault's genealogies lies in literary works which illustrate and elaborate or oppose and transgress them.[52] I suggest, by contrast, that the literary import of Foucault's work lies in such genealogies of aesthetic regimes.

To sum up, critics have revived the aesthetics of Adorno because it opposes literary theory and cultural movements and practices and justifies close textual analysis and aesthetic negativity. Despite Adorno's criticism of Heidegger he, like Heidegger (but not Lukács), argues that art preserves its autonomy and reveals socio-historical truth as well. Like Heidegger as well, Foucault grants that equipmental or technological reason constitutes the subject, but he shows that changing historical conditions, not what Kant called the transcendental forms of human understanding, explain the changing modes of discourse. Derrida criticizes Foucault's historical method as well as the Kantian notion of aesthetic autonomy. His critique of Kant's and Heidegger's aesthetics suggests that the frames of a text are philosophical constructs, not truths. In light of the parallels of Adorno's and Heidegger's aesthetics, this critique also suggests that, to preserve the formal autonomy and the realist insights of a text, Adorno treats its frames as sociohistorical truth. In a post-Marxist fashion, John Frow grants, by contrast, that the frames are constructs, as Derrida shows, but in keeping with Foucault's genealogical methods, he argues that they are actually situated in diverse cultural institutions, regimes, or formations whose historical evolution explains readers' changing constructions of a text. While this approach does not reconcile or resolve the sharp differences of Derrida and Foucault, it opens texts to the interpretive practices and socio-historical contexts of their readers, viewers, audiences, or fans.

## NOTES

1. For an early version of this essay, see "Marxist Theory: From Aesthetic Critique to Cultural Politics," *A Left Ontology*, edited by Carsten Strathausen (Minneapolis: University of Minnesota Press, 2009), 152–81.

2. See "Engaging the Aesthetic," *The Aesthetics of Cultural Studies*, edited by Michael Bérubé (Oxford: Blackwell, 2005), in which Bérubé says that the "backlash" to those studies "presented itself as the Next Big Thing, and the next Big Thing was the aesthetic" (2); "Tasks of Critical Reading Today" (Unpublished presentation, the Modern Language Association, 2010), in which Vincent Leitch says, "various backlashes have called for returns to the common reader, to close reading, to appreciative criticism, and to limited critical pluralism" (1); *Revenge of the Aesthetic: The Place of Literature in Theory Today*, edited by Michael Clark (Berkeley: University of California Press, 2000), in which Michael Clark says that the critical examination of "aesthetic values and formal characteristics specific to literary texts . . . has taken on a contrarian quality today, as aesthetic issues have often been displaced from a field that only twenty years ago could still be called 'literary' theory" (1). For the contrary view, see "Running and Dodging: The Rhetoric of Doubleness in Contemporary Theory," *New Literary History* 41, no. 2 (Spring 2010), in which Timothy Brennan grants that the decline of theory has led to a "new formalism" but argues that the decline was also theory's way of reinventing itself as political (279–80), and "The Death of Deconstruction, the End of Theory, and Other Ominous Rumors," *Narrative* 4, no. 1 (January 1996), in which Jeffrey Williams also grants that theory underwent a decline but attributes it to several causes, including the revelation of Paul de Man's Nazi past (28).

3. As of a search last conducted March 2018 using the broadest possible search parameters.

4. In *The Radical Aesthetic* (Oxford: Blackwell, 2000), Isabel Armstrong, who favors an affective sort of close textual analysis rather than the cool rationality of literary theory, says that Adorno's aesthetics did much more than "give the old bourgeois humanist terms, the traditional nineteenth-century aesthetics, a Marxist gloss" (175). See also Terry Eagleton, *The Ideology of the Aesthetic* (Cambridge, MA: Basil Blackwell, Inc., 1990), 334–35 and 354–55; Fredric Jameson, *Late Marxism: Adorno, or The Persistence of the Dialectic* (New York: Verso, 1990), 248–49; Steven Best and Douglas Kellner, *Postmodern Theory: Critical Interrogations* (New York: Guilford, 1991), 229; Emory Elliott, "Introduction: Cultural Diversity and the Problem of Aesthetics," *Aesthetics in a Multicultural Age,* edited by Emory Elliott, Louis Freitas, and Jeffrey Rhyne (Oxford: Oxford University Press, 2002), 5; and John J. Joughin and Simon Malpas, "Introduction," *The New Aestheticism*, edited by John J. Joughin and Simon Malpas (Manchester: Manchester University Press, 2003), 1, 7.

5. Theodor Adorno, *Aesthetic Theory*, edited by Gretel Adorno and Rolf Tiedemann, trans. C. Lenhardt (1970; London: Routledge & Kegan Paul, 1984), 25.

6. In *Lukács, Marx and the Sources of Critical Theory* (Lanham, MD: Rowman & Littlefield, 1981), Andrew Feenberg says that "Adorno himself acknowledged that Lukács' concept of reification" led to the Frankfurt School's modern view of capitalism (165).

7. See J. M. Bernstein, *The Philosophy of the Novel: Lukács, Marxism, and the Dialectics of Form* (Minneapolis: University of Minnesota Press, 1984), 82; Susan Buck-Morss, *The Origin of Negative Dialectics: Theodor W. Adorno, Walter Benjamin, and the Frankfurt Institute* (Hassocks: Harvester, 1977), 25; and Brian O'Connor, *Adorno* (New York: Routledge, 2013), 179.

8. Theodor Adorno and Max Horkheimer, *Dialectic of Enlightenment*, trans. John Cumming (1944; New York: Continuum Press, 1972), 27.

9. Peter Uwe Hohendahl, "The Theory of the Novel and the Concept of Realism in Lukács and Adorno," *George Lukács Reconsidered*, edited by Michael J. Thompson (New York: Continuum, 2011), 81.

10. See Adorno and Horkheimer, 94–136; Eagleton, 356–57; and Brian O'Connor, *Adorno* (New York: Routledge, 2013), 179.

11. Hohendahl, 81.

12. Adorno, 113.

13. Peter E. Gordon, *Adorno and Existence* (Cambridge: Harvard University Press, 2016), 90.

14. In *The Theory of Communicative Action*, vol. 1, trans. Thomas McCarthy (Boston: Beacon Press, 1981), Jürgen Habermas rightly says, "As opposed as the intentions behind their respective philosophies of history are, Adorno is in the end very similar to Heidegger as regards his position on the theoretical claims of objectivating thought and reflection" (385). See also "The Rage against Reason," *Philosophy and Literature*, 1986, 10 (2), in which Richard Bernstein maintains that in "Heidegger's fateful, strong reading of the 'history of being' . . . we find a thematic affinity with Adorno's claim" that the roots of Enlightenment reason "with its hidden will-to-mastery are to be found in the very origins of Western rationality" (198). For thorough discussions of these similarities, see Fred Dallmayr, "Adorno and Heidegger," *Diacritics* 19, nos. 3–4 (Fall-Winter 1989), 82–100; David Roberts, "Art and Myth: Adorno and Heidegger," *Thesis Eleven* 58 (August 1999), 19–34; Mario Wenning, "Heidegger and Adorno: Opening up Grounds for Dialogue," *Gnosis* VI, 1 (2002): http://artsandscience.concordia.ca/philosophy/gnosis/vol_vi/index.html#toc; and Krzysztof Ziarek, "Mimesis in Black and White: Feminist Aesthetics, Negativity and Semblance," *The New Aestheticism*, edited by John J. Joughin and Simon Malpas (Manchester: Manchester University Press, 2003), 51–67. For a dismissal of these similarities, see Jameson, who says, "I have been surprised by the increasing frequency of comparisons with his arch-enemy Heidegger (whose philosophy, he once observed, 'is fascist to its innermost core')" (9).

15. Heidegger, Martin, *Being and Time*, trans. John Macquarrie and Edward Robinson (San Francisco: HarperSanFrancisco, 1962).

16. Gordon, 146.

17. Deborah Cook, "Theodor W. Adorno: An Introduction," *Theodor Adorno: Key Concepts*, edited by Deborah Cook (Stocksfield, UK: Acumen, 2008), 21.

18. Adorno, 128–29.

19. Eagleton, 356–57; Hauke Brunkhorst, "Irreconcilable Modernity: Adorno's Aesthetic Experimentalism and the Transgression Theorem," *The Actuality of Adorno: Critical Essays on Adorno and the Postmodern*, edited by Max Pensky (Albany: State University of New York Press, 1997), 126.

20. Martin Heidegger, *Poetry, Language, Thought*, trans. Albert Hofstadter (New York: Harper & Row, 1975), 36.

21. Barbara Bolt, *Heidegger Reframed* (New York: L. B. Taurus & Co., 2011), 44.

22. Heidegger, *Poetry, Language, Thought*, 59–63.

23. Bolt, 48.

24. Adorno, 330.

25. See also Adorno and Horkheimer, who maintain that, divided and contradictory, high art accepts and subverts established aesthetic practices and ruling ideologies, resists its commodified character and, as a negative moment projecting a utopian vision, reaffirms the totality (120–67).

26. Alan Milchman and Alan Rosenberg, "Toward a Foucault / Heidegger *Auseinandersetzung*," *Foucault and Heidegger Critical Encounters*, edited by Alan Milchman and Alan Rosenberg (Minneapolis: University of Minnesota Press, 2003), 3.

27. Gilles Deleuze, *Foucault* (Paris: Les Éditions de Minuit, 1986), 120

28. Michael Schwartz, "Epistemes and the History of Being," in *Foucault and Heidegger: Critical Encounters*, edited by Alan Milchman and Alan Rosenberg (Minneapolis and London: University of Minnesota Press, 2003), 165–67.

29. Marcello Hoffman, "Disciplinary Power," in *Michel Foucault: Key Concepts*, edited by Dianna Taylor (Durham, England: Acumen Pub., 2011), 34.

30. Michel Foucault, *History of Sexuality, Vol. 1: An Introduction*, trans. Robert Hurley (New York: Vintage Books, 1980), 25.

31. Foucault, 105.

32. Colin Koopman, *Genealogy as Critique: Foucault and the Problems of Modernity* (Bloomington: Indiana UP, 2013), 30–1; see also "Reading Genealogy as Historical Ontology," *Mapping the Present: Heidegger, Foucault and the Project of a Spatial History* (London: Continuum Press, 2001), in which Stuart Elden considers the archaeology and the genealogy "two halves of a complementary approach" (198).

33. For an account of how Nietzsche and Heidegger interpret Kant and influence Foucault, see Stuart Elden, "Reading Genealogy as Historical Ontology," *Foucault and Heidegger Critical Encounters*, edited by Alan Milchman and Alan Rosenberg (Minneapolis: University of Minnesota Press, 2003), 187–205.

34. Ibid., 196–97.

35. Michael Schwartz, 163–186; see also Jana Sawicki, *Disciplining Foucault: Feminism, Power, and the Body* (New York: Routledge, 1991), 56.

36. Leslie Paul Thiele, "The Ethics and Politics of Narrative: Heidegger + Foucault," *Foucault and Heidegger Critical Encounters*, edited by Alan Milchman and Alan Rosenberg (Minneapolis: University of Minnesota Press, 2003), 207.

37. Jacques Derrida, "Cogito and the History of Madness," in *Between Foucault and Derrida*, edited by Yubraj Aryal et al. (Edinburgh: Edinburgh University Press, 2016), 29.

38. Ibid. See also Michel Foucault, "My Body, This Paper, This Fire," *Aesthetics, Method, and Epistemology*, edited by James D. Fabion, trans. Robert Hurley et al. (New York: The New Press, 1998), 394–417.

39. Pierre Macherey, "The Foucault-Derrida Debate on the Argument Concerning Madness and Dreams," in *Derrida / Foucault Fifty Years Later: The Futures of Genealogy, Deconstruction, and Politics*, edited by Olivia Custer et al. (New York: Columbia University Press, 2016), 18–19.

40. Heidegger, *Poetry, Language, Thought*, 36.

41. Jacques Derrida, "Differance," in *Speech and Phenomena* (Evanston: Northwestern Univ. Press, 1973), 147.

42. Jacques Derrida, *The Truth in Painting*, trans. Geoff Bennington and Ian McLeod (Chicago: The University of Chicago Press, 1987), 54.

43. Simone Heller-Andrist, *The Friction of the Frame: Derrida's Parergon in Literature* (Tubingen: Francke, 2012), 34.

44. Derrida, *Truth in Painting*, 73.

45. David Carroll, *Paraesthetics: Foucault, Lyotard, Derrida* (New York: Methuen, 1987), 136.

46. Derrida, *Truth in Painting*, 363.

47. See John Frow, *Marxism and Literary History* (Cambridge, MA: Harvard University Press, 1986).

48. Stuart Sim, *Post-Marxism: An Intellectual History* (New York: Routledge, 2000), 5.

49. Louis Althusser, *For Marx*, trans. Ben Brewster (New York: Random House, 1969), 182–93.

50. John Frow, *Cultural Studies and Cultural Value* (Oxford: Clarendon Press, 1995), 301

51. John Frow, "On Literature and Cultural Studies," *The Aesthetics of Cultural Studies*, edited by Michael Bérubé (Oxford: Blackwell, 2005), 53. See also *Culture: A Reformer's Science* (St. Leonard's, Australia: Allyn & Unwin, 1998), 69–70, in which Tony Bennett also maintains that a "reading formation" is established in educational or cultural institutions, but he claims that their various technologies produce various cultural resources and impose equally various forms and kinds of discipline or governmental organization.

52. For a Foucauldian approach which treats literature as transgressive, see Simon During, *Foucault and Literature Towards a Genealogy of Writing* (London and New York: Routledge, 1992), and Timothy O'Leary, *Foucault and Fiction: The Experience Book* (London: Continu-

um, 2009). For accounts in which literature illustrates and elaborates Foucault's work, see *Genealogy and Literature*, edited by Lee Quinby (Minneapolis: U of Minnesota P, 1995).

*Chapter Eight*

# Judith Butler

## *A Livable Life*

## Darcie Rives-East

Judith Butler is best known for her work in queer theory, especially her 1990 study, *Gender Trouble: Feminism and the Subversion of Identity*. In it, she argues that sex and gender are not innate but continually created through a cultural matrix and normalized via the repetition of acceptable gestures, actions, and thought (what Butler terms "performativity").[1] However, beginning with her dissertation on philosopher G. W. F. Hegel and continuing throughout her career, Butler's interest has not only been in queer identity per se, but also in larger questions of who is counted as human and who is deemed recognizable as a subject in society. These fundamental questions have constantly guided her thought, and she has applied them not only to issues of gender and sexuality, but also more broadly to ideas about government, obscenity, speech, violence, and media. Butler and her work must be considered through the framework of these larger questions rather than understood solely through the lens of queer theory. For Butler, these questions of who counts and who can be a subject force us to interrogate how we form our identities within social restrictions and also how we can exceed those restrictions. Ultimately, focusing on these questions allows Butler to argue that all subjects should be allowed what she terms a "livable" life: a life not consigned to "social death" in which a person is not recognized as human and whose death and loss is never grieved.

Further, we should approach Butler's oeuvre with the knowledge that it is necessarily bound up with her own negotiation of her personal identities as lesbian, Jewish, and feminist, and the larger social-historical context in which her writing emerged. Butler would agree that one can never fully divorce the personal from the social.[2] Rather, the "I" who speaks and writes is tensely conjoined with larger social forces that delimit the subject even as the "I" contests and pushes the boundaries of these social limits.[3] Therefore, Butler's work also needs to be considered alongside the writings of other theorists, such as Hegel, Michel Foucault, and Jacques Derrida, who have influenced her thought and with whom she dialogues in her studies.

After discussing key aspects of Butler's personal background, this essay will use this context to situate Butler's major studies in three parts to argue that we should understand Butler's ethics of gender and queer theory as more broadly applicable to larger questions of how we culturally define human beings and who counts as a subject. Part 1: Gender and the Body will focus on her publications *Gender Trouble* and *Bodies that Matter: On the Discursive Limits of "Sex"* (1993). Part 2: Language and the State will cover *Excitable Speech: A Politics of the Performative* (1997). Finally, Part 3: Mourning and the Media will examine *Precarious Life: The Powers of Mourning and Violence* (2004) and *Frames of War: When is Life Grievable?* (2009). The essay then concludes with a brief discussion of Butler's most recent work. While this chronological schema is created for convenience and clarity, we should be mindful that Butler's work cannot truly be "divided" into phases of work. As Butler herself notes, she does not attempt to reconcile the different trajectories and foci of her work, but instead acknowledges that she applies the same frames and questions to various topics to illuminate how we are continually in the process of forming our subjectivities.[4]

## THE PERSONAL AND THE POLITICAL SUBJECT

Butler's engagement with subjectivity and who counts as human has its roots in her upbringing. Born in Cleveland, Ohio, in 1956, Butler is currently the Maxine Elliot Professor in the Departments of Rhetoric and Comparative Literature at the University of California, Berkeley. Butler's Jewish family background and education in Ohio would become one of the primary influences on her critical thought, particularly her interest in and development of her theories regarding subjectivity. Butler states that her "family was from Hungary and from Russia. And they maintained ties to Europe. And many of my family lived here through the [19]30s and died in the [Second World] War."[5] During her childhood, she observed her family attempting to assimilate into an American society predominated and delimited by Anglo identity.[6] This "ideal subject" (white, Christian, heterosexual) as constructed by the dominant culture was ethnic and racial as well as gendered and sexual.[7] Anglo society demanded a certain way of acting and being that had become what Roland Barthes terms "naturalized;"[8] and so, in Butler's words, her family members gained "entrance into American society"[9] by emulating the dominant culture's standards of gender and ethnicity that were disseminated through popular culture, particularly film. [10] For example, Butler humorously remarks that her grandmother "slowly but surely became Helen Hayes" and her mother "slowly but surely became . . . Joan Crawford." [11]

However, what was important for Butler as a child was observing the ways that her family *failed* to successfully enact such identity. In this way, the loss (of Jewish identity) reemerged in this failure and produced what Butler terms "excess." [12] For Butler, then, this excess or failure gained her attention, since it indicated to her that identity formation cannot be natural; if so, no one would have problems meeting the ideal demanded by society. [13] But since we all do fail in various ways, it must follow that identity is created by society, and we as subjects respond to this interpellation. We sometimes succeed in our response but often we do not—we exceed those limits, and that excess can be threatening to society, to its definition of lives that matter, and even to oneself. This realization would eventually become foundational to her understanding of gender and sex as performative in *Gender Trouble* and *Bodies that Matter*, and, later, to her arguments of what it means to have a "liveable life" (i.e., be recognized as a subject who matters). But, for Butler, this awareness was also profoundly personal: "I grew up understanding something of the violence of gender norms: an uncle incarcerated for his anatomically anomalous body . . . gay cousins forced to leave their homes because of their sexuality . . . [and] my own tempestuous coming out at the age of 16." [14]

Equally important for Butler was her Jewish education through which she developed her interest in critical theory and philosophy. She remembers that she was an outlier not only because of her ethnicity and sexuality, but also because she was a "problem child"; she did not do well in school and constantly rebelled against rules and restrictions to the point that she was not allowed to continue as a student in her Jewish school. [15] However, Butler was extremely intelligent, and in lieu of school became a personal tutee of her rabbi who helped her explore and study philosophical questions she had as early as age fourteen: "I explained that I wanted to read existential theology focusing on Martin Buber. . . . I wanted look at the question of whether German idealism could be linked with National Socialism. . . . My third question was why Spinoza was excommunicated from the synagogue. I wanted to know what happened and whether the synagogue was justified." [16] These questions reveal that early on Butler was interested in how the individual subject can be formed within larger social forces, and how the subject both can agree to and contest those limits.

Butler's philosophical curiosity would lead her to Yale, where she earned a PhD in Continental philosophy, writing a dissertation that explored the influence of Hegel on contemporary French critical theory. [17] Hegel's argument that the subject is formed in relation to others would become a crucial influence on Butler's own thought. Later, Butler also studied in Germany, which her grandmother encouraged despite Butler's Jewish identity: "My grandmother was always very clear that I should go back to Europe to study, and so I came to study in Heidelberg in 1979. My mother and her generation were worried whether I should go to Germany and that could be difficult being Jewish. But my grandmother said: 'Yes, you go to Germany. Jews always went to study in Prague, in Berlin, yes, you go!'"[18] As we shall see, Butler would add to Hegel's concept of the subject the post-structuralist language theories of Jacques Derrida; Michel Foucault's theorization of power in the relationship between the social and the subject; the feminist theories of Simone de Beauvoir and Monique Wittig; and her own personal life experience to create her particular understanding of how we become subjects, who counts as one, and who determines which subjectivities are valued and which are not.

## PART 1: EARLY AUTHORSHIP: GENDER, THE BODY, AND LIVES THAT MATTER

We can see how these trajectories of Butler's early personal experiences with larger questions of who counts as human, as well as her work with Hegel, become influential in Butler's most famous work, *Gender Trouble* (*GT*). Drawing on Hegel's idea that the subject forms through a dialectical relationship with others[19] as well as Foucault's contention that social discourses and power relations precede the subject (rather than vice versa),[20] Butler argues in *GT* that any attempt to find the origin of a subject is impossible. The parameters of who a subject can be (the "I") are formed socially before the subject even exists. Our identity is both limited by and challenges those parameters, such that the subject is never "finished" but is always in process.

Butler uses this moment to consider this idea of "becoming" through the lens of gender (masculine and feminine social roles ostensibly derived from biological sex) and sexuality (sexual practices). Turning to de Beauvoir's famous assertion that "one is not born, but rather becomes, a woman,"[21] Butler introduces her profound insight that gender has "neither origin nor cause"[22] and is the result of performativity and process rather than an identity that is innate and unchanging. This concept of performativity is frequently misunderstood. Butler does not argue that we consciously assume or "put on" gender each day, as if gender were a theatrical performance or a costume one chooses from a wardrobe.[23] Rather, what gender means and how it is constituted are already socially determined before one becomes conscious and develops a sense of self (the "I"). These social forms become naturalized by repeated performance—it is the repetition of a set of accepted codes, actions, gestures, and thoughts that legitimize the social parameters of gender and sexuality.[24] This is what Butler means by performativity and that we "perform" gender: our gender and sexual identities *are* the repetitions in which we participate. These reiterations work to establish dyadic gender (man / woman) and heterosexuality, and hence an illusion of "primary and stable identity."[25]

But, as she was in her teenage years, Butler is here compelled by ways in which this supposedly stable identity fails, and the notion of failure is central to her theory of performativity. The relationship between failure and repetition reveals two points. First, something innate, natural, and impervious to failure would not have to repeat itself again and again to establish its legitimacy (it would simply "be"). Thus, the performative aspect of gender exposes anxiety and panic at the heart of the normalization of dyadic gender and heterosexual identities, fears that these norms will be exposed as constructs if the performance is not repeated satisfactorily. Second, the fact that the performance is often a "failure" (as indicated by those who do not conform to dyadic gender or whose sexuality is not heterosexual) demonstrates that gender and sexuality are indeed performances and not innate ways of being.[26]

Another key element Butler employs to underscore the performativity of gender is drag. Butler's theorization of drag is likewise misunderstood. Drag is not about choosing or creating one's own gender, but, rather, through its performance of masculinity or femininity, it allows us insight into the ways in which what is considered "natural" gender (man / woman) or sexuality (heterosexuality) is also a structure or performance built up via the repetition of a set of gestures or actions: "*In imitating gender, drag implicitly reveals the imitative structure of gender itself—as well as its contingency.*"[27] Despite the constructed nature of gender and sexuality, Butler cautions that none of us have the ability to "create" a gender or sexual identity ex nihilo, nor to reject the constructs that are already in place; instead, we can only work within the social matrix that surrounds us and adopt, adapt, and exceed what already exists.

Gender "trouble" therefore occurs through such adaptations and excesses—the failures— which expose the narrowness of "naturalized" gender and sexuality. It is at this "limit of intelligibility"[28] that the dominant culture will often attempt to curtail or erase those excesses (i.e., those who do not conform to gender or sexual norms) by making certain people invisible and forcing them into a "social death" (or, worse, physical death by violence) in which they do not count as legitimate subjects in society. For instance, Butler writes of the invisibility of herself and others who identify as lesbian: "Lesbianism is not explicitly prohibited [by law] in part because it has not even made its way into the thinkable, the imaginable, that grid of cultural intelligibility that regulates the real and the nameable."[29] In this way, Butler's argument for the performativity of gender introduces a call for tolerance that will become a pervading theme of her career. Since there is no right way to "do" gender (or any identity), everyone's subjectivity should be respected such that they have access to "livable life": the ability to exist and be recognized in society.

*Gender Trouble* grew out of a larger post-structuralist critical movement in the 1980s and 1990s that became known as "queer theory." Building on feminist and gay and lesbian critiques of patriarchal and heterosexual norms, queer theory emphasizes the fluid and complex nature of gender and sexuality; queer theory maintains that people's identities cannot be constrained within limited categories such as "man," "woman," "gay," "straight," and so on.[30] In so doing, queer theory itself engages with how cultures define subjectivity and who "counts" in society. By arguing that people should not be so easily divided up into strict categories, queer theory maintains that non-normative bodies, sexualities, and identities must be recognized as lives that matter. Queer theory and the queer movement began also in large part as a response to the cultural presence of AIDS. As Butler writes, those with the illness became stigmatized as "polluted" in terms of the virus and their sexuality, given that at the time (and still today) AIDS was considered primarily a "gay disease."[31] In this way, non-normative sexuality became constructed, paradoxically, as "*both* uncivilized and unnatural."[32] Those with the disease, to use Butler's ideas from later works like *Frames of War* and *Precarious Life*, were not recognized by society as subjects because they were not "mourned" by the dominant culture; as such they were not granted "liveable life" because they did not count as lives that mattered. The purpose of queer theory, then, was and is to interrogate the idea of normative subjectivity and to demonstrate that the norm itself is a construct to which no identity can fully conform.

Butler would develop these ideas further in *Bodies That Matter* (*BTM*). One question often asked of Butler following the publication of *Gender Trouble* was, "What about the materiality of the body, *Judy*?"[33] In other words, even if we concede that gender is constructed, is not one "born with a sexed body, i.e. with recognizably male or female genitalia"[34] such that one's sex is fixed before birth? Butler answers this question by deconstructing the "naturalness" of biological sex; she argues that while bodies are real, how we understand and view those bodies is as socially constructed as gender. As Matt Waggoner notes, "What was mistaken by many as an idealized version of the socially constructed body in *Gender Trouble* is in fact an effort on Butler's part to acknowledge that it is precisely the materiality of the body that accounts for the fact that we are more than our bodies, or that bodies are not self-evident."[35] In making this argument, Butler concurs with Wittig's contention that our culture emphasizes and elevates the importance of certain body parts versus others (such as genitalia rather than ears or noses) and uses these features as a means of categorizing people as either male or female.[36] Butler adds that those male / female categorizations force us down different paths that lead to certain life outcomes while foreclosing other possibilities.[37] Like Wittig, she cites the moment of the doctor pronouncing, after birth, whether the infant is a "boy" or a "girl": "in the naming the girl is 'girled' . . . [and] that founding interpellation is reiterated by various authorities and throughout the various intervals of time to reinforce or contest this naturalized effect. The naming is at once the setting of a boundary, and also the repeated inculcation of a norm."[38]

Two key points arise from this observation. First, the medical interpellation of the subject's body does not allow for any other choice or possibility other than male or female; yet, not all bodies conform strictly to either category at birth, and technology makes it possible for us to alter our bodies if we so choose. Second, nothing about the body must inevitably give rise to certain social roles or behaviors (i.e., gender). As Butler notes in *Undoing Gender* (2004), she does not directly address the issue of those who are intersex or transgender in *BTM*, given that these identities gained greater visibility and cultural presence after its publication.[39] However, *BTM* certainly anticipates those subjects who challenge how we correlate bodily sex with gender and sexuality, and how we divide bodies up into only two categories. The body is a fact, but that fact becomes interpreted and made to mean through a complex cultural framework. In understanding the body in this way, a view we can trace back to how she saw her uncle institutionalized and punished for his physical "deviance," Butler legitimizes and dignifies all variations of the human form. She makes visible bodies that are otherwise relegated by the dominant culture to erasure and social death. In other words, Butler more broadly argues that all bodies matter and that all bodies should be recognized as human.

## PART 2: AFTER GENDER: CRITIQUING LANGUAGE, THE STATE, AND SUBJECTIVITY

From a focus on gender and sexuality, in 1997 Butler expanded her questions about who is allowed subjectivity and a livable life to the relationship of government, language, censorship, and obscenity. Butler turned to these issues in the wake of two Supreme Court decisions regarding free speech, *R.A.V. v. St. Paul* (1992) and *Wisconsin v. Mitchell* (1993),[40] as well as Jesse Helms's attempts in 1989 to cut Congressional funding for the NEA (National Endowment for the Humanities) because of its financial support of artist Robert Mapplethorpe's controversial photography.[41] In these cases, Butler reveals how the state controls and frames language; it determines what constitutes free speech and obscenity and who can speak and who cannot. These concerns form the basis for Butler's *Excitable Speech* (*ES*), so named after a "US legal term defining a confession made when a person is not in possession of their faculties, and therefore invalid."[42] However, Butler argues, "Since utterances take place within discursive contexts which precede and exceed the utterer, [she] asserts that all speech is excitable."[43] Because we are created as subjects through language, and because we have no choice but to use the language available to us, Butler claims that the state cannot and should not legislate what is or is not hate speech or obscenity. To do so would be to legislate who counts as a subject and who does not.

Language, according to Derrida, is hard to control and contain; language is grounded in history, and yet meaning proliferates in unexpected and surprising ways. As such, language is also contingent and contextual.[44] Turning to Derrida's observations, Butler contends that attempts to legislate and define language are necessarily failures that often result less in the protection and more in the foreclosing of possibilities for sexual, gender, and racial minorities. For example, she carefully reads two Supreme Court cases, one (*R.A.V. v. St. Paul*) in which a burning cross in front of an African-American family's home is ruled free speech and another (*Wisconsin v. Mitchell*) in which the words of a black man prior to his assault on a white male is deemed not protected by the First Amendment. Butler notes here the inconsistency in the Court's determination of hate speech versus free speech, and opines that the decisions were influenced by the racially charged atmosphere and rioting in Los Angeles in response to the acquittal of four white policemen in the beating of African American Rodney King: "And so the High Court might be understood in its decision of June 22, 1992, to be taking its revenge on Rodney King, protecting itself against the riots in Los Angeles and elsewhere which appeared to be attacking the system of justice itself."[45] It would seem that language which threatens racial minorities becomes free speech when the subject of articulation is white; but, when the speaking subject is a minority, then the speech becomes threatening. Butler argues, therefore, that the power of the state results in foreclosure of speech by those whom the state does not consider viable subjects (i.e., racial, sexual, and gender minorities). In this way, "hate speech" and "free speech" become contingent terms marshaled by the state to reinforce normative subjectivity; as a result, to advocate for the elimination or prosecution of hate speech can paradoxically lead to increasing state power to regulate and foreclose those very subjectivities that feel threated.

Butler continues this point by examining Helms's offensive against the NEA. She notes that the basis of Helms's obscenity charge stems from Mapplethorpe's gay male identity.[46] In other words, state regulation of obscenity, like that of hate speech, is contingent on who is speaking. Because Mapplethorpe was gay, and his photography reflected homoerotic themes, his work was deemed threatening and obscene because it challenged dominant cultural norms regarding gender, the body, and sexuality. Had Mapplethorpe been a straight male and his photography expressed heterosexual eroticism, one wonders if there would have been any controversy at all. Butler argues that if there is a perpetrator of obscenity, it is the state (via Helms) for articulating and perpetuating in the Congressional amendment its own fantasies about the correlation of homosexuality, sadomasochism, and pedophilia: "In a sense, the Helms amendment in its final form can be read as precisely the kind of pornographic exercise that it seeks to renounce."[47] In this way, the obscenity charges revealed panic and anxiety about art that exposes the performativity of normative heterosexuality.

Discussions regarding hate speech and obscenity were prominent in the 1990s, as many groups called for banning or making criminal those speech acts that could cause emotional injury or be perceived as threatening or offensive.[48] Butler draws on the linguistic analyses of J. L. Austin and Derrida[49] to argue that the line between perlocution (speech that produces an effect, such as fear or happiness) and illocution (speech that is the act itself, such as a warning or a promise) is "tricky, and not always stable."[50] Butler therefore reasons that "treating a speech act as illocutionary [as do those who advocating banning pornography and hate speech], and then censoring it, only means people will talk about it more, so that whatever such laws seek to forbid becomes part of common parlance."[51]

Butler acknowledges that words can wound, and that we need to be mindful of this fact; however, she argues that the best way to deal with hate speech is not to legislate it (which would give the state more power) but to counter it with "insurrectionary speech in spite of the risk that such repetition involves."[52] An example would be the GLBTQ community's re-appropriation of derogatory labels such as "queer" or "dyke" to make them signify in new and powerful ways. While Butler recalls that at first she balked at using such terms in the early days of the queer movement, she "did note that using the word *queer* again and again as part of an affirmative practice in certain contexts helped take it out of an established context of being exclusively injurious."[53] Though a derogatory word can never completely divest itself of its historically deleterious meaning, Butler suggests that there still remains "a certain kind of opening up of the term. . . . A possibility of transforming stigmatization into something more celebratory."[54]

For Butler, the debates in the 1990s regarding free speech were personal as well as academic. For example, Butler writes that her own work is endangered by legislation of what is hate speech and what is obscenity. She writes in "The Force of Fantasy" that her publications in gender and sexuality studies could be considered "obscene": "anyone in academics and in the arts, who wishes to study representations of homosexuality or homoeroticism . . . as I am doing now, will likewise be ruled out of NEA and NEH [National Endowment for the Humanities] funding."[55] One of Butler's conditions for a livable life is that a subject is able to have access to the forms of expression they require in order to make visible and legitimate their subjectivity. Therefore, the risks of censorship outweigh the harm or injury speech may cause, since censorship, as legislated by the government, can relegate to social death and silence those identities who do not conform to normative paradigms.

## PART 3: LATER WRITING: MOURNING AND THE MEDIA

The notion of social death and the question of who counts as a subject became particularly acute for Butler in the wake of the September 11, 2001, terrorist attacks and the U.S. response that followed. Butler responded with two works, *Precarious Life* (*PL*) and *Frames of War* (*FW*) in which she theorizes that our ability and willingness to mourn a life means that we recognize the importance and subjectivity of that life. Mourning also means acknowledging that all lives are precarious and vulnerable, and so they must be approached with empathy. However, if we refuse to recognize a life as grievable, then we have denied that life recognition and personhood. In other words, we deny them livable life. If we do so, we are able to kill and perpetrate violence with much more ease and complacency than we would otherwise.

In *PL*, Butler reads America's response to 9/11 in two related ways. First, rather than mourn our own loss as well as the losses of the Other (i.e., decades of punitive American foreign policy in Muslim cultures and nation states) that prompted the attacks and acknowledge the subjectivity and vulnerability of people from both cultures, this opportunity was missed in favor of violence and erasure of the Other. We as a nation state refused to accept that the Other necessarily forms a part of us and our subjectivity (a point she derives from Hegel). Butler argues that acknowledging ours and others' vulnerability in this way helps us to humanize the Other and mitigate violence: "If we are interested in arresting cycles of violence to produce less violent outcomes, it is no doubt important to ask what, politically, might be made of grief besides a cry for war."[56] Secondly, Butler observes in *PL* as well as in *FW* that the erasure of the Other takes place in particular through the media, which delimits who we make visible and thus who is allowed subjectivity. For example, Butler notes that in the "war on terror" that followed 9/11, we recognized as grievable American lives lost but not those whom we were fighting: "I argue that . . . a disavowed mourning . . . follows upon the erasure from public representations of the names, images, and narratives of those the U.S. has killed. . . . Some lives are grievable, and others are not."[57] In this way, she accuses the United States of refusing livability and subjectivity to those with whom we are in conflict.

In both *PL* and *FW*, she further illustrates this point by focusing specifically on the ongoing Israeli-Palestinian conflict which is central to the animosity between Western and Muslim cultures. She notes that in this conflict, the Israeli media constructs who can be perceived as a subject (Israelis) and who cannot (Palestinians), so that Palestinian deaths go unmourned. For example, she notes that during Israeli army operations in Gaza in 2008 and 2009, the Israeli media constructed Palestinians, including women and children, as military apparatuses rather than as subjects; in so doing, the media justified Palestinian deaths: "If the Palestinian children who are killed by mortar and phosphorous bombs are human shields, then they are not children at all, but rather bits of armament, military instruments and material, aiding and abetting an assault on Israel."[58] In this way, Butler argues that the media visually and rhetorically frames war and conflict such that we are primed to accept war. The rationale for war and its context is already outlined for us so that we understand the conflict in a certain way, and this framing relies on who counts as visible and mournable subjects in a conflict.

This subject is one that Butler engages in not only critically but also politically and personally. She derives her ideas about grieveability and subjectivity in part from her early grounding in Jewish practice and thought: "For me . . . one of the most valuable things about Judaism has always been its insistence on public grieving, and its insistence that an entire community needed to come together to grieve. It won't do just to grieve one's own."[59] From this position, she has publicly condemned Israel for its occupation of Palestine and has suffered criticism as a result, particularly because of her Jewish identity: "as a Jew one is under obligation to criticize excessive state violence and state racism—then one is in a bind, because one is told that one is either self-hating as a Jew or engaging anti-Semitism. And yet for me, it comes out of a certain Jewish value of social justice."[60] Her insistence on the importance of subjectivity and livable life, issues that have been central to her work since *Gender Trouble*, drive her to critique the delimiting of Palestinian subjectivity.

Further, Butler does not divorce queer theory and politics from her activism regarding the Israeli-Palestinian conflict. For instance, in 2012 she refused the "Civil Courage Prize" from the organizers of the German Christopher Street Day (CSD), a gay pride parade, because they had opposed Muslim practices as being discriminatory of gays and lesbians. Butler states, "The CSD is linked with several groups and individuals who engage in a very strong anti-immigrant discourse, referring to people from North Africa, Turkey, and various Arab countries as less modern or more primitive."[61] Drawing on Hegel's theory of subjectivity, Butler contends that one must look to the Other and work in dialectic with him or her, rather than rejecting the Other outright.

In the case of the CSD, its Islamophobia is as problematic for Butler as is homophobia, and she insists that both problems require dialogue and the acknowledgment of connections among sexism, racism, and homophobia: "Although we can find homophobia in many places, including those of religious and racial minorities, we would be making a very serious error if we tried to fight homophobia by propagating stereotypical and debasing constructions of other minorities."[62] In addition, Butler points out that Islamophobia in the Western queer movement does not account for queerness in Muslim culture and how its presence is constructed and articulated: "My view is that the struggle against homophobia must be linked with the struggle against racism, and that subjugated minorities have to find ways of working in coalition."[63] As always, Butler eschews attempts to foreclose possibilities of identity in favor of opening up the potential for new and complex ways of forming subjectivity.

## MOST RECENT WORK AND LEGACY

Butler's influence within critical theory and beyond cannot be overestimated. Her critique of normative categories of gender, sex, and subjectivity have led us, even outside academia, to what Gary A. Olson and Lynn Worsham call "a more nuanced understanding of identity."[64] The significance of her work was recognized in 2012 when she was presented with the Theordor W. Adorno Award, which recognizes "outstanding performances in the fields of philosophy, theater, music, and film."[65] Yet, it would be a mistake to speak of Butler in the past tense or to perceive her as moving on from the concerns which prompted *Gender Trouble*. Butler's most recent major publications, *Parting Ways: Jewishness and the Critique of Zionism* (2013), *Dispossession: The Performative in the Political* (2013, with Athena Athanasiou), *Senses of the Subject* (2015), *Notes toward a Performative Theory of Assembly* (2015), and *Vulnerability in Resistance* (2016, coedited with Zeynep Gambetti and Leticia Sabsay) demonstrate that her abiding questions remain: Who counts as a subject? How do loss, the body, vulnerability, and social norms work in the process of subject formation? What does it mean that one is never finished "becoming"? How can we all access a livable and grievable life? These questions also informed her response to the Black Lives Matter movement. She understands the movement as one that recognizes, protests, and makes visible that "[t]he [Black] lives taken in this way [police shootings] are not lives worth grieving; they belong to the increasing number of those who are understood as ungrievable, whose lives are thought not to be worth preserving."[66] Butler's insistence on continually thinking about the process and nature of subjectivity stands in stark contrast to the recent discontinuation of some queer theory journals and to sweeping pronouncements that we are "done" with queer and gender studies.[67] For Butler, we can never be finished with any of these interrogations. Given Butler's statements about continual doing and undoing of gender, sexuality, and subjectivity, we can anticipate that she will herself continue to ask and re-ask questions even if others might consider such issues out of "vogue." For many in our culture and others, these issues are not passé but are crucial questions of day-to-day survival, of demanding a livable life, even if a small segment of academia does not consider it so. Butler notes that "we're struggling for all kinds of people who for whatever reason are not immediately captured or legitimated by the available norms."[68] For Butler, the political, the critical, and the academic are not separable; her work and activism in how and who is allowed livability and subjectivity will continue.

## NOTES

1. This essay will refer to three terms which are often conflated in public discourse: gender (social roles), sex (the body), and sexuality (sexual practices). Butler, along with other queer and feminist theorists, disabuses the notion that these aspects of identity necessarily correlate. For example, we often think that females (sex) are women (gender) who engage in heterosexual practices (sexuality). However, as Butler notes, identity is far more complex and varied: "Sexuality does not follow from gender in the sense that what gender you 'are' determines what kind of sexuality you will 'have'" (*Undoing Gender*, New York: Routledge, 2004, Kindle edition, "Introduction"). A male might identify both as a woman and a heterosexual, for instance.

2. Judith Butler, preface to the Anniversary Edition, *Gender Trouble: Feminism and the Subversion of Identity* (New York: Routledge, 1999), Kindle edition. Originally published in 1990 by Routledge, New York.

3. Judith Butler, "Changing the Subject: Judith Butler's Politics of Radical Resignification," interview by Gary A. Olson and Lynn Worsham, in *The Judith Butler Reader*, edited by Sarah Salih with Judith Butler (Malden, MA: Blackwell, 2004), Kindle edition. Originally published in *jac* 20, no. 4 (2000), 731–65.

4. *Judith Butler: Philosophical Encounters of the Third Kind*, DVD, directed by Paule Zadjermann (New York: First Run/Icarus Films, 2006).

5. Judith Butler, "The Desire for Philosophy," interview by Regina Michalik, in *LOLA Press*, May 2001, accessed June 20, 2012, http://www.lolapress.org/elec2/artenglish/butl_e.htm.

6. *Philosophical Encounters*.

7. Indeed, Butler will contend in chapter 8 of *Bodies that Matter* that it becomes impossible to separate race and gender when considering the function of social forces in subject formation.

8. Barthes theorizes that ideology (what he calls "myth") becomes effective through its ability to make itself seem natural and not a construct that perpetuates the power of the dominant culture. See especially Barthes's *Mythologies*, edited and translated by Annette Lavers (New York: Hill and Wang, 1983).

9. *Philosophical Encounters*.

10. Butler reveals that her mother's family owned several movie theaters in Cleveland (see *Philosophical Encounters*).

11. Ibid.

12. Butler explains that in performing our identities, we always go beyond those limits that are set on subjectivity by social norms; hence, our identities are failures due not only to falling short of the ideal, but also of going beyond it (the "excess"). See especially Butler's "Imitation and Gender Subordination" in *Inside Out: Lesbian Theories, Gay Theories*, edited by Diana Fuss (New York: Routledge, 1991), 13–31.

13. *Philosophical Encounters*.

14. Butler, "Preface."

15. *Philosophical Encounters*.

16. Judith Butler, "Judith Butler: As a Jew I Was Taught it Was Ethically Imperative to Speak Up," interview by Udi Aloni, in *Haaretz.com*, February 24, 2010, accessed June 22, 2012, http://

www.haaretz.com/misc/article-print-page/judith-butler-as-a-jew-i-was-taught-it-was-ethically-imperative-to-speak-up-part-ii-1.266244?trailingPath=2.169%2C2.216%2C.

17. Later published as *Subjects of Desire: Hegelian Reflections in Twentieth-Century France* (New York: Columbia University Press, 1987).

18. Butler, "The Desire for Philosophy."

19. In this way, Hegel disagrees with the Cartesian idea that the subject is self-formed (i.e., "I think, therefore, I am"). See Hegel's 1807 work *Phenomenology of Spirit*, trans. A. V. Miller (Oxford: Oxford UP, 1979).

20. Foucault's formulation that the social precedes and determines the subject can be found throughout his oeuvre, but see especially *The Birth of the Clinic: An Archeology of Medical Perception* (1973; New York: Vintage, 1994) and *Discipline and Punish: The Birth of the Prison* (1977; New York: Vintage, 1995).

21. Beauvoir makes this assertion in her 1949 *The Second Sex*, trans. H. M. Parshley (New York: Vintage, 1989). Butler notes that while Beauvoir "does not claim to be describing a theory of gender identity or gender acquisition in *The Second Sex* . . . yet her formulation of gender as a project seems to invite speculation on just such a theory" ("Variations"). It is this theorization of gender as a continual process that becomes the focus of Butler's *Gender Trouble*.

22. Sarah Salih, introduction to chapter 3, in *The Judith Butler Reader*, edited by Sarah Salih with Judith Butler (Malden, MA: Blackwell, 2004), Kindle edition.

23. Salih, introduction to chapter 5, in *The Judith Butler Reader*, edited by Sarah Salih with Judith Butler (Malden, MA: Blackwell, 2004), Kindle edition.

24. Butler, *Gender Trouble*, chapter 3.

25. Ibid.

26. Ibid.

27. Ibid., italics original.

28. Butler, *Undoing Gender*, chapter 3.

29. Judith Butler, "Imitation and Gender Insubordination," in *The Judith Butler Reader*, edited by Sarah Salih with Judith Butler (Malden, MA: Blackwell, 2004), Kindle edition. Originally published in *Inside Out: Lesbian Theories, Gay Theories*, ed. Diana Fuss (New York: Routledge, 1991), 13–31.

30. The use of the term "queer," as Butler notes, was to reclaim a derogatory term for those who are not heterosexual (see "Changing the Subject"). "Queer" is also used to refer more broadly to any identity or practice that might fall outside traditional norms of gender and sexuality.

31. Butler, *Gender Trouble*, chapter 3.

32. Ibid., italics original.

33. Salih, chapter 5, italics original.

34. Ibid.

35. Matt Waggoner, "Judith Butler's *Senses of the Subject*," *JCRT* 16, no. 1 (Winter 2016), 95–108.

36. Judith Butler, "Variations on Sex and Gender: Beauvoir, Wittig, Foucault," in *The Judith Butler Reader*, edited by Sarah Salih with Judith Butler (Malden, MA: Blackwell, 2004), Kindle edition. Originally published in *Feminism as Critique: Essays on the Politics of Gender in Late Capitalist Societies*, edited by Seyla Benhabib and Drucilla Cornell (Oxford: Polity Press, 1987), 128–42. For more on Wittig's point, see especially her essay, "One is Not Born a Woman" in *Feminist Theory Reader: Local and Global Perspectives*, edited by Carole R. McCann and Seung-Kyung Kim (New York: Routledge, 2003), 249–254.

37. Ibid.

38. Judith Butler, *Bodies that Matter: On the Discursive Limits of "Sex"* (New York: Routledge, 1993), Kindle edition, chapter 1.

39. The idea that bodies are not easily categorizable gained national attention with the release of *Boys Don't Cry*, a 1999 film which dramatized the life and murder of Brandon Teena, a transgendered man in Nebraska. The film also brought attention to the violence to which those who do not conform to bodily sex and gender norms are subjected.

40. In *R.A.V. v. St. Paul*, 112 S. Ct. 2538, 120 L. Ed. 2d 305 (1992), a teenager was charged with violating the St. Paul (Minnesota) Bias-Motivated Crime Ordinance for burning a cross in front of a home belonging to an African-American family. The conviction was overturned by the Supreme Court on the grounds that the act was protected by the First Amendment. In *Wisconsin v. Mitchell*, 113 S. Ct. 2194, 14 L. Ed. 2d 436 (1993), the Supreme Court upheld the sentencing of a black man, Todd Mitchell, for beating a white male, Gregory Reddick, after viewing the film *Mississippi Burning* (1988) and supposedly saying to friends, "Do you all feel hyped up to move on some white people?" Mitchell had appealed his conviction, arguing that it was based on the words he said prior to his attack; his sentence had been raised to seven years based on a Wisconsin statute that increased penalties if it could be shown a victim had been singled out for their race, gender, religion, sexual orientation, or national origin. The Court ruled that the conviction was permissible and not a violation of Mitchell's First Amendment rights.

41. The controversy began with the refusal of The Corcoran Gallery of Art in Washington, D.C. to host Mapplethorpe's posthumous photography exhibition, *Robert Mapplethorpe: The Perfect Moment* (1989), due to objections by some members of Congress to the exhibit's themes of homoeroticism and sadomasochism.

42. Kate Worsley, "Spastic, Paki, Abortion, Queer, Faggot, Sperm," *Times Higher Education*, May 16, 1997, accessed July 31, 2012, http://www.timeshighereducation.co.uk/story.asp?storyCode=100832&sectioncode=26.

43. Sarah Salih, introduction to chapter 8, in *The Judith Butler Reader*, edited by Sarah Salih with Judith Butler (Malden, MA: Blackwell, 2004), Kindle edition.

44. See especially Jacques Derrida, *Writing and Difference*, trans. Alan Bass (London: Routledge, 1978).

45. Judith Butler, *Excitable Speech: A Politics of the Performative* (New York: Routledge, 1997), 59. On March 3, 1991, Rodney King, an African American, was pulled over by Los Angeles police for a traffic stop. Accounts differ regarding if King resisted arrest; the officers claim he did and beat him in an incident that was videotaped by George Holliday from his apartment balcony. Four white officers were later tried for their conduct but were acquitted by an all-white jury. Rioting in Los Angeles and other cities ensued and reflected the anger of African Americans (and other minorities) concerning their perception of racism inherent in the U.S. law enforcement and judicial system.

46. Butler, *Excitable Speech*, 65–69, and "The Force of Fantasy: Feminism, Mapplethorpe, and Discursive Excess," in *The Judith Butler Reader*, edited by Sarah Salih with Judith Butler (Malden, MA: Blackwell, 2004), Kindle edition. Originally published in *differences: A Journal of Feminist Cultural Studies* 2, no. 2 (1990), 105–25.

47. Butler, "The Force of Fantasy." The Helms amendment, eventually approved by Congress with modifications as Public Law 101–121, reads that federal funding would be prohibited from being used to "promote, disseminate or produce obscene materials, including but not limited to depictions of sadomasochism, homoeroticism, the exploitation of children, or individuals engaged in sex acts." This version of the amendment was accepted by the NEA and NEH, and currently remains in place.

48. For example, in the 1980s and 1990s, many campuses in the U.S. began to institute "speech codes" that "regulated potentially offensive or bigoted speech among students and faculty" (Sanne Seinstra, "Evaluating Hate Speech Codes," *Lewis and Clark Pioneer Log*, 2009, accessed July 31, 2012, http://aclu-or.org/content/evaluating-hate-speech-codes-editorial-lewis-clark-pioneer-log). Also, certain feminist critics, such as Catharine MacKinnon (in her 1993 *Only Words*) and Andrea Dworkin (in her 1981 *Pornography: Men Possessing Women*) argued that pornography's visual and linguistic signification directly harmed women and as such should be banned.

49. See J. L. Austin, *How to Do Things with Words*, second edition, edited by J.O. Urmson and Marina Sbisà (1955; Boston: Harvard UP, 1975), and Jacques Derrida, *Limited INC.* (Evanston, IL: Northwestern UP, 1988).

50. Butler, *Excitable Speech*, 44.

51. Worsley, "Spastic."

52. Salih, chapter 8.

53. Butler, "Changing the Subject."

54. Ibid.

55. Butler, "The Force of Fantasy."

56. Butler, *Precarious Life: The Powers of Mourning and Violence* (London: Verso, 2004), xii.

57. Ibid., xiv.

58. Judith Butler, *Frames of War: When is Life Grievable?* (London: Verso, 2010), xxvi.

59. Judith Butler, "Peace is a Resistance to the Terrible Satisfactions of War," interview by Jill Stauffer, in *The Believer*, May 2003, accessed June 20, 2012, http://www.believermag.com/issues/200305/?read=interview_butler.

60. Butler, "Judith Butler: As a Jew."

61. Judith Butler, "AVIVA-Interview with Judith Butler," interview by Undine Zimmer, Marie Heidingsfelder, and Sharon Adler, in *AVIVA-Berlin.de*, June 2012, accessed June 21, 2012, http://www.aviva-berlin.de/aviva/content_Interviews.php?id=1427323.

62. Ibid.

63. Ibid.

64. Butler, "Changing the Subject."

65. "Theodor-W.-Adorno-Prize," *Das Kulturportal der Stadt Frankfurt*. Her reception of the award was not without controversy. The University of Frankfurt prize committee was criticized by some Israeli officials and others for giving the award to Butler, who has been an outspoken critic of Israel's actions and policies towards Palestinians (Benjamin Weinthal, "Envoy to Germany: Awardee Ignores Terror on Israel," *The Jerusalem Post*, Aug. 28, 2012).

66. George Yancy and Judith Butler, "What's Wrong with 'All Lives Matter'," *The New York Times*, Jan. 12, 2015.

67. See especially Michael Warner, "Queer and Then?" in *The Chronicle of Higher Education*, Jan. 1, 2012, accessed July 30, 2012, http://chronicle.com/article/QueerThen-/130161/.

68. Butler, "Changing the Subject."

*Chapter Nine*

# Networking the Great Outdoors

*Object-Oriented Ontology and the Digital Humanities*

Roger Whitson

One way to understand the allure of Object-Oriented Ontology (OOO) and Digital Humanities (DH) is to examine the conversion narratives on their blogs. Most major scholars from both movements have them. Video-game guru and *Alien Phenomenology* author Ian Bogost mentions in 2009 a "flurry of interest" bubbling up over a blog post he wrote about creating a metaphysical video game "like the filling of a blueberry pie."[1] Patrick Murray-John, Omeka specialist at the Roy Royzenzweig Center for History and New Media, mentions how his Digital Humanities job and the shift in focus from teaching to coding "left me with a chance to try something new and see what happened."[2] Levi Bryant, author of *The Democracy of Objects* and editor of *The Speculative Turn*, describes a feeling during the aftermath of the 2008 Obama election as an "odd way in which I feel all my old assumptions falling away one by one and being replaced by something else; yet I do not know what this new thing is."[3] Finally, #altac coiner and Scholar's Lab director Bethany Nowviskie mentions a "palpable sense" during a 2009 Scholarly Communication Institute summit "that the plans we were hatching could change the way the business is done in the humanities, digital and otherwise."[4]

If we were to adapt a quote by Virginia Woolf used to describe the emergence of Modernist literary and visual culture, we could say that somewhere in or around November 2008, the character of academia started to change. To be sure, both object-oriented ontology and the digital humanities have much longer histories than the one sketched above. Most digital humanities scholars mark the beginning of their field in 1949, with Father Robert Busa's *index verborum* of the work of St. Thomas Aquinas. This work, according to Susan Hockey, included a "lemmatization of 11 million words . . . completed in a semi-automatic way" and eventually appeared in 1992 as a "CD ROM."[5] Further, the digital humanities also collaborates and mingles with other schools of thought: new media studies, computers and writing, and humanities computing. OOO scholars have identified a concern with objects in the work of Deleuze, Heidegger, Husserl, and a tradition of philosophy going back to Aristotle. The critique of correlationism, the idea that the only important philosophical relationship is between subject and object or human and world, also exists in the work of Speculative Realists like Quentin Meillassoux, Ray Brassier, and Ian Hamilton Grant. And the structure of OOO is constantly changing. Graham Harman wrote an oft-cited blog post about the differences between OOO and Speculative Realism, and Levi Bryant later distanced Harman's version of OOO from his and Jane Bennett's own version.[6]

Yet I argue that several factors conspired to cause a more fundamental change that dramatically shifted the identity of both schools of thought. First, the late 2000s brought with them a growing awareness of a crisis in academic funding, which was heightened by the economic recession of 2008–2011 and the publication of exposés uncovering the oppression of adjunct teachers and the economic bubble in higher education. Second, the emergence of academic blogging and other applications of digital technology as viable forms of scholarly communication started to accelerate the sharing of ideas and awakened academics to audiences beyond the ivory tower. In *After Finitude*, considered by many a foundational text of Speculative Realism and Object Oriented Ontology, Meillassoux argues that philosophers have "lost the great outdoors, the *absolute* outside of pre-critical thinkers [where] thought could explore with the legitimate feeling of being on foreign territory—of being entirely elsewhere."[7] All three of the conditions outlined above have caused humanists, tenure-track and otherwise, to start venturing into another outdoors: that *great* beyond of new scholarly associations and networks.

This chapter will examine, in parallel, a set of scholars in Object-Oriented Ontology and the Digital Humanities. I gather several scholars from both camps for each section, showing how their work connects to one of the historical events I articulated earlier. I do so to argue that both DH and OOO have changed in tandem with the shifts currently happening in academia. Their popularity is, moreover, largely based upon their embrace of these changes, as well as their willingness to act collaboratively across networks of scholars, new funding models, and digital media tools. Above all, I suggest that DH and OOO mark a turning point in theory and cultural studies where neither the theory, nor the individual thinkers, nor the technology, nor the history are predominant: rather each emerges as a node with the others. In other words, both movements have foundational texts and ideas, but they focus more on loose affiliations and interconnections than specific histories and discourses. What follows might be best construed as what Walter Benjamin calls a "constellation": a network sketched among very different thinkers and ideas, held together by a shared historical desire to think the great outdoors of traditional academic disciplinary structures.[8]

## LABOR, ECOLOGY, AND FUNDING

Different but related moves toward the great outdoors can be seen by the very different career trajectories of Tim Morton and Brian Croxall. Tim Morton began his academic career studying Percy Shelley's vegetarianism and its impact on food studies, and he has published widely and been promoted several times since his graduation from Oxford.[9] While he enjoyed a certain amount of success, Morton's tenure at UC-Davis was marked by infamous budget cuts occurring across the UC system. Jaime Applegate of *The Daily Californian* reports that over $1.5 billion was cut from California higher education between the 2010–2011 and 2011–2012 fiscal year.[10] Morton was, in fact, on campus during the infamous pepper-spray incident on November 18, 2011. Students protesting the California budget cuts and associating themselves with the Occupy Wall Street movement were pepper-sprayed by University police, who cited a need to maintain civility on campus. Photographs and videos of the incident were posted on Facebook, quickly went viral, and ignited further protests across the country.

Morton posted several articles on his blog *Ecology without Nature* during the days and weeks that followed. He related the event to the massacre at Peterloo and Shelley's reaction to it in "The Mask of Anarchy," calling upon his readers to "Rise like lions after slumber."[11] He admonished the "thuggery" of the UCD police, mentioning the contrast between their supposed concern about civility and their failure to investigate "the vandalism of the LGBT resource center" and "swastikas scrawled on the doors of Jewish students."[12] He even published details about a meditation course offered for protesters and a homeopathic pepper spray remedy recipe from his father including "euphrasia, sol, carbo vegetalis, cantharis, and urtica urens." Morton mentions that the remedy should be prepared by combining the ingredients "in the 200c potency and make into a tincture in a dropper bottle, which is easier to administer."[13]

Morton's commitment to an engaged community informs his groundbreaking work on object-oriented ecology. Morton's two books devoted to ecology, *Ecology without Nature: Rethinking Environmental Ethics* (2007) and *The Ecological Thought* (2010), reject nature as an essence and embrace ecology as a way of thinking and living together. In *Ecology without Nature*, Morton argues that the idea of nature as essence "impedes a proper relationship with the earth and its life forms" since conceptualizing nature as essence puts it over there "on a pedestal" and admires it "from afar."[14] Morton sees this act as "a paradoxical act of sadistic admiration" in which people ignore the environment while admiring it (4–5).[15] Morton's *The Ecological Thought* calls nature "a plastic knockoff of the real thing" filled with "giant, abstract versions of the products hanging in mall windows," while ecology is "the thinking of interconnectedness" that is also an "ecological project" in which we are "becoming fully aware of how human beings are connected with other beings—animal, vegetable, or mineral."[16]

Morton's work on ecology is an interesting case study in the historical development of object-oriented ontology, since both of his books were written before he "converted" to OOO. In the post "All You Need is Love," Morton says that he initially had reservations about OOO, "[b]ut I gradually realized, thanks to the infinite patience of Levi Bryant, that I was already thinking OOO things. It was like looking at one of those magic eye pictures. (I am very bad at that). At first you see nothing, then suddenly your perspective shifts."[17] This moment is telling because it demonstrates how the collaborative nature of OOO establishes an alternative to correlationism. As I briefly mentioned above, OOO primarily argues against correlationism, the emphasis of one particular relationship (human and world, or subject and object) above all others. Correlationism is not idealism; rather as Robin Mackay defines it in the introduction to *Collapse II*, it is "the injunction that, unable to know things 'in themselves,' philosophy must limit itself to the adumbration of 'conditions of experience'" which to correlationists from Kant to certain practitioners of cultural studies is "unassailable, something that only the most unsophisticated, 'pre-critical' thinker would seek to challenge."[18] Imagining nature as an essence is a form of correlationism, since it elevates the human as the only being with agency and denigrates nature to being a "mere" object—something that is thoughtless, passive, and weak. For Morton, the interinstitutional blogging network emerging from OOO is a form of solidarity and provides a powerful counterexample to traditional academic work, one in which individual scholars work on projects largely divorced from the rest of the world, and this world consequently becomes a passive object.

Apart from publishing versions of his work on his blog "Ecology without Nature," Morton also distributes .mp3s of his conference talks and provides videos of his class lectures. In an introductory lecture on OOO delivered at UC Davis in the spring of 2012, he draws a historical connection between the publication of Kant's *Critique of Pure Reason* and the beginning of the anthropacy in 1790 which he defines as an era following a geological period marked by the deposit of a thin layer of carbon in Earth's crust. The anthropacy is, according to Morton, the moment where "human history intersects with geological time." Correlationism divorces people from talking about things; it only allows us to speak about our access to those things. And,

Morton argues, the Industrial Revolution gives rise to both anthropacy and correlationism. "The fact," Morton says, "that you can't talk about reality directly, and the fact that you are f'ing with it, directly, seem to be part of the same syndrome to me."[19]

The historical connection Morton draws is striking, and yet correlationism also extends to very different facets of contemporary academic life. It should be remembered that Kant, the high priest of correlationism according to OOO, also published *Conflict of the Faculties* in which he argues that scholars should have the freedom "to evaluate everything" without interference from the government.[20] Kant mentions that the freedom of the professor to create more graduates is different from the freedom of the *intelligentsia*, which may be educated by the University, but remain under the auspices of the government and can, moreover, "have legal influence on the public."[21] Kant's argument creates a correlationist space for freedom of speech: the University has the freedom to study and research what it wants as long as it confines itself to the space afforded by the University campus. What matters here is that University space is separated from public space, and Kant's professors are encouraged to engage in academic freedom to the degree that they do not cross into public space. Professors can only speak about public space; they can't speak directly to the public. Brian Croxall, whose article on "The Absent Presence" called attention to the plight of adjuncts in 2009, epitomizes a hybrid-scholar that challenges Kant's correlationist approach to higher education. These hybrid scholars are referred to as #altac, or "Alternative Academics," professionals who have received the PhD, expect academic freedom, and yet do not work in the clean spaces demarcated by Kant in *The Conflict of the Faculties*.

Croxall's 2009 article "The Absent Presence," delivered in absentia at the MLA conference and posted on his blog, acted as a call to action for the adjunct instructors who teach "most of the students in America" and who were "not at the MLA" that year.[22] Indeed a 2012 survey conducted by the MLA and published on *The Chronicle of Higher Education* found that over seventy percent of teachers in academia are "off the tenure-track" and that "during the period of 2007–2010" the number of non-tenure-track professors with PhDs who received welfare jumped from "9,776 to 33,665."[23] Marc Bousquet's *How the University Works* points out that the vast majority of teachers in the University have no benefits and no reasonable sense that they can expect future employment. This "system of disposable faculty," Bousquet argues, "replaces its *most* experienced and accomplished teachers with persons who are *less* accomplished and *less* experienced."[24]

Bethany Nowviskie coined the #altac movement partly as a response to the crisis Bousquet identified, and Croxall has emerged as a major figure within that movement. Nowviskie points out that there is a larger range of potential careers waiting for PhDs outside of the tenure-track. These include

administrators with varied levels of responsibility for supporting the academic
enterprise; instructional technologists and software developers who collaborate on scholarly projects; journalists, editors, and publishers; cultural heritage
workers in a variety of roles and institutions; librarians, archivists, and other
information professionals; entrepreneurs who partner on projects of value to
scholars, program officers for funding agencies and humanities centers, and
many more.[25]

While Croxall would be the first to argue that #altac is not limited to the
digital humanities, DH has certainly taken advantage of the #altac movement
to suggest different funding models and more flexible professional careers
that have become central to its approach towards digital scholarship. As
Matthew Kirschenbaum argues in "What is Digital Humanities and What is it
Doing in English Departments," DH is "publicly visible," "bound up with
infrastructure," and "collaborative and depends upon networks of people . . .
that live an active 24/7 life online."[26] Croxall has argued that #altac is "the
most likely track for most positions in the digital humanities—and probably
for the University as a whole," yet has also suggested (along with William
Pannapacker and Nowviskie), that new professional models are needed to
address the very different professional lives of #altacs.[27] Departments, according to Croxall, "should look elsewhere in the university—libraries, administration, research-only positions—for helping us structure these career
paths."[28]

#altac has profoundly affected how Croxall approaches his own scholar-
ship. Croxall's dissertation is on technology in American literature concerning trauma, but he has also embraced digital projects ranging from postcolonial literature to digital maps of Rome and Atlanta.[29] He is known primarily
for his work in pedagogy and works tirelessly to promote teaching as a viable
form of scholarship. He's experimented with fellow DHers Mark Sample,
Zach Whalen, Erin Templeton, and Paul Benzon to create an interinstitutional teaching network around Mark Danielewski's novel *House of Leaves*, he
taught one of the first "Introduction to Digital Humanities" courses in the
United States, and he also writes frequently for *ProfHacker*—a blog on
teaching and technology hosted by *The Chronicle of Higher Education*.
There, he has published articles on GoogleDrive, Forking Syllabi, Dropbox,
and CharacterPal, to name only a few.

Both Croxall and Morton respond to the academic crisis occurring in
higher education from very different vantage points: Croxall advocates for
#altac positions and greater use of technology to multiply the opportunities
for newly minted PhDs, while Morton rethinks philosophy and theory for an
age when practicing new ecologies and interrelationships are becoming increasingly vital. Both also, however, practice the humanities in ways that
take advantage of new forms of relation and association. Many of these

forms are enabled by not only the networks emerging in social media venues, but the values of movements like open access.

## SOCIAL MEDIA AND OBJECT-ORIENTED COLLABORATION

Kathleen Fitzpatrick, in her book advocating for post-publication and peer-to-peer review *Planned Obsolescence*, urges academics to "rethink our authorship practices and our relationships to ourselves and our colleagues as authors" because "new digital technology becoming dominant within the academy are rapidly facilitating new ways of working and of imagining ourselves as we work."[30] Fitzpatrick has emerged as a central figure in the digital humanities movement, primarily because she has become a tireless advocate for embracing digital technology and its potential for changing scholarly debate.[31] She has worked not only as an Associate Professor of English and Media Studies at Pomona College, but also as coordinating editor and press director for the open access and experimental publication site *MediaCommons* and as Director of Scholarly Communication at the Modern Language Association.

Fitzpatrick's first book, *The Anxiety of Obsolescence: The American Novel in the Age of Television*, explores the "ways in which the novel has suggested its own demise through the representations of television and other modes of late-twentieth century communication."[32] In a most revealing chapter, she argues how the work of Thomas Pynchon and Don DeLillo use anxieties surrounding new technologies in order to mask more complicated forms of social obsolescence: "the perceived dominance of the contemporary literary scene of fiction by women and racial and ethnic minorities."[33] More broadly, obsolescence works here to shore up specific types of cultural hierarchy in order to "create an elite cadre of cultural producers and consumers" in the wake of changing media forms.[34] *Planned Obsolescence* extends this insight about the cultural reaction surrounding changing technology to anxieties about scholarly communication by arguing that scholars have a choice: "we can shore up the boundaries between ourselves and the open spaces of intellectual exchange on the Internet . . . [but] unless we can find ways to speak with that culture, to demonstrate the vibrancy and the value of the liberal arts, we run the risk of being silenced altogether."[35]

Peter Suber, director of Harvard's Open Access project, defines open access as literature that is "digital, online, free of charge, and free of most copyright and licensing restrictions."[36] This ideal has led to several controversies and new opportunities in academia. Take, for example, HathiTrust: a consortium of libraries that work to archive and make available most of their collections. Hathitrust works like a large digital library, and indeed it advertises itself as a Digital Library. They have also worked with the University of

Michigan Press, another advocate for Open Access, to develop jPatch: an easy-to-use modular platform for the inclusion of open access journals in the HathiTrust repository. HathiTrust had been sued by the Author's Guild for their publication of so-called orphan works. Orphan works are texts that are still under copyright, not being published, and the owner of the copyright cannot be found. HathiTrust listed several benefits of being part of the repository, including "be[ing] more readily shared with our community, who increasingly expect their research materials to be available in digital form, and they can also provide a trove of data, both humanistic and scientific, that will help scholars and researchers discover and create new knowledge."[37]

The benefit of using open-access scholarly communication to create new knowledge is also a concern for scholars associated with object-oriented ontology. Steven Shaviro, though he lives on the margins of the movement, actively refuses to publish in venues that have strict policies on their book contracts. He once rejected a contract offered by Oxford University Press that would have listed his book as "work-for-hire," meaning that OUP would claim copyright to all aspects of Shaviro's work from its inception. "It is obvious," Shaviro explains, "were this to become the norm in academic publishing, then intellectual inquiry and academic freedom, as we know them, would cease to exist."[38] Many OOO scholars, and the publishers disseminating their work, advocate for open-access. The journal *Collapse*, managed by Urbanomic and featuring many of the articles defining the early Speculative Realism movement, periodically makes their earlier issues available for free. Graham Harman published his book on Bruno Latour, *Prince of Networks*, with a known OA publisher called re.press. Open Humanities Press publishes a series of OOO works called *The New Metaphysics* and makes them available as hypertexts. Levi Bryant published *The Democracy of Objects* in this manner. Finally, Punctum Books publishes OA books associated with OOO and a slew of journals: from *Speculations* to *Helvete: A Journal of Black Metal Theory* and the more recent *O-Zone: a Journal of Object-Oriented Studies*.

Punctum's director, Eileen Joy, has worked to combine OOO with medieval literary study and applies her interests in OA with her theoretical reflections on collaboration, making, and non-human networks. She also runs the BABEL working group, where she invites scholars to "PLEASE SHUT UP AND START DOING AND MAKING THINGS,"[39] and experiments with new forms of thought (Youngsterism). In her contribution for Jeffrey Cohen's *Animal, Vegetable, Mineral: Ethics and Objects*, Joy identifies literature as a

> *living* and open signaling system, an endlessly looping reel-to-reel tape-feed (even when interrupted by static, worms chewing on the wires, bad translators, fire, and floods), that could also be described, as Fradenburg suggested in

Siena, as a "territorial assemblage," one that enables an endless series of parallel relations within and across various temporal zones that are, in some sense, always here with us now and also located in the Great Outdoors of a forest of textual data that may or may not always be accessible to us (or to our particular questions).[40]

Joy's conception of literature as a system accords with her work on Punctum to make texts more accessible. The literary text emerges as a kind of collaboration between different zones and actors, relaying and changing its content depending on the environment. Further, Joy imagines the question of access to be a complicated one. Things are not simply openly accessible as a "forest of textual data"; they may be forever withdrawn from view.[41] Access, in Joy's work, emerges as an ideal that is forever enmeshed in endless loops of objects and assemblages, relations and temporal zones, each of which allows certain perspectives to emerge and represses others.

But objects work in collaboration just as much as they isolate, individualize, and withdraw. Joy's work expresses a form of this collaboration in terms of the poet's address with reference to Harman's notion of the allure. Using the example of Medieval poet Spencer Reece, she argues that poetic addresses "perform the office of yawping across the silence, and re-filling the world with the sounds of things, with their names, which is a form of loving the world, however ridiculous."[42] While she mentions the relation between "man and the world" in reference to Reece's own poetic project, in fact we find that all objects yawp—albeit in profoundly different ways and in different languages. The ontological tension Joy identifies here has analogues with what Jane Bennett identifies in *Vibrant Matter: A Political Ecology of Things* as bodies enhancing their power by being in an assemblage with other objects. "What this suggests about the concept of agency," Bennett argues, "is that efficacy or effectivity . . . becomes distributed across an ontologically heterogeneous field, rather than being localized in a human body or in a collective produced (only) by human efforts."[43] Open access and social media reveal the network of bodies and texts that make up the assemblage labeled as "literature" while simultaneously relaying that assemblage across different audiences and in different environments.

If Joy and Bennett mark an ontological space where the tension between open access and closed publication operate, then Fitzpatrick, Suber, and Shaviro identify the ethics of opening the relay points that have traditionally confined scholarly publication into specific tunnels of dissemination. These seemingly different approaches mask a more compelling reality: scholars and philosophers are finding that collaborative, open, and flexible forms of scholarly communication are necessary in a world that is increasingly losing traditional borders. In a way, the ontological maps conceptualized by open access and drawn by Joy and Bennett eschew the traditional narratives of nationalist identity that have marked both literary study and literary theory. If we are to understand how academia has changed in an age where nationalism is disappearing, we'll need to understand OOO and DH in the realm of globalization.

## GLOBALIZATION AND WITHDRAWAL

Graham Harman's first post about the Arab Spring of 2011 on January 26, 2011, indicates that "there may be delays from me as well," referring to a possible delay in his blogging.[44] What follows is a powerful example of how Harman's position at the University of Cairo, along with his embrace of social media, impacted the development of object-oriented ontology. Harman delivered quotations from the protestors, providing a vital inside perspective to the uprisings. January 31, for example, notes that a friend of a friend said, "when I watch the media, I am afraid. when I go onto the streets with the people, I feel secure."[45] He also created a moving list of "Egypt's heroic dead," including pictures and personal stories of people dying in the protests. The February 14 entry features a story on Mohammad Ali Abd El Megeed who was "33 years old, and a graduate of Cairo University. He was shot and killed near Tahrir Square on Friday, February 28. Married just two years ago, he leaves behind a 1-year-old son named Ali."[46]

Harman's posts about the final days of the Spring are particularly compelling. On the 8th he mentions that "thousands of people have poured into the Square. This isn't going away."[47] When Mubarak resigned on February 11, Harman is literally speechless.

> We can only salute their intelligent and flexible planning, their sense of humor amidst adversity, their organizational skill in the neighborhoods after the police disappeared, the profound sense of unity among different religions and social classes, and above all—the courage of those who remained in Tahrir amidst barbaric camel attacks and sniper fire.[48]

He compares the uprising to the 1989 fall of the Berlin Wall and says that it is "[h]ard to fight back tears at the moment."[49] While philosophers have covered political events in the past, I'm thinking about Slavoj Žižek's response to Occupy Wall Street and how Harman's coverage illustrated his humility regarding political events.[50] In the past few decades, theorists have made an industry out of proclaiming themselves the next big thing in understanding the very violent and complex political events occurring across the world. Shannon Mattern has argued that often the collaborative aspect of theory production is erased in the act of marking the next great name in philosophy. People who create useful theory are "more often than not, *groups* of people who develop their ideas collaboratively, over time, through processes that likely won't bring glory to any one of them or to any dynamic duos (e.g., Deleuze and Guattari, Hardt and Negri, Adorno and Horkheimer)."[51]

We can push Mattern's point even further to suggest that, more often than not, the theorists used to understand globalization are Westerners, loudly proclaiming what large groups of people in countries wildly different from theirs should be doing. In the introduction to their Kindle single on the occupy movement titled *Declaration*, for example, Michael Hardt and Antonio Negri claim that they aren't writing a manifesto. Nevertheless, they say, "the multitudes must discover the passage from declaration to constitution."[52] OOO develops out of a much more humble, and I would argue courageous, approach to theoretical and philosophical reflection. Bruno Latour has shown how political theory frequently makes politicians become the scapegoats of policy failure: "We deride, despise, and hate them. We compete to denounce their venality and incompetence, their blinkered vision, their schemes and compromises, their failures, their lack of realism, or their demagoguery."[53] What separates the political approach of thinkers who to celebrate direct action and sometimes violence (Hardt and Negri, Žižek) from those who understand the compromise that often characterizes politics (Harman, Mattern, and Latour) is an approach to globalization that I will identify, following Harman, as vicarious causation.[54]

Harman derives vicarious causation from his reading of Martin Heidegger's understanding of phenomenological withdrawal and, I argue, from the mechanisms of globalization that he experiences as a Dean and a Professor at the University of Cairo. In *Heidegger Explained*, Harman defines withdrawal as the basic ontological situation where "[t]hings are always partly concealed from us": in other words, we will never have a full experience of any object in the world.[55] Further, withdrawal doesn't just happen between humans and the world (and here is Harman's intervention into Heideggerian thought and his contribution to object-oriented ontology), but also between different objects. "[J]ust as we never grasp the being of two pieces of rock," Harman suggests, "neither do they fully unlock the being of *each other* when they slam together in distant space."[56] Harman's object-oriented ontology also depends upon the irreductive ontology of Latour, a point he makes in *Prince of Networks*: "the mission of the intellect" (Harman is clearly agreeing with his paraphrase of Latour here), "is to make things more real rather than less real—the very opposite method of the overrated 'critical thinking.'"[57] Critical reduction for Harman strips an object of its hidden depths while having fun by playing "a self-proclaimed radical, bursting the bubbles of gullible dupes."[58] Vicarious causation, on the other hand, presumes that any encounter between two objects is incomplete and "forms do not touch one another directly, but somehow melt, fuse, and decompress in a shared common space from which all are partially absent."[59]

Harman is elucidating not only an ontological theory but also, I would argue, a vision of politics that is often absent in other accounts of globalization. Contrast Harman's idea of a shared but partially absent common space as a vision of globalization with Frederic Jameson's sense that globalization is simply a newer form of the Marxist dialectic.[60] "The much repeated dialectic of global and local," Jameson argues, "is just that, a dialectic, even though it has rarely been seriously analyzed in those terms, which involve the interrelationship between a totality and a set of empirical particulars."[61] What's missing in this passage is a sense of the role of causation in the interrelationships Jameson outlines and the role of withdrawal in establishing political conflict, dominance, and cooperation. Does the globe as a totality, if it is indeed a totality, withdraw from analysis? Harman is a philosopher of globalization, perhaps without knowing it, since he has experienced important global events and incorporated them into his work. Vicarious causation is an important addition to the Marxist studies investigating globalization, because it theorizes the role of indirect and mediated action in the emergent global world.

Vicarious causation is also at work in the development of hardware and software studies. The growing awareness of globalization in software studies reacts to both Jameson's notion of the dialectic of globalization and Harman's withdrawn totality by exploring how objects and communities "withdraw from human view into a shadowy subterranean realm."[62] Neither thinkers have the first-hand experience that Harman has, yet their interests in networks coincide with imagining newer forms of association that also influence recent developments in the digital humanities. Kirschenbaum's *Mechanisms: New Media and the Forensic Imagination* devotes a chapter to what he calls "A Grammatology of the Hard Drive," in which he explores the hard drive as "almost always automated textuality—which is to say that most of the textual events in a modern operating system, or network, occur without the impetus of a human agency."[63] Automated electronic textuality is a heavily mediated activity, depending upon the cooperation of many very different non-human actors. Kirschenbaum critiques what Nick Montfort calls "screen essentialism," the idea that electronic textuality is ephemeral because it is easy to erase things on a graphical user interface.[64] On the other hand, he points out that most computers are black boxes: "*Most users will never see their hard drive during the life of their computer. As a writing instrument it thus remains an abstraction—presented as a pie chart to show disk space remaining—or else apprehended through aural rather than visual cues (the drive is audible as it spins up or down).*"[65]

Globalization operates in *Mechanisms* as a shadowy presence lurking throughout Kirschenbaum's discussions of screen-essentialism and the labor of mechanical tools. As a word or a concept, it only appears in the book once. Kirschenbaum describes different methods of versioning, or marking iterations in the process of producing knowledge (i.e., *Wikipedia*) or producing tools (i.e., computers). Versioning provides an important way of identifying the collaborative work of hard drive design. "[I]n an era of globalization," Kirschenbaum notes, "they [software projects] are frequently distributed, with people in different physical places inhabiting different time zones and adapting different rhythms of work."[66] The task of versioning requires a more networked understanding of globalization, where critics can understand the interaction between the non-human mechanisms within the computer and the versioning left behind by the very different spaces within the globalized world where these parts were first created. Wendy Chun's *Programmed Visions: Software and Memory*, on the other hand, illuminates how software obscures global relations and nonhuman operations—something she identifies as "sourcery." Sourcery is the movement, Chun argues, that functions to imagine programmers and software developers as contemporary wizards, and it emerges at the precise moment that we "become incapable of 'understanding'—of seeing through—the machine."[67]

Miriam Posner has interrogated how sourcery works in the development of Steve Jobs's mystique as a guru in the history of the Apple corporation. She notes how Walter Issac's biography of Jobs elevates his individual persona and simultaneously relegates "a complicated history of race, power, and labor [to] the distant past, courtesy of a new device or business model."[68] More recently, Tara McPherson has expanded this critique by identifying "emerging modes of computation [as] symptoms and drivers of our 'post-racial moment,' [that] refract . . . in some way national anxieties (or hopes) about a decreasing 'white' America."[69] However much we want to embrace the post-racial or globalized environment of computation, digital humanities scholars show that it always comes at the price of transforming complicated networks of associations to black boxes. The black box phenomenon also fetishizes the work of gurus as embodying direct action: where the messy realities of culture and nature seemingly give way to a utopian space in which everyone, excluding those invisible workers who actually make our digital devices or those poor children who cannot afford them, can connect directly with everyone else.

## WHAT HAPPENED?

As I argued in the beginning of this chapter, both object-oriented ontology and digital humanities have complicated histories that cannot be adequately represented here. On the other hand, both schools of thought have participated in larger historical shifts in academia inspired by the depreciation of academic labor and a dependence on adjunct instructors, the emergence of open access scholarship and social media as viable forms of scholarly communication, and the complicated racial and political terrain of globalization. In many cases, as seen from the stories outlined above, these forces have intermingled. Fitzpatrick's call for open access publishing thrives in an environment where #altac positions have found a need for different forms of evaluation. Morton's interest in object-oriented ontology found a voice only because he was able to connect to Levi Bryant through social media. Finally, the depreciation of fields like English and the humanities themselves are enabled by a globalized world in which it is no longer enough to simply discuss nationalist literatures or Western philosophers.

More generally, I would say that the great outdoors offers a new set of challenges. David Weinberger argues that the internet has shown us that knowledge is not "an unshaken house based on the foundation of facts"; moreover, we probably previously thought this was the case because print culture simply gave "the clamorous disagreement no public voice."[70] Both OOO and DH have demonstrated that grand theories and individual perspectives are less important than finding ways to connect with one another and combine our insights into more effective ways of instituting progressive change. But we also have to be wary of how these changes occur. The same network that gave Mike Daisey an enormous audience for his exposé of FoxConn and Apple also made it easier for the producers of *This American Life* to ignore the story's holes, which lead to a very public retraction.[71] The whole Mike Daisy incident undermines the core truth at the center of that story: the great price we enjoy for our iPads and iPhones very probably relies upon cheap, backbreaking, depression-inducing labor. The same networks that helped publicize Brian Croxall's article, and connected Tim Morton to all of those philosophers chatting about speculative realism, also rely upon a history of racism, sexism, and oppression which still lurks in the dark, subterranean realities that withdraw from the lives of academics, adjuncts, and #altac professionals. The point is not that we can uncover all of these realities or that we should get rid of all of our technology and strut around like "beautiful souls."[72] Rather, both OOO and DH have the potential to help us, in small ways, become stewards of the emergent global ecology. As in all relationships, this is a messy process, and most of us will need to forgive and be forgiven, expose and rethink our assumptions, work to open lines of building and communication, and generally be humble in the face of a global infrastructure that is bigger than any one of our articles, books, or theories.

## NOTES

1. Ian Bogost, "The Metaphysics Video Game," web log post, *Bogost.com*. Web. July 24, 2009. Accessed May 9, 2012. See also *Alien Phenomenology, Or, What It's like to Be a Thing* (Minneapolis: University of Minnesota, 2012).

2. Patrick Murray-John, "The 'Life of the Mind' Lost?" *Alt-Academy* (2011). Web. Accessed May 9, 2012.

3. Levi Bryant, "Post-Identity Politics?" weblog post. *Larval Subjects.* November 8, 2008. Accessed May 9, 2012.

4. Bethany Nowviskie, "Introduction: Two Tramps in Mud Time," *Alt-Academy* (2011). Web. Accessed May 9, 2012.

5. Susan Hockey, "The History of Humanities Computing," *A Companion to the Digital Humanities* (Oxford: Blackwell, 2004).

6. See Harman's "brief SR/OOO tutorial," in which he argues that "OOO can be seen as one of the 'states' within a larger speculative realist union," at Graham Harman, "Brief SR/OOO Tutorial," weblog post, *Object-Oriented Philosophy.* July 23, 2010. Web. Accessed May 9, 2012. See also Levi Bryant's sympathetic discussion of Jane Bennett's thought: "Bennett MOO (Materialist Oriented Ontology)" where he says "[w]ith Bennett (and Lucretius) and in contrast to Harman, I am a staunch materialist," at Levi Bryant, "Post-Identity Politics?" weblog post, *Larval Subjects.* November 8, 2008. Web. Accessed May 9, 2012.

7. Quentin Mellaisoux, *After Finitude: An Essay on the Necessity of Contingency*, trans. Ray Brassier (London: Continuum, 2010).

8. It's worth mentioning Eugene Thacker and Alexander Galloway's foundational work *The Exploit*, in which they argue that the network as a political concept "has infected broad swaths of contemporary life" (25–6.). By invoking Benjamin's constellation, which appears in a good portion of his work but primarily in "Theses on the Philosophy of History" and *The Origin of German Tragic Drama*, I hope to link his notion that "ideas are to objects as constellations are to stars" to the theories of networking and objects presented by both Thacker and Galloway and OOO philosophers (34). See Alexander R. Galloway and Eugene Thacker, *The Exploit: A Theory of Networks* (Minneapolis, MN: University of Minnesota Press, 2007). See also Walter Benjamin, *The Origin of German Tragic Drama* (London: Verso, 2009); and Walter Benjamin, "Theses on the Philosophy of History," *Illuminations*, edited by Hannah Arendt, trans. Harry Zohn (New York: Harcourt, Brace & World, 1968), 253–64.

9. See Morton's dissertation "Re-Imagining the Body: Shelley and the Languages of Diet," which he has made available on the website *academia.edu*, for more information about his work on the Romantic poet and vegetarianism. See "Reimagining the Body: Shelley and the Languages of Diet." Diss. Oxford University, 1992.

10. Jaime Applegate, "Study: State Suffered Dramatic Drop in Funding for Higher Education," *The Daily Californian.* January 1, 2012. Web. Accessed May 9, 2012.

11. Timothy Morton, "Peterloo Revisited," weblog post. *Ecology without Nature.* November 19, 2011. Web. Accessed May 9, 2012.

12. Timothy Morton, "The Bigger Picture: Race Issues and Thuggery," web log post, *Ecology without Nature.* November 20, 2011. Web. Accessed May 9, 2012.

13. Timothy Morton, "Homeopathic Pepper Spray Remedy," web log post, *Ecology without Nature.* November 24, 2011. Web. Accessed May 9, 2012.

14. Timothy Morton, *Ecology without Nature: Rethinking Environmental Aesthetics* (Cambridge, MA: Harvard University Press, 2007).

15. Ibid. By describing Nature in this way, Morton invokes the work of Simone de Beauvoir and her argument in *The Second Sex* that such fantasies transform women into fetish objects. See Simone De Beauvoir, *The Second Sex* (New York: Knopf, 1953).

16. Timothy Morton, *The Ecological Thought* (Cambridge, MA: Harvard University Press, 2010).

17. Bryant also mentions being indebted to Morton's work several times in *The Democracy of Objects*. For example, Bryant argues that being is flat "in the precise sense that all beings are characterized by withdrawal and othering," and he mentions that his conception of flat ontology is "deeply indebted to Alain Badiou's *Logics of Worlds* and Timothy Morton's *dark ecology* proposed in *Ecology without Nature*" (269–70). See Levi Bryant, *The Democracy of Objects* (Ann Arbor, MI: Open Humanities, 2011).

18. Robin Mackay, "Editorial Introduction," *Collapse* 2 (2007), 3–13.

19. Timothy Morton, "OOO Class #1 (Embedded Video and MP3)," video blog post, *Ecology without Nature.* April 2, 2012. Web. Accessed May 9, 2012.

20. Immanuel Kant, *The Conflict of the Faculties / Der Streit Der Fakultaten* (New York: Abaris, 1979).

21. Ibid., 25.

22. Brian Croxall, "The Absent Presence: Today's Faculty," web log post, *Briancroxall.net*. December 27, 2009. Web. Accessed May 9, 2012.

23. Stacy Patton, "The Ph.D. Now Comes with Food Stamps," *The Chronicle of Higher Education* (2012). May 6, 2012. Web. Accessed May 9, 2012.

24. Marc Bousquet, *How the University Works: Higher Education and the Low-Wage Nation* (New York: New York University Press, 2008), 42.

25. Nowviskie, "Introduction."

26. Matthew G. Kirschenbaum, "What Is Digital Humanities and What's It Doing in English Departments," *ADE Bulletin* 150 (2010), 1–7.

27. See, for example, Nowviskie's "It Starts on Day One," which argues that humanities departments should "kill the grad-level methods course" and focus instead upon "new research methodologies and corpora. . . that address hitherto unanswerable questions about history, the arts, and the human condition" and "new-model scholarly communications platforms." See Bethany Nowviskie, "It Starts on Day One," web log post, ProfHacker, *The Chronicle of Higher Education*, January 12, 2012. Web. Accessed May 10, 2012. Also see Pannapacker's "Alt-Ac is the Future of the Academy" where he argues that the "academe's 'angry generation' is being replaced by academe's 'service generation'" and that this is "a positive development." See William Pannapacker, "Pannapacker at the MLA: Alt-Ac Is the Future of the Academy," web log post, *Brainstorm, The Chronicle of Higher Education*. January 8, 2012. Web. Accessed May 10, 2012.

28. Brian Croxall, "Five Questions and Three Answers about Alt-Ac," web log post, *Briancroxall.net*, January 7, 2012. Web. Accessed May 9, 2012.

29. Croxall's work at the Digital Scholarship Commons at Emory University includes projects like *Commonwealth*, which revamps "the infrastructure" of Deepika Bahri's "renowned Introduction to Postcolonial Studies resource" and *Views of Rome*, which focuses on "Pirro Ligorio's 1561 map of Ancient Rome." See Brian Croxall, "Commonwealth: A Postcolonial Studies Community," web log post, *Digital Scholarship Commons*, Emory University, September 12, 2011. Accessed May 12, 2012; and "Views of Rome," web log post, *Briancoxall.net*. December 12, 2011. Web. Accessed May 10, 2012.

30. Kathleen Fitzpatrick, *Planned Obsolescence: Publishing, Technology, and the Future of the Academy* (New York: New York University Press, 2011).

31. In an article for *The Chronicle of Higher Education*, Fitzpatrick urged graduate students to "Do the 'Risky Thing' in Digital Humanities," by which she means that they "should take a chance on an innovative project," and that faculty "must support her in doing the risky thing." See Kathleen Fitzpatrick, "Do the 'Risky Thing' in the Digital Humanities," web log post, *The Chronicle of Higher Education*, September 25, 2011. Web. Accessed May 10, 2012.

32. Kathleen Fitzpatrick, *The Anxiety of Obsolescence: The American Novel in the Age of Television* (Nashville: Vanderbilt University Press, 2006), 50.

33. Ibid.

34. Ibid., 2

35. Fitzpatrick, *Planned Obsolecence*.

36. Peter Suber, "Open Access Overview (definition, Introduction)." Peter Suber. Earlham College, April 2010. Web. Accessed May 9, 2012.

37. HathiTrust Digital Library. "Information about the Authors Guild Lawsuit." *Hathitrust.org*. Web. May 9, 2012.

38. Steven Shaviro, "Work for Hire?" Web log post. *The Pinocchio Theory*. January 11, 2012. Web. Accessed May 9, 2012.

39. Eileen Joy, "Fuck Pessimism: Embrace Youngsterism," *Babel Working Group*. January 27, 2012. Web. Accessed May 9, 2012.

40. Eileen Joy, "You Are Here: A Manifesto," *Animal, Vegetable, Mineral: Ethics and Objects*, edited by Jeffrey Jerome Cohen (Brooklyn: Punctum, 2012), 166.

41. Ibid.

42. Eileen Joy, "All That Remains Unnoticed I Adore: Spencer Reece's Addresses," *Glossator* 5 (Fall 2011), 69–84.

43. Jane Bennett, *Vibrant Matter: A Political Ecology of Things* (Durham: Duke University Press, 2010), 23.

44. Graham Harman, "Egypt," web log post, *Object-Oriented Philosophy*. January 26, 2011. Web. Accessed May 10, 2012.

45. Graham Harman, "What I'm Hearing from Many Egyptians," web log post, *Object-Oriented Philosophy*. January 31, 2011. Web. Accessed May 10, 2012.

46. Graham Harman, "Mohamed Ali Eid Abd Megeed," web log post, *Object-Oriented Philosophy*. February 14, 2011. Web. Accessed May 10, 2012.

47. Graham Harman, "Biggest Tahrir Protests So Far," web log post, *Object-Oriented Philosophy*. February 8, 2011. Web. Accessed May 10, 2012.

48. Graham Harman, "A Congratulations to the Egyptian People," web log post, *Object-Oriented Philosophy*. February 11, 2011. Web. Accessed May 10, 2012.

49. Harman, "What I'm Hearing from Many Egyptians."

50. See Žižek's address to Occupy Wall Street when he tries to identify what the occupiers are doing, and says, "There is a danger. Don't fall in love with yourselves. We have a nice time here. But remember, carnivals come cheap. What matters is the day after, when we will have to return to normal lives." The point is well-taken, and yet also reinscribes Žižek as someone who stands above the crowd and directs their movements. See Sarahana, "Slavoj Žižek Speaks to Occupy Wall Street: A Transcript," web log post, *IMPOSE Magazine*. Web. Accessed May 10, 2012.

51. Shannon Mattern, "Theoretical Humility," web log post. *Words in Space*. May 7, 2012. Web. Accessed May 10, 2012.

52. Michael Hardt and Antonio Negri. *Declaration* (Hardt and Negri, 2012).

53. Bruno Latour, *The Pasteurization of France* (Cambridge, MA: Harvard University Press, 1988), 210.

54. Hardt and Negri are particularly problematic on this point. In *Commonwealth*, they critique "Leftists today who talk of a new fascism" for their "moral outrage and resignation rather than calls for armed struggle" and say that "there can be no political engagement with a sovereign fascist power; all it knows is violence" (5). See Michael Hardt and Antonio Negri, *Commonwealth* (Cambridge, MA: Belknap of Harvard University Press, 2009).

55. Graham Harman, *Heidegger Explained* (Chicago, IL: Open Court, 2007), 177.

56. Graham Harman, *Tool-being: Heidegger and the Metaphysics of Objects* (Chicago: Open Court, 2002), 5.

57. Graham Harman, *Prince of Networks: Bruno Latour and Metaphysics* (Prahran, VIC: Re.press, 2009), 196.

58. Ibid., 199.

59. Graham Harman, "On Vicarious Causation," *Collapse* 2 (2007), 190.

60. This common space can never be fully present to any actor, a point he makes in *The Quadruple Object*, when he notices that "[n]o matter how hard I work to become conscious of things, environing conditions still remain of which I never become fully aware" (39). See Graham Harman, *The Quadruple Object* (Winchester, UK: Zero, 2011).

61. Fredric Jameson, *Valences of the Dialectic* (London: Verso, 2009), 67.

62. Matthew G. Kirschenbaum, *Mechanisms: New Media and the Forensic Imagination* (Cambridge, MA: MIT, 2008).

63. Ibid., 83.

64. Ibid.

65. Ibid., 75.

66. Ibid., 202.

67. Wendy Hui Kyong Chun, *Programmed Visions: Software and Memory* (Cambridge, MA: MIT, 2011), 33.

68. Miriam Posner, "Reading Steve Jobs: Labor, Race, and Growing Up in the Bay Area," web log post, *Miriamposner.com*. December 6, 2011. Web. Accessed May 10, 2012.

69. Tara Mcpherson, "U.S. Operating Systems at Mid-Century: The Intertwining of Race and Unix," *Race After the Internet*, edited by Lisa Nakamura and Peter Chow-White (New York: Routledge, 2012), 33

70. David Weinberger, *Too Big to Know: Rethinking Knowledge Now That the Facts Aren't the Facts, Experts Are Everywhere, and the Smartest Person in the Room Is the Room* (New York: Basic, 2011), 41.

71. See the two *This American Life* episodes devoted to Daisy's story—"Mr. Daisey and the Apple Factory" and "Retraction"—for more information about the FoxConn story and the approach of the show when it came to light that Daisy had fabricated parts of it. See Tim Morton, "Mr. Daisy and the Apple Factory," audio blog post, *This American Life*, January 6, 2012. Web. Accessed May 10, 2012; and "Retraction." Audio blog post, *This American Life*, March 16, 2012. Web. Accessed May 10, 2012.

72. Tim Morton identifies "beautiful soul syndrome" as the belief that "you've exited consumerism." See Tim Morton, "Beautiful Soul Syndrome," web log post, *Ecology without Nature*. May 16, 2009. Web. Accessed May 10, 2012. Since consumerism and capitalism are identified as bad, "[y]ou, having exited that world, are good. Over there is the evil object, which you shun or seek to eliminate. Over here is the good subject, who feels good precisely insofar as he or she has separated from the evil world" (14). See Morton, *The Ecological Thought*.

# Bibliography

Adorno, Theodor and Max Horkheimer, *Dialectic of Enlightenment*, trans. John Cumming. New York: Continuum Press, 1972.

Adorno, Theodor. *Aesthetic Theory*, edited by Gretel Adorno and Rolf Tiedemann, trans. C. Lenhardt. London: Routledge & Kegan Paul, 1984.

Althusser, Louis. *For Marx*, trans. Ben Brewster. New York: Random House, 1969.

Anderson, Devery S. *Emmett Till: The Murder that Shocked the World and Propelled the Civil Rights Movement*. Jackson: University Press of Mississippi, 2015.

Applegate, Jaime. "Study: State Suffered Dramatic Drop in Funding for Higher Education," *The Daily Californian*. January 1, 2012. Web. Accessed May 9, 2012.

Balibar, Étienne, *The Philosophy of Marx*. London: Verso, 1995.

Barber, Karen. "Michel Foucault and the Specters of War," in *Historicizing Theory*, edited by Peter Herman. Albany, NY: SUNY Press, 2003.

Beck, Charlotte. *Robert Penn Warren: Critic*. Knoxville: University of Tennessee Press, 2006.

Bennett, Jane. *Vibrant Matter: A Political Ecology of Things*. Durham: Duke University Press, 2010.

Bennington, Geoffrey and Jacques Derrida. *Jacques Derrida*. Chicago: The University of Chicago Press, 1997.

Bergson, Henri. *Time and Freedom: An Essay on the Immediate Data of Consciousness,* translated by F.L. Pogson. London: George Allen and Unwin, 1910.

Berthold-Bond, Daniel."Hegel's Eschatological Vision: Does History Have a Future?" *History and Theory* 27, no. 1 (February 1988).

Bloom, Harold. *Poets and Poems*. New York: Chelsea House, 2005.

Boehner, Charles. *Robert Penn Warren*. New Haven: Twayne Publishers, 1964.

Bogost, Ian. "The Metaphysics Video Game," web log post, *Bogost.com*. Web. July 24, 2009. Accessed May 9, 2012.

Bolt, Barbara. *Heidegger Reframed*. New York: L. B. Taurus & Co., 2011.

Booth, Wayne. Foreword to *Literature as Exploration,* 5th edition. New York: MLA, 1995.

Bousquet, Marc. *How the University Works: Higher Education and the Low-wage Nation*. New York: New York University Press, 2008.

Brandom, Robert. "Reason, Genealogy, and the Hermeneutics of Magnanimity," November 21, 2012, http://www.pitt.edu/~brandom/downloads/RGHM%20%2012–11–21%20a.docx.

Brill, Susan B. *Wittgenstein and Critical Theory: Beyond Postmodern Criticism and Toward Descriptive Investigations*. Athens: University of Ohio Press, 1995.

Bryant, Levi. "Post-Identity Politics?," weblog post. *Larval Subjects*. November 8, 2008. Accessed May 9, 2012.

Bush, Douglas. "The Humanist Critic," *The Kenyon Review* 13, no. 1 (Winter 1951).

Butler, Judith *Gender Trouble: Feminism and the Subversion of Identity*. New York: Routledge, 1999.
———. "AVIVA-Interview with Judith Butler," interview by Undine Zimmer, Marie Heidingsfelder, and Sharon Adler, in *AVIVA-Berlin.de*, June 2012, accessed June 21, 2012,
http://www.aviva-berlin.de/aviva/content_Interviews.php?id=1427323.
———. "Judith Butler: As a Jew I Was Taught it Was Ethically Imperative to Speak Up,"
interview by Udi Aloni, in *Haaretz.com*, February 24, 2010, accessed June 22, 2012, http://
www.haaretz.com/misc/article-print-page/judith-butler-as-a-jew-i-was-taught-it-was-ethi-
cally-imperative-to-speak-up-part-ii-1.266244?trailingPath=2.169%2C2.216%2C.
———. "Peace is a Resistance to the Terrible Satisfactions of War," interview by Jill Stauffer,
in *The Believer*, May 2003, accessed June 20, 2012, http://www.believermag.com/issues/
200305/?read=interview_butler.
———. "The Desire for Philosophy," interview by Regina Michalik, in *LOLA Press*, May
2001, accessed June 20, 2012, http://www.lolapress.org/elec2/artenglish/butl_e.htm.
———. *Bodies that Matter: On the Discursive Limits of "Sex."* New York: Routledge, 1993.
———. *Excitable Speech: A Politics of the Performative*. New York: Routledge, 1997.
———. *Frames of War: When is Life Grievable?* London: Verso, 2010.
———. *Precarious Life: The Powers of Mourning and Violence*. London: Verso, 2004.
Büttner, Stefan. "The Tripartition of the Soul in Plato's *Republic*," in *New Essays on Plato:
Language and Thought in Fourth-Century Greek Philosophy*, edited by Fritz-Gregor Her-
mann. Swansea, UK: The Classical Press of Wales, 2006.
Calvino, Italo. *If on a winter's night a traveler*, trans. William Weaver. New York: Harcourt
Brace Jovanovich, Publishers, 1981.
Carroll, David. *Paraesthetics: Foucault, Lyotard, Derrida*. New York: Methuen, 1987.
Carton, Evan. "The Holocaust, French Poststructuralism, the American Literary Academy, and
Jewish Identity Poetics," in *Historicizing Theory*, edited by Peter Herman. Albany, NY:
SUNY Press, 2003.
Carvallo, Guglielmo and Roger Chartier, eds., *A History of Reading in the West*, trans. Lydia G.
Cochrane. Amherst, MA: University of Massachusetts Press, 1999.
Champagne, Roland A. *Jacques Derrida*. New York: Twayne Publishers, 1995.
Clark, Meredith. "U.S. More Oligarchy than Democracy, Study Suggests," *MSNBC*, April 19,
2014, accessed June 17, 2018, http://www.msnbc.com/msnbc/the-us-no-longer-democra-
cy#51760.
Cole, Andrew. *The Birth of Theory*. Chicago: Chicago University Press, 2015.
Comay, Rebecca. *Mourning Sickness: Hegel and the French Revolution*. Stanford: Stanford
University Press, 2011.
Cook, Deborah. "Theodor W. Adorno: An Introduction," *Theodor Adorno: Key Concepts*,
edited by Deborah Cook. Stocksfield, UK: Acumen, 2008.
Cotter, Jennifer et al. *Human, All Too (Post)Human: The Humanities after Humanism*. London:
Lexington, 2016.
Crowe Ransom, John. "Criticism, Inc.," *Virginia Quarterly Review* (Autumn 1937).
Croxall, Brian. "The Absent Presence: Today's Faculty," web log post, *Briancroxall.net*. De-
cember 27, 2009. Web. Accessed May 9, 2012.
Croxall, Brian."Five Questions and Three Answers about Alt-Ac," web log post, *Briancrox-
all.net*, January 7, 2012. Web. Accessed May 9, 2012.
Culler, Jonathan. "New Literary History and European Theory," *New Literary History* 25, no. 4
(1994).
de la Piedra, Benji. "Fifty Years Later: Robert Penn Warren's *Who Speaks for the Ne-
gro?*" *Oral History Review* 42, no. 2 (2015).
Deleuze, Gilles. *Foucault*. Paris: Les Éditions de Minuit, 1986.
"Democracy Index 2016," *The Economist*, accessed June 17, 2018, https://www.eiu.com/pub-
lic/topical_report.aspx?campaignid=DemocracyIndex2016.
Derrida, Jacques. *Disseminations*, translated by Barbara Johnson. London: The Athlone Press,
1981.
———. *Edmund Husserl's Origin of Geometry: An Introduction*, translated by John P. Leavy
Jr. Lincoln, NE: University of Nebraska Press, 1989.

————. *The Problem of Genesis in Husserl's Philosophy*, translated by Martin Hobson. Chicago: University of Chicago Press, 2003.

————. "Cogito and the History of Madness," in *Between Foucault and Derrida*, edited by Yubraj Aryal et al. Edinburgh: Edinburgh University Press, 2016.

————. "Differance," in *Speech and Phenomena*. Evanston: Northwestern Univ. Press, 1973.

————. "Letter to a Japanese Friend," *Everything2*, April 25, 2002, accessed June 22, 2018, https://www.everything2.com/title/Letter+to+a+Japanese+Friend+by+Jacques+Derrida.

————. *Of Grammatology*, translated by Gayatri Chakravorty Spivak. Chicago: The Johns Hopkins University Press, 1974, 1976.

————. *The Truth in Painting*, trans. Geoff Bennington and Ian McLeod. Chicago: The University of Chicago Press, 1987.

————. *Writing and Difference*, trans. Alan Bass. Chicago: The University of Chicago Press, 1978.

Dudley, Will. *Hegel, Nietzsche, and Philosophy: Thinking Freedom*. Cambridge: Cambridge University Press, 2002.

Eldridge, David. *American Culture in the 1930s*. Edinburgh: Edinburgh University Press, 2008.

Fikri Alican, Necip. *Rethinking Plato: A Cartesian Quest for the Real Plato*. Rodopi: New York, 2012.

Fish, Stanley E. "Literature in the Reader: Affective Stylistics." *Reader-Response Criticism: From Formalism to Post-Structuralism,* edited by Jane P. Tompkins. Baltimore: Johns Hopkins University Press, 1980.

Fitzpatrick, Kathleen. *Planned Obsolescence: Publishing, Technology, and the Future of the Academy*. New York: New York University Press, 2011.

————. *The Anxiety of Obsolescence: The American Novel in the Age of Television*. Nashville: Vanderbilt University Press, 2006.

Foa Dienstag, Joshua. "Building the Temple of Memory: Hegel's Aesthetic Narrative of History," *The Review of Politics* 56, no. 4 (Autumn 1994).

Forster, Richard. *The New Romantics*. Bloomington, IN, 1962.

Foucault, Michel. *History of Sexuality, Vol. 1: An Introduction*, trans. Robert Hurley. New York: Vintage Books, 1980.

"'Friedrich Engels to Eduard Berstein,' 2–3 November 1882," in *Marx-Engels Collected Works* (*MECW*) vol. 46. New York: International Publishers, 1992.

Frow, John. "On Literature and Cultural Studies," *The Aesthetics of Cultural Studies*, edited by Michael Bérubé. Oxford: Blackwell, 2005.

Frow, John. *Cultural Studies and Cultural Value*. Oxford: Clarendon Press, 1995.

Fukuyama, Francis. *The End of History and the Last Man*. New York: Free Press, 2006.

Gee, James. *Social Linguistics and Literacies: Ideology in Discourses*, 4th edition. New York: Routledge, 2012.

Gilens, Martin and Benjamin I. Page, "Testing Theories of American Politics: Elites, Interest Groups, and Average Citizens," *Perspectives on Politics* vol. 12, issue 3, September 2014, pp. 564–581, doi:https://doi.org/10.1017/S1537592714001595.

Goldin, Claudia and Lawrence F. Katz. "Human Capital and Social Capital: The Rise of Secondary Schooling in America, 1910–1940." *The Journal of Interdisciplinary History* 29, no. 4, 1999.

Goldstein, Leon J. "The Meaning of 'State' in Hegel's Philosophy of History," *The Philosophical Quarterly (1950-)* 12, no. 46 (January 1962).

Gordon, Peter E. *Adorno and Existence*. Cambridge: Harvard University Press, 2016.

Gormley, Steven. "Rearticulating the Concept of Experience, Rethinking the Demands of Deconstruction," in *Research in Phenomenology* vol. 42 (2012): 374–407.

Habermas, Jürgen. *Knowledge and Human Interests*, trans. Jeremy J. Shapiro. Boston: Beacon Press, 1971.

Hamilton, Edith and Huntington Cairns, eds., *The Collected Dialogues of Plato, Including the Letters*, Bollingen Series LXXI. Princeton: Princeton University Press, 1961.

Harman, Graham. "What I'm Hearing from Many Egyptians," web log post, *Object-Oriented Philosophy*. January 31, 2011. Web. Accessed May 10, 2012.

————. *Prince of Networks: Bruno Latour and Metaphysics*. Prahran, VIC: Re.press, 2009.

————. *Tool-being: Heidegger and the Metaphysics of Objects*. Chicago: Open Court, 2002.

————. "Egypt," web log post, *Object-Oriented Philosophy*. January 26, 2011. Web. Accessed May 10, 2012.

————. "A Congratulations to the Egyptian People," web log post, *Object-Oriented Philosophy*. February 11, 2011. Web. Accessed May 10, 2012.

————. "Biggest Tahrir Protests So Far," web log post, *Object-Oriented Philosophy*. February 8, 2011. Web. Accessed May 10, 2012.

————. "Mohamed Ali Eid Abd Megeed," web log post, *Object-Oriented Philosophy*. February 14, 2011. Web. Accessed May 10,2012.

————. "On Vicarious Causation," *Collapse* 2 (2007).

————. *Heidegger Explained*. Chicago, IL: Open Court, 2007.

Harris, H. S., *Hegel's Development: Toward the Sunlight, 1770–1801*. Oxford: The Clarendon Press, 1972.

Hartman, Geoffrey. "Preface" to *Deconstruction and Criticism*, edited by Harold Bloom, Paul de Man, Jacques Derrida, Geoffrey Hartman, and J. Hillis Miller. New York: Continuum, 1979.

HathiTrust Digital Library. "Information about the Authors Guild Lawsuit." *Hathitrust.org*. Web. May 9, 2012.

Havelock, Eric A. *Preface to Plato*. Cambridge, MA: The Belknap Press of Harvard University Press, 1963.

Hegel, Georg Wilhelm Friedrich, *The Philosophy of Right,* trans. Alan White. Indianapolis: Focus Publishing, 2002.

Heidegger, Martin. *Being and Time*, translated by John Macquarrie and Edward Robinson. San Francisco: HarperSanFrancisco, 1962.

————. *Poetry, Language, and Thought*, trans. Albert Hofstadter. New York: Harper & Row, 1975.

Heller-Andrist, Simone, *The Friction of the Frame: Derrida's Parergon in Literature*. Tubingen: Francke, 2012.

Herman, Peter. ed., *Historicizing Theory*. Albany, NY: SUNY Press, 2003.

Hockey, Susan. "The History of Humanities Computing," *A Companion to the Digital Humanities*. Oxford: Blackwell, 2004.

Hodgson, Peter C. *Shapes of Freedom: Hegel's Philosophy of World History in Theological Perspective*. Oxford: Oxford University Press, 2012.

Hoffman, Marcello. "Disciplinary Power," in *Michel Foucault: Key Concepts*, edited by Dianna Taylor. Durham, England: Acumen Pub., 2011.

Hui Kyong Chun, Wendy. *Programmed Visions: Software and Memory*. Cambridge, MA: MIT, 2011.

Jameson, Fredric. *Valences of the Dialectic*. London: Verso, 2009.

Janik, Allan and Stephen Toulmin. *Wittgenstein's Vienna*. Chicago: Elephant, 1996.

Joy, Eileen. "All That Remains Unnoticed I Adore: Spencer Reece's Addresses," *Glossator* 5 (Fall 2011).

Joy, Eileen. "Fuck Pessimism: Embrace Youngsterism," *Babel Working Group*. January 27, 2012. Web. Accessed May 9, 2012.

————. "You Are Here: A Manifesto," *Animal, Vegetable, Mineral: Ethics and Objects*, edited by Jeffrey Jerome Cohen. Brooklyn: Punctum, 2012.

*Judith Butler: Philosophical Encounters of the Third Kind*, DVD, directed by Paule Zadjermann. Brooklyn, NY: First Run/Icarus Films, 2006.

Kainz, Howard P. *G. W. F. Hegel: The Philosophical System*. New York: Twayne Publishers, 1996.

Kant, Immanuel. *The Conflict of the Faculties / Der Streit Der Fakultaten*. New York, NY: Abaris, 1979.

Karolides, Nicholas and Louise Rosenblatt, "Theory and Practice: An Interview with Louise M. Rosenblatt," *Language Arts* 77, no. 2.

Kierkegaard, Søren. *The Concept of Anxiety: A Simple Psychologically Orienting Deliberation on the Dogmatic Issue of Original Sin*, ed. and trans. Reidar Thomte. Princeton, NJ: Princeton University Press, 1980.

"King Me." *Time* vol. 191, no. 23, June 18, 2018, accessed June 17, 2018, http://time.com/5304206/donald-trump-discredit-mueller-investigation/.

Kirschenbaum, Matthew G. "What Is Digital Humanities and What's It Doing in English Departments," *ADE Bulletin* 150 (2010).

Kirschenbaum, Matthew G. *Mechanisms: New Media and the Forensic Imagination*. Cambridge, MA: MIT, 2008.

Kojève, Alexandre. *Introduction to the Reading of Hegel: Lectures on the* Phenomenology of Spirit, *Assembled by Raymond Queneau*, edited by Allan Bloom, trans. James H. Nichols, Jr. Ithaca: Cornell University Press, 1980.

Koopman, Colin. *Genealogy as Critique: Foucault and the Problems of Modernity*. Bloomington: Indiana University Press, 2013.

Küng, Hans. *The Incarnation of God: An Introduction to Hegel's Theological Thought as Prolegomena to a Future Christology*. Edinburgh: T. & T. Clark, 1987.

Latour, Bruno. *The Pasteurization of France*. Cambridge, MA: Harvard University Press, 1988.

Leitch, Vincent, et. al., eds., *The Norton Anthology of Theory and Criticism*. New York: Norton, 2010.

Lesko, Nancy. *Act Your Age: A Cultural Construction of Adolescence*, 2nd edition. New York, Taylor & Francis, 2012.

Lewis, Nathaniel. "David Milch at Yale: An Interview," in *Dirty Words in Deadwood: Literature and the Postwestern,* edited by Melody Graulich and Nicolas S. Witschi. Lincoln: University of Nebraska Press, 2013.

Llewelyn, John. "Approaches to (Quasi) Theology via Appresentation," *Research in Phenomenology* 39 (2009).

Losonsky, Michael. *Linguistic Turns in Modern Philosophy*. Cambridge: Cambridge University Press, 2006.

Lukács, Georg. *History and Class Consciousness*, trans. Rodney Livingstone. London: Merlin Press, 1971.

Macherey, Pierre. "The Foucault-Derrida Debate on the Argument Concerning Madness and Dreams," in *Derrida / Foucault Fifty Years Later: The Futures of Genealogy, Deconstruction, and Politics*, edited by Olivia Custer et al. New York: Columbia University Press, 2016.

Mackay, Robin. "Editorial Introduction," *Collapse* 2 (2007).

Magee, Glenn Alexander. "Hegelian Panentheism," in *Models of God and Alternative Ultimate Realities*, edited by Jeanine Diller and Asa Kasher. Dordrecht: Springer, 2013.

Malabou, Catherine and Lisabeth During. "The Future of Hegel: Plasticity, Temporality, Dialectic," *Hypatia* 15, no. 4 (Autumn 2000).

Marcuse, Herbert. *Hegel's Ontology and the Theory of Historicity*, trans. Seyla Benhabib. Cambridge, Massachusetts: The MIT Press, 1987.

Marx, Karl. "Direct Results of the Production Process," in *MECW* vol. 34. New York: International Publishers, 1994.

———. *Capital*, vol. 1, in *MECW* vol. 35. New York: International Publishers, 1996.

———. *The Communist Manifesto*, in *MECW* vol. 6. New York: International Publishers, 1976.

———. "Critique of the Hegelian Dialectic and Philosophy as a Whole," in *MECW* vol. 3. New York: International Publishers, 1975.

———. "The Eighteenth Brumaire of Louis Bonaparte," in *MECW* vol. 11. New York: International Publishers, 1979.

———. *The German Ideology*, in *MECW* vol. 5. New York: International Publishers, 1976.

Mattern, Shannon. "Theoretical Humility," web log post. *Words in Space*. May 7, 2012. Web. Accessed May 10, 2012.

McCarney, Joseph. *Hegel on History*. London: Routledge, 2000.

McGann, Jerome. *The Romantic Ideology: A Critical Investigation*. Chicago: Chicago University Press, 1983.

Mcpherson, Tara. "U.S. Operating Systems at Mid-Century: The Intertwining of Race and Unix," *Race After the Internet*, edited by Lisa Nakamura and Peter Chow-White. New York: Routledge, 2012.

Mellaisoux, Quentin. *After Finitude: An Essay on the Necessity of Contingency*, trans. Ray Brassier. London: Continuum, 2010.

Merklinger, Philip M. *Philosophy, Theology, and Hegel's Berlin Philosophy of Religion*. Albany: State University of New York Press, 1993.

Meynell, Hugo. "Doubts about Wittgenstein's Influence," *Philosophy* 57, no. 220 (Apr. 1982).

Milchman, Alan and Alan Rosenberg. "Toward a Foucault / Heidegger *Auseinandersetzung*," *Foucault and Heidegger Critical Encounters*, edited by Alan Milchman and Alan Rosenberg. Minneapolis: University of Minnesota Press, 2003.

Miller, Mark D. "Faith in Good Works: The Salvation of Robert Penn Warren," in *Mississippi Quarterly* 48, no. 1 (Winter 94/95).

Monk, Ray. "One of the Great Intellects of His Time," *The New York Review of Books*, December 22, 2016, http://www.nybooks.com/articles/2016/12/22/frank-ramsey-great-intellects/.

Morris, Michael. "A Review of *The Dimensions of Hegel's Dialectic*," *Notre Dame Philosophical Reviews: An Electronic Journal*, 21 September 2010, http://ndpr.nd.edu/news/the-dimensions-of-hegel-s-dialectic/.

Morton, Timothy. *The Ecological Thought*. Cambridge, MA: Harvard University Press, 2010.

———. "The Bigger Picture: Race Issues and Thuggery," web log post, *Ecology without Nature*. November 20, 2011. Web. Accessed May 9, 2012.

———. *Ecology without Nature: Rethinking Environmental Aesthetics*. Cambridge, MA: Harvard University Press, 2007.

———. "Homeopathic Pepper Spray Remedy," web log post, *Ecology without Nature*. November 24, 2011. Web. Accessed May 9, 2012.

———. "OOO Class #1 (Embedded Video and MP3)," video blog post, *Ecology Without Nature*. April 2, 2012. Web. Accessed May 9, 2012.

———. "Peterloo Revisited," weblog post. *Ecology without Nature*. November 19, 2011. Web. Accessed May 9, 2012.

Mowitt, John. "Reason thus Unveils Itself," *Mosaic* 40, no. 2 (June 2007).

Murray-John, Patrick. "The 'Life of the Mind' Lost?," *Alt-Academy* (2011). Web. Accessed May 9, 2012.

"Nixon: 'I Am Not a Crook." *History.com*, accessed June 17, 2018, https://www.history.com/topics/us-presidents/richard-m-nixon/videos/nixon-i-am-not-a-crook.

Nietzsche, Friedrich. "On Truth and Lies in a Nonmoral Sense," *The Nietzsche Reader*, edited by Keith Ansell Pearson and Duncan Large. Malden, MA: Blackwell, 2006.

Nowviskie, Bethany. "Introduction: Two Tramps in Mud Time," *Alt-Academy* (2011). Web. Accessed May 9, 2012.

O'Brien, George Dennis. "Does Hegel Have a Philosophy of History," *History and Theory* 10, no. 3 (1971).

O'Regan, Cyril. *The Heterodox Hegel*. Albany: State University of New York Press, 1994.

Patton, Stacy. "The Ph.D. Now Comes with Food Stamps," *The Chronicle of Higher Education* (2012). May 6, 2012. Web. Accessed May 9, 2012.

Peeters, Benoit. *Derrida: A Biography*. Cambridge, UK: Polity Books, 2016.

Peirce, Charles S. *Selected Writings: Values in a Universe of Chance,* edited by Philip P. Wiener. New York: Dover, 1958.

Penn Warren, Robert. "The Uses of the Past," *New and Selected Essays*. New York: Random House, 1989.

———. "When Life Begins," *The Collected Poems of Robert Penn Warren*, edited by John Burt. Baton Rouge: Louisiana State University Press, 1998.

———. *Democracy and Poetry*. Cambridge: Harvard University Press, 1975.

———. *Segregation: The Inner Conflict in the South*. Athens, GA: University of Georgia Press, 1994.

———. *Selected Essays*. New York: Random House, 1958.

Petrucci, Armando. "Reading to Read: A Future for Reading," in *A History of Reading in the West*, edited by Guglielmo Carvallo and Roger Chartier, translated by Lydia G. Cochrane. Amherst, MA: University of Massachusetts Press, 1999.

Pinkard, Terry. *Hegel's Dialectic: The Explanation of Possibility*. Philadelphia: Temple University Press, 1988.

Posner, Miriam. "Reading Steve Jobs: Labor, Race, and Growing Up in the Bay Area," web log post, *Miriamposner.com*. December 6, 2011. Web. Accessed May 10, 2012.

Pulido, Martin. "The Place of Saying and Showing in Wittgenstein's *Tractatus* and Some Later Works," *Aporia* 19.2 (2009).

Riedel, Manfred. *Between Tradition and Revolution: The Hegelian Transformation of Political Philosophy*. Cambridge: Cambridge University Press, 1984.

Rijksbaron, Albert. *Plato.* Ion, *or: On the* Iliad. Boston: Brill, 2007.

Ritter, Joachim. *Hegel and the French Revolution: Essays on the* Philosophy of Right, trans. Richard Dien Winfield. Cambridge, MA: The MIT Press, 1982.

Roberts, Clayton. *The Logic of Historical Explanation*. University Park, PA: The Pennsylvania State University Press, 1996.

Rosenblatt, Louise. *Literature as Exploration*, first edition. New York: Appleton-Century-Crofts,1938.

Rovira, James. *Blake and Kierkegaard: Creation and Anxiety*. London: Continuum, 2010.

————. "Subverting the Mechanisms of Control: Baudrillard, *The Matrix Trilogy*, and the Future of Religion," *The International Journal of Baudrillard Studies* 2, no. 2 (July 2005): https://www2.ubishops.ca/baudrillardstudies/vol2_2/rovirapf.htm.

Rury, John. *Education and Social Change: Themes in the History of American Schooling*, 2nd edition. Mahwah, New Jersey: Lawrence Erlbaum, 2005.

Salih, Sarah, ed. with Judith Butler, *The Judith Butler Reader*. Malden, MA: Blackwell, 2004.

Schwartz, Michael. "Epistemes and the History of Being," in *Foucault and Heidegger: Critical Encounters*, edited by Alan Milchman and Alan Rosenberg. Minneapolis and London: University of Minnesota Press, 2003.

Shaviro, Steven. "Work for Hire?" Web log post. *The Pinocchio Theory*. January 11, 2012. Web. Accessed May 9, 2012.

Sim, Stuart. *Post-Marxism: An Intellectual History*. New York: Routledge, 2000.

Sluga, Hans. "Hans Sluga on the Life and Work of Wittgenstein," *Entitled Opinions (about Life and Literature)*, Stanford University Radio, October 7, 2015, accessed September 23, 2016, http://french-italian.stanford.edu/opinions.

Smith, Adam. *Lectures on Jurisprudence* (1763), edited by R. L. Meek, D. D. Raphael, and Peter Stein. Oxford: Oxford University Press, 1978.

Smith, Steven B. "Hegel's Discovery of History," in *The Review of Politics* 45, no. 2 (April 1983).

Southern Regional Council, the American Friends Service Committee, and the Churches of Christ, *Intimidation, Reprisal and Violence in the South's Racial Crisis*. Atlanta: Southern Regional Council, 1960.

Spender, Stephen. "On the Function of Criticism," *The Kenyon Review* 13, no. 2 (Spring 1951).

Stöltzner, Michael. "Vienna Indeterminism: Mach, Boltzmann, Exner," *Synthese* 119, no. 1/2 (1999): 85–111. http://www.jstor.org/stable/20118164 , 85.

Suber, Peter. "Open Access Overview (definition, Introduction)." Peter Suber. Earlham College, April 2010. Web. Accessed May 9, 2012.

Svenbro, Jesper. "Archaic and Classical Greece: The Invention of Silent Reading," in *A History of Reading in the West*, edited by Guglielmo Carvallo and Roger Chartier, trans. Lydia G. Cochrane. Amherst, MA: University of Massachusetts Press, 1999.

Tate, Allen. "The Profession of Letters in the South," in *On the Limits of Poetry*, edited by Allen Tate, 265–281. New York: Morrow Press, 1948.

Taylor, Charles . *Hegel and Modern Society*. Cambridge: Cambridge University Press, 1979.

Thiele, Leslie Paul. "The Ethics and Politics of Narrative: Heidegger + Foucault," *Foucault and Heidegger Critical Encounters*, edited by Alan Milchman and Alan Rosenberg. Minneapolis: University of Minnesota Press, 2003.

Tibebu, Teshale. *Hegel and the Third World: The Making of Eurocentrism in World History.* Syracuse: Syracuse University Press, 2011.

Toulmin, Stephen. *Cosmopolis: The Hidden Agenda of Modernity.* Chicago: University of Chicago Press, 1990.

———. *Return to Reason.* Cambridge: Harvard University Press, 2001.

Trompf, G.W. *The Idea of Historical Recurrence in Western Thought: From Antiquity to the Reformation.* Los Angeles: University of California Press, 1979.

Trüper, Henning, Dipesh Chakrabarty, and Sanjay Subrahmanyam. *Historical Teleologies in the Modern World.* New York: Bloomsbury, 2015.

Uwe Hohendahl, Peter. "The Theory of the Novel and the Concept of Realism in Lukács and Adorno," *George Lukács Reconsidered,* edited by Michael J. Thompson. New York: Continuum, 2011.

Voegelin, Eric. "The Irish Dialogue with Eric Voegelin," *VoegelinView,* lecture transcription, http://voegelinview.com/the-irish-dialogueue-with-eric-voegelin-pt1/.

Waggoner, Matt. "Judith Butler's *Senses of the Subject,*" *JCRT* 16, no. 1 (Winter 2016): 95–108.

Watkins, Floyd, John T. Heirs, and Mary Louise Weaks, eds. *Talking with Robert Penn Warren.* Athens: University of Georgia Press, 1990.

Weinberger, David. *Too Big to Know: Rethinking Knowledge Now That the Facts Aren't the Facts, Experts Are Everywhere, and the Smartest Person in the Room Is the Room.* New York: Basic, 2011.

West, Cornel. "Theory, Pragmatisms, and Politics," *Consequences of Theory,* edited by Jonathan Arac and Barbara Johnson. Baltimore: Johns Hopkins University Press, 1991.

Wittgenstein, Ludwig. "Review: P. Coffey, *The Science of Logic,*" *The Cambridge Review* 34, no. 853 (March 6, 1913).

———. *Culture and Value,* trans. Peter Winch. Chicago. University of Chicago Press, 1980.

———. *Lectures and Conversations on Aesthetics, Psychology, and Religious Belief,* edited by Cyril Barrett. Oxford: Basil Blackwell, 1966.

———. *Philosophical Grammar.* Oxford: Blackwell, 1974.

———. *Philosophical Investigations,* trans. G.E.M. Anscombe. New York: Macmillan, 1953.

———. *Tractatus Logico-Philosophicus,* trans. C.K. Ogden. New York. Barnes & Noble, 2003.

Wordsworth, William. "The Tables Turned," *The Poetry Foundation,* August 13, 2017, https://www.poetryfoundation.org/poems/45557/the-tables-turned.

Worsley, Kate. "Spastic, Paki, Abortion, Queer, Faggot, Sperm," *Times Higher Education,* May 16, 1997, accessed July 31, 2012, http://www.timeshighereducation.co.uk/story.asp?storyCode=100832&sectioncode=26.

Yancy, George and Judith Butler, "What's Wrong with 'All Lives Matter,'" *The New York Times,* January 12, 2015.

Young, Thomas Daniel. *Gentleman in a Dustcoat: John Crowe Ransom.* Baton Rouge: Louisiana State Press, 1976.

# Index

# About the Editor

Dr. James Rovira is a scholar, an author, and the founder and owner of *Bright Futures Educational Consulting*. He holds a PhD and MPhil from Drew University and a BA from Rollins College. His most recent publications include *Rock and Romanticism: Post-Punk, Goth, and Metal as Dark Romanticisms* (Palgrave Macmillan, 2018) and *Rock and Romanticism: Blake, Wordsworth, and Rock from Dylan to U2* (Lexington Books, 2018). In addition to his first book, *Blake and Kierkegaard: Creation and Anxiety* (Continuum/Bloomsbury 2010), he has published book chapters, poetry, short stories, creative non-fiction, journal articles, and reviews, and he has received grants from the NEH and from the Ohio Council for the Arts. He is currently working on the anthologies *David Bowie and Romanticism* and *Women in Rock/Women in Romanticism* as well as on the first-year writing text *Writing for College and Beyond*. He currently lives on Florida's Space Coast with his wife Sheridan and their children.

# About the Contributors

**Dr. Cassandra Falke** is Professor of English Literature at UiT—The Arctic University of Norway and President of the American Studies Association of Norway. She is the author of *Literature by the Working Class: English Autobiography, 1820–1848* (2013) and *The Phenomenology of Love and Reading* (2016), and she is the editor of *Intersections in Christianity and Critical Theory* (2010) and *The Phenomenology of the Broken Body* (2019; with Dahl and Eriksen). She has received grants from the NEH, the Fulbright Foundation, and the Nordic Councils in the Humanities and Social Sciences and has published 25 book chapters and journal articles about Romanticism, phenomenology, working-class writing, and liberal-arts education.

**Dr. Philip Goldstein** earned a BA in English from Columbia University in 1966, an MA in Philosophy from Temple University in 1970, and a PhD in English from Temple University in 1984. From 1977 to 2012, when he retired, he taught English and philosophy at the University of Delaware, where he was promoted to Associate Professor in 1990 and to Professor in 2001. He has published *The Politics of Literary Criticism: An Introduction to Marxist Cultural Theory* (University of Florida Press, 1990), *PostMarxism: An Introduction* (SUNY-Albany Press, 2005), and *Modern American Reading Practices* (Palgrave-MacMillan, 2008). With James Machor, he has edited *Reception Study: Theory, Practice, History* (Routledge, 2000) and *New Directions in Reception Study* (Oxford, 2008). He is presently finishing *Reading Race and Gender: The Theory and Practice of Reception Study.*

**Dr. Eric Hood** is an Assistant Professor at Michigan State University and holds a PhD in English from the University of Kansas. His research interests include cultural theory and British Romanticism, particularly epic poetry. His study of Elizabeth Barrett Browning, affect, and "free love" socialism appears in the collection, *"A Tribe of Authoresses": Women's Literary Networks and Romanticism* (2017). He is also a Founding Editor at *The Digital Mitford, the Mary Russell Mitford Digital Archive.*

**Dr. Darcie Rives-East** is Associate Professor of English at Augustana University in Sioux Falls, South Dakota. Her research and teaching specializations include American literature, critical theory, gender and ethnic studies, surveillance studies, and popular culture. She is the author of "Haunted by Violence: Edith Wharton's *The Decoration of Houses* and Her Gothic Fiction" in *The Edith Wharton Review*; "Watching the Detective: Sherlock, Surveillance, and British Fears Post-7/7" in *The Journal of Popular Culture*; "Charlotte Perkins Gilman's *Herland*, Race, and the California and the Suffrage and Women's Club Movements, 1896–1911," in *Left in the West: Literature, Culture, and Progressive Politics in the American West* (ed. Gioia Woods, The University of Nevada Press); and *Surveillance and the State in Post-9/11 British and American Television*, forthcoming from Palgrave Macmillan.

**Dr. Meredith N. Sinclair** is Assistant Professor of English Education in the English Department at Southern Connecticut State University. Her research and teaching interests include critical, anti-racist pedagogy; critical literacy as a component of social justice education for adolescents and pre-service teachers; secondary English curriculum; and young adult literature. Recent publications address reader agency in the age of spectacle, the use of young adult fiction to decolonize secondary English classrooms, and reimagining transcription in exploring phenomenological questions.

**Dr. Aglaia Maretta Venters**'s thesis title is "Makers of Men: Jesuit-Indian Relations, Philosophes, and Paternalistic Vision," which was approved December 2002. Her dissertation is entitled "Creativity through Destructive Tendencies: Utopian Designs in Early Modern French Travel Literature on Louisiana," approved in December 2011. She has taught Western Civilization, World History, American History, African-American History, and Louisiana History at Tulane University, Baton Rouge Community College, Dillard University, and South Louisiana Community College, where she still teaches. She was a research assistant at the NEH Deep South Regional Humanities Center from 2000–2001 and worked for the Writing Workshop at Tulane University from Fall 2004 to Spring 2005.

**Dr. Steve Wexler** is Professor of English at California State University, Northridge, where he teaches courses in history of rhetoric, rhetoric of science, critical theory, and popular culture. His work examines the intersections of rhetoric, epistemology, labor, and political theory, including essays and reviews published in *Science & Society*, *College Composition and Communication*, *Workplace: A Journal for Academic Labor*, *Works & Days*, and *Kairos*. He is currently working on a monograph titled *The Dialectics of Information*.

**Dr. Roger Whitson** is Associate Professor of English at Washington State University, where he also teaches in the Digital Technology and Culture program. He works in the fields of digital humanities, nineteenth-century media archaeology, and British Romantic and Victorian literary studies. He received his MA from Saint Louis University and his PhD from the University of Florida in Gainesville.